The Confederate Negro

JAMES H. BREWER

The Confederate Negro

Virginia's craftsmen and military laborers, 1861–1865

Duke University Press   Durham, N.C.   1969

To ZADYE, BERTHA, ANNA, *and* ISABELL

The women in my life

Contents

List of tables

x *List of tables*

Foreword

This thoughtful and moving book opens an almost wholly unexplored subject in its detailed account of Virginia's Negro "Craftsmen and Military Laborers" during the Civil War. It follows Professor Frank Vandiver's pioneer *Ploughshares into Swords: Josiah Gorgas and Confederate Ordnance* and gives much-needed detail to some of Professor E. Merton Coulter's insights, in his *Confederate States of America, 1861–1865*, into the political, economic, and morale problems of the Confederacy. What Professor Brewer does is to study the last two of these for a key group in the most important Confederate state. His results are as convincing in their massive documentation as in the skill with which he interprets them.

Brewer's treatment is necessarily functional and statistical, after an introductory chapter on the mobilization of Negro labor and before his conclusions. Between these he has studied the Virginia Negro's contribution to supply, logistics, manufacturing, transport, and medicine, before going into that vast fortifications network which was one of the factors in the Confederacy's astounding success in defending its strategically ill-placed capital. But was this capital as badly placed as most historians have assumed? Brewer shows that the Virginia Negro was not only "an inseparable part" of the Confederacy's "general economic machinery," but that he was also, from his previous role in one of the few "protoindustrial" areas of the Confederacy, particularly well-suited to making an especially valuable contribution.

Until similarly detailed studies are made for New Orleans and Tennessee, Dr. Brewer's distinction between craftsmen and common laborers cannot be applied to the whole Confederacy, but we may guess that even New Orleans, the only major American city in the Confederacy, did not have more skilled and semi-skilled Negroes in a wider variety of industries than Brewer has found in Richmond and the smaller towns of Virginia. Virginia had more free Negroes and slaves of both sexes whose skills could be upgraded to meet the demands of this first total war of the industrial era. Their presence will force many military historians to revise their earlier judgments of the "bad luck" which placed the Confederate capital within a hundred miles of that of the Union.

The first of Brewer's fascinating tables (Table 1.1) shows the concentration of free Negro craftsmen in the "developed" Tidewater, where long settlement and soil exhaustion had forced economic specialization in craft and industrial production and in the export of slaves to plantation markets. The house servants and craftsmen who were left behind were surely more skilled and more adaptable and more "loyal" than many of the others. Table 1.2 shows that less than a third of the conscripted free Negroes were laborers. We will never know how many craftsmen were exempted, under the protection of some white patron, over and above the 50 percent who were known to be employed in war industry and transport. The great majority of the hospital employees were skilled or semiskilled workers. Similar striking differences emerge in Dr. Brewer's studies of the Negroes in war industry, supply, and essential transport, from the men who worked on the 1861 James River batteries, Table 6.1.

The tragic story of the Engineer Labor Corps, Chapter 6, has been known, but has never been told in such convincing detail. Whether they were working on Confederate or Union engineering projects, the living and working conditions of these day laborers were almost equally dreadful. They were the Civil War equivalents of the labor armies which saved both Moscow and Leningrad under similarly desperate conditions three quarters of a century later. And the necessity of depending on both groups of Negro laborers, as well as the heroism of the Negroes themselves, led to a "degree of racial tolerance" within Virginia which increasingly contrasted with the legal and racial dogmas for which the Confederacy was fighting. Again Dr. Brewer's evidence is most impressive. The services of these Negroes served to force the recognition of the Negro as a man, in perhaps the only way that this can be done, by working for some common cause: that of healing the sick, comforting the dying, and mastering the techniques on which all modern societies depend. As Zambia's President Kenneth D. Kaunda has recently put it, "The only meaningful development, whether it be economic, social, cultural, scientific or anything else, is one that acknowledges and enhances the importance of Man . . . particularly the weaker members of any given society."*

This recognition of the Negro as a person had already begun in Virginia in 1865. It was surely the source of some of the attitudes expressed by some Confederate veterans during the tragedy of Reconstruction. What Brewer has been unable to do in this superb study is to speculate on the next chapter of his story. What happened to these thousands of skilled Negro workers? How many did the Union's destruction of Virginia's industry and transport force back to farming? Who went on and to what kind of jobs in other parts of the country? Why did the giants of Northern business and transportation —who were scouring Europe for labor of all kinds—not use these men? Or did war, their loss of capital, and Northern competition ruin those local employers who might have given these skilled Negroes employment? When the New South arose in the underdeveloped Piedmont, with its supply of cheap white labor, what was the process by which the untrained children of these skilled Negroes were denied entrance to the very jobs which their slave and free fathers had done so well? This is, finally, one of those rare works which not only answer fundamental questions about the events with which they deal but also raise equally disturbing questions about the whole historical process of "modernization" after a catastrophic military defeat. The Smithsonian Institution, one can add, is to be wholeheartedly congratulated for its support of this superb work in the social history of American industry and technology.

THEODORE ROPP

Duke University

* "Zambia's Aim—Loyalty Between Government and People," *Optima*, Vol. XVI, No. 2 (June 1966), 59–64.

Preface

The omission of the Confederate Negro from the pages of history seems like a striking instance of the death of the unfit in the struggle for historical survival. However, fitness to live for human service is quite another matter than fitness to survive in the rugged contest for meaningful identification in a nation's history. The legacy of the Negro, free and slave, in the War for Southern Independence has too often been ignored by the historian. Scholars have avoided the un-savory task of linking the Negro to the Confederate war effort, a cause generally interpreted as one designed to sustain his enslavement and degradation.

Yet worthy of interpretation are innumerable manuscripts which clearly set forth the vast responsibilities assumed by Virginia Negroes. Unfortunately many records are missing, presumably destroyed by fire which swept through Richmond on the morning of its occupation by Federal troops, or deliberately destroyed at Charlotte, North Carolina, and Fort Mill, South Carolina, during the retreat of the Confederate government. Other records have been partially destroyed by later fires, by pests, and by time. The manuscripts are widely scattered in Virginia's libraries, historical societies, universities, and other public depositories. At times custodians of Civil War records are totally unaware of their presence. Consequently, what may appear to be merely random samples of Negro activities in that war are actually fortunate discoveries of missing and hitherto unpublished documents.

This book sets forth the extensive involvement of the Virginia Negro in the South's war efforts. It shows how Negro manpower was used to close a huge gap in Virginia's technological labor needs. The Negro's brawn and his skill were key elements in the mechanism of Confederate technology, logistics, transportation, and fortification. Bell Irvin Wiley's definitive study, *Southern Negroes, 1861–1865*, probes the war experiences of the Negro in the Confederate States of America. The present writing, however, is concerned solely with the distinctive character of the war experiences of the Negro in Virginia, the major battlefield of the Civil War. For four years this Negro, whether free or slave, sometimes by choice and other times by necessity, contributed a sustaining effort to the War for Southern Independence.

At first encounter, the Confederate Negro appears invidiously as chattel, to be used—not as a person, to be respected. His actions are characterized by paradoxes and contradictions. In his history one finds frustratingly intricate webs and countless unintelligible events. The laws under which he lived were repressive, and the South made no apologies for them. Yet thousands ignored the beckoning of their Yankee liberators. Though enslaved in a land of freedom, the Negro quickly responded to the rebel yell. Though denied the right of bearing arms, he bore them for the Confederacy. Though in fiction and in legend he twanged a banjo, sang melodious spirituals, and labored in the field, he was in fact an integral part of the entire Virginia war effort.

When considered only in context of the restrictions circumscribing his life, Negro support of the Southern war presents an illogical picture. Yet it must be remembered that the firing upon Fort Sumter marked the beginning of an era characterized by a higher level of racial tolerance (not a change of racial attitude about his innate inferiority) within Virginia. Consequently the Negro's war response must be weighed carefully against his more favorable war environment.

A topical rather than a chronological method of presentation predominates in this study. Within topical groupings, however, the chronological organization is generally followed. To present fuller documentation, and at the expense of being repetitious, I have offered data in descriptive rather than in tabular form. The latter procedure would greatly have reduced the volume of evidence submitted. This was not considered desirable or requisite in light of the need to document conclusively the extensive services performed by the Virginia Negro. I have also judged it expedient to use with great liberality in many cases the exact words, phrases, extracts of letters, and contexts of orders, circulars, and commands of military authorities. Likewise, both the laws of the General Assembly of Virginia and the Confederate Congress have been cited.

In the preparation of this book, I have incurred obligations that I gladly take this opportunity to acknowledge. I am indebted to the Smithsonian Institution for the award of a Senior Research Associateship in 1965, which made possible an entire year of uninterrupted writing. Financial assistance by the Richmond Area University Center and Virginia State College made possible the completion of portions of the research for this book.

I should also like to note special obligations to Mrs. Sarah D. Jackson of the National Archives and to the staffs of the libraries of the Smithsonian Institution, Virginia State College, North Carolina College, the Virginia Historical Society, and the State Library of Virginia at Richmond.

To Mr. Roger Pineau of the Smithsonian Institution I am indebted for helpful suggestions regarding the presentation. Likewise to Dr. Philip W. Bishop and Dr. John N. Hoffman, many thanks for encouragement and valuable suggestions. The kindness of Mrs. Dorothy E. Young and her assistance at the Smithsonian Institution made my stay there most rewarding.

I wish especially to express my sincere appreciation to Professors Theodore Ropp of Duke University and James Hugo Johnston of Virginia State College for convincing me that this study should be made. To Dr. Robert P. Daniel, President, and Dr. John M. Hunter, Dean, of Virginia State College I am thankful for assistance. I wish to acknowledge the courtesies of many others not listed.

Finally, to my wife Zadye Carter Brewer, I offer a special acknowledgement for her patience, sacrifice, and encouragement.

J. H. B.

Durham, North Carolina
April 1969

The Confederate Negro

CHAPTER ONE

Negro Mobilization: Impressment laws and voluntary hiring-out

The presence of over 500,000 Negroes in Virginia at the outset of the Civil War raises the question of their involvement in and their importance to the Confederate war effort. Part of the answer is to be found in legislation enacted by both the General Assembly of Virginia and the Confederate Congress; and part of the story is told in Confederate war records which reflect the extent to which Negroes, with their brawn and skills, were effectively mobilized to meet the Confederacy's technological, military, and agricultural demands.[1]

As an auxiliary labor force, the total slave population of Virginia on the eve of the Civil War numbered over 491,000, while the state's free Negro population numbered only some 58,000. Translated into percentages of the total white population 1,048,000 Negroes equaled approximately 51 per cent of the white population in Virginia. An estimate of the geographical distribution of the state's Negro population is shown in Table 1.1.

The immense demands of armed conflict were such that they could not be borne by whites alone. Many skilled laborers, for example, were needed to fabricate the weapons of war in machine shops, arsenals, and ironworks. Many other workers were needed to procure

Table 1.1 *Distribution of Negro population in Virginia on the eve of the Civil War*

Section	Free Negroes	Slaves
Tidewater	59%	39%
Piedmont	30%	46%
Appalachian	11%	15%

raw materials. Building new transportation lanes, or improving upon existing ones, to facilitate the movement of troops, war materials, and other supplies essential to the war effort demanded a number of laborers. Likewise, Virginia's vulnerability necessitated the extensive use by Confederate engineers of a massive labor force for the construction of fortifications and defensive works to protect industrial centers, strategic areas, and the endangered routes of communication within the state. Finally, an ample supply of labor was imperative to sustain and to increase the production of foodstuffs and to make possible the wholesale conversion of the use of land to corn, wheat, potatoes, and cereal grains such as oats and barley. Black manpower throughout the war was called upon not only by military authorities but by private industry as well to offset the dwindling pool of white civilian war workers.

By the late fall of 1862 Virginia was confronted with a serious problem. The impressment of slaves and free Negroes to labor on fortifications and river batteries, coupled with the slaveowners' practice of hiring out a large percentage of their slaves to the quartermaster, ordnance, and other bureaus of the War Department, tended to exhaust the supply of available Negro manpower which was necessary for the agricultural and industrial needs of the state. This labor shortage was one of the knottiest problems facing Confederate and state authorities. As the war became more critical, open conflict ensued between these two groups, even though it was apparent that if the South were to increase its military potential, Virginia would have to commit to the Confederate government as noncombat workers an even larger proportion of its Negro population.

II

Negro labor had been used extensively in Virginia's industrial growth for several decades before the conflict of 1861.[2] In the forties and fifties, for example, the expanding practice of slave hiring was exceptionally well suited for supplying labor force to meet the mounting needs of manufacturing, transportation, mining, and public works.[3] There emerged a new class of brokers, usually known as "agents," who specialized in hiring and supplying slaves for industrial and urban employment. In the tobacco-growing regions they also supplied slaves to serve as a supplementary labor force during both the planting and harvesting seasons. The agent's fees were usually 7½ per cent for "hiring-out, bonding, collecting the hire, and attention to the physical needs of the slave during the period of hire." Throughout Virginia many owners had hired out their slaves for annual payments, according to Clement Eaton, that averaged "from 10 to 15 per cent of their value." This practice permitted employers to secure the labor of slaves by hire instead of investing money to purchase them. The state's businessmen considered this a sound procedure; and Richmond, Petersburg, Danville, and Lynchburg became the principal centers for slave hiring. The practice afforded profitable returns to Tidewater and Piedmont slaveowners.

Prewar Virginia history, especially during the 1850's, includes typical scenes in which slaves were hired out by their owners as sawyers, coopers, quarrymen, millers, wheelwrights, and wagonmakers; they were also hired to mine coal, limestone, lead, salt, and iron ore; and they worked as pilots, boathands, and fishermen. Hundreds of slaves were employed in the construction and maintenance of canals and railroads. Town slaves were hired out to work in flour mills, tobacco factories, shoe shops, foundries, sawmills, and stores. On the docks they labored as stevedores, and at railroad depots they loaded and unloaded freight. There were hundreds of slave and free Negro craftsmen engaged in such trades as boatmaker, ropemaker, caulker, blacksmith, shoemaker, and carpenter. Virginia's railroads procured a large labor force of slaves to work as firemen, track hands, brakemen, machinists, boilermakers, and blacksmiths.

According to Clement Eaton, "the growing practice of obtaining the service of slave labor by hire instead of by purchase" was an important aspect of the institution in the upper South.[4] It was inevitable that the condition of servitude would be affected by the nature of the bondsman's employment. Some slaves were permitted to receive wages, make contracts, and maintain their own homes.[5] Urban slaves possessed a greater degree of mobility and quite often at least a limited choice as to the place of their employment. Increasing numbers of slaves were allowed to hire their own time and to pay their masters an annual fee from their wages.

Prewar slave hiring, with its greater flexibility of labor supply, contributed to the upgrading of slave labor and was an important factor in the industrial development of ante-bellum Virginia. In 1846, for example, there were 5,667 slaves employed in Richmond's business enterprises such as cotton and flour mills, and a decade later the number had increased to 6,326. In many instances such slaves were hired rather than owned by manufacturers.[6]

III

Prewar slave hiring not only contributed to the upgrading of slave labor, it also augmented the industrial development of the state. Ante-bellum slave hiring also greatly increased the number of slave technicians who were to be available for service as war workers, thereby contributing to the success of the state's program of mobilization of Negro labor for the Civil War.

The responsibility for effectively assembling Negro manpower became that of the Virginia lawmakers and the Confederate Congressmen. Speaking on this point, President Jefferson Davis stated, "Much of our success was due to the much abused institution of African servitude." This opinion was shared by General Ulysses S. Grant, who was well aware of the need to remove from the South her vast army of Negro noncombatants. Grant said, "The 4,000,000 colored noncombatants were equal to more than three times their numbers in the North, age for age, sex for sex." Both President Davis and General Grant early recognized that the mobilization of the Negro constituted an extremely valuable military resource. The Virginia legislature found it necessary, however, to pass impressment laws forcing slaveholders to send their chattel to labor for the military. Statutes were also enacted to draft free Negroes for military work.

From February 1862 to February 1864, five impressment laws constituted the most significant acts dealing with the mobilization of Virginia's Negro population for noncombat purposes. Three of the five laws were passed by the General Assembly of the state, while the other two were enacted by the Confederate Congress. The first state law subjected the free Negro to the draft as a laborer, the second placed a ceiling on the number of slaves that could be impressed, and the third exempted the slaves from counties where impressment would materially affect agricultural production. The two wartime regulations passed by the Confederate Congress not only made provision for tapping Virginia's Negro reservoir but were also designed to minimize conflicts between Confederate and state authorities over the impressment of slaves and to correct glaring defects of state impressment laws.

Such impressment legislation was prompted by the collapse, nine months after the beginning of hostilities, of the voluntary recruiting efforts for Negro labor. At the call to repel the Yankee invaders, for example, Virginia looked to its Negro population as a major source of civilian workers. Yet, by the late fall of 1861 the fervor of free Negroes for volunteering had largely subsided. The early months of war had also taught the folly of depending upon slaveholders to comply willingly with military requisitions for the labor of their slaves. Consequently, the state by January 1862 was in no mood to continue its voluntary recruiting efforts for Negro workers. Nevertheless the hiring-out of slaves and the hire of free colored persons by contracts with military authorities and private war industries were to continue throughout the war. This was particularly true with respect to the state's railroads, ironworks, factories, and public works. Likewise the majority of Negroes employed by the quartermaster, ordnance, niter and mining bureaus, and military hospitals were hired through voluntary contracts with free Negroes and the owners of bondsmen.

The realities of war and the mounting demands of the Confederate armies forced Virginia actively to recruit Negroes as military laborers. At first, legal provision was made for tapping only the free Negro reservoir. In February 1862 the state legislature passed an act which required the local courts to register all male free Negroes within their jurisdiction who were between the ages of eighteen and fifty. Such registration lists were to be sent to the Adjutant General, and whenever a commanding officer of any post or department wanted laborers he was to submit his requisition to the local court. A board of three justices was authorized to select the workers from the registration list. The local sheriff was responsible for notifying the free Negroes of their call, and if he failed to perform his duty he was subject to a fine of from $50 to $100. The selected free persons were not required to serve longer than 180 days without their consent. They were also entitled to such compensation, rations, quarters, and medical attention as any white laborers of similar character. Their pay, rations, and allowances were borne by the Confederate States, unless the services rendered were exclusively for the state.[7]

After authorizing the impressment of free Negroes for military service, Virginia lawmakers next considered the slave. By the late summer of 1862, it was apparent that ample slave labor could not be obtained without specific legislative action. Therefore, on October 3, 1862, the legislature passed an act providing for the public defense of the state. The act required that a census be taken of all slaves between the ages of eighteen and forty-five. Upon requisition from the President of the Confederate States, the Governor of Virginia would impress slaves to work on entrenchments and to do other labor necessary for the defense of the state. The number that could be impressed should not exceed 10,000 or more than 5 per cent of the slave population from any county, city, or town. The sheriff was to receive the slaves from their masters for delivery to the proper government agents. Such slaves were not allowed to remain in the employment of the government longer than sixty days. A penalty of thirty days was invoked for cases in which steps had to be taken against the local authorities who refused to comply with the act. The law further provided that $16 per month was to be paid to the slaveowner, plus a soldier's ration, medicine, and medical care for the slave. All expenses were to be borne by the Confederate States government. If the owner furnished his slaves' subsistence he would be given 60 cents per day for each one. Slaves working on farms devoted exclusively to the production of grains were to be exempt from impressment. Owners were to be paid by the government for the loss of bondsmen who escaped to the Union lines, were killed by the enemy, or were injured because of negligence on the part of the military.[8]

Military officers violated this law from time to time. Occasionally military commanders took steps to impress more slaves after receiving all that had been made available for public defense. Governor Letcher accordingly turned down a request by Major General Jones to draft slaves to work at Saltville in the salt mines. The governor also received protests from many owners about the seizure of their slaves by military officers without the owners' authorizations. The Virginia lawmakers finally made unauthorized impressment a misdemeanor, and the violator was subject to a fine double the value of the slave impressed.

In March 1863 the General Assembly passed a third act which exempted agricultural counties where slave impressment would materially affect production. This law also increased to $20 per month the maximum pay to owners. Any owner sending thirty to forty slaves to a receiving station was expected to provide an overseer to guard his property. Legal exemption was expanded to include counties near the enemy lines, where owners could prove to the court that they had lost one third of their slaves through escape. Still other exemptions from impressment included any soldier in the army having only one slave, and a widow having a son in the army or whose husband had died in the service. The act of 1863 also extended to fifty-five the age limit for the impressment of slaves. Any owner who refused to send a slave was subject to a maximum fine of $10 for each day of recalcitrance. Failure of the sheriff to deliver a drafted bondsman carried a fine of from $50 to $200. Thus in 1862 and in 1863 the state's lawmakers enacted these laws to put a portion of its large Negro labor market in readiness for effective war service.

As the conflict entered the twenty-third month, the Confederate Congress was forced to take more drastic steps to procure Negro labor. On March 26, 1863, it passed its first significant act to achieve access to the Confederacy's Negro military labor force. No longer was the state governor to be the chief enforcing agent in procuring Negro labor, but instead he was to be replaced by President Davis. The act of March 1863, designed to correct the defects of state impressment laws, specifically legalized slave impressment by Confederate authorities "according to the rules and regulations provided in the laws of the state wherein they are impressed."[9] At times, however, military officers were obliged to find ways to evade the more annoying state provisions. For example, one section of the law of 1863 gave army officers the right to impress "other property" whenever the exigencies were such as to make impressment absolutely necessary. Supported by this "other property" phrase, military commanders resorted to impressment of slaves, in some instances in violation of Virginia law. Such action, however, was immediately challenged by state officials. During the months to follow, Virginia lawmakers wrote to the Secretary of War protesting such action. J. B. Baldwin of Staunton urged the importance of returning slaves and free Negroes to the Valley district to aid in harvesting the large crop. Virginia lawmakers openly questioned the legality of "any law authorizing a draft of slaves in the state except according to state law and through the Governor and the county courts."[10] Early in 1864 a joint resolution of the General Assembly directed the Confederate government to refrain, if possible, from drafting slaves from agricultural areas because they were needed for food production.

Throughout 1863 demands to impress or conscript free blacks as military laborers were intensified. Occasionally a military officer expressed similar sentiments. On November 11, 1863, Major Samuel W. M. Melton, the Assistant Adjutant General, suggested to War Secretary Seddon that conscription might be extended to free Negroes. He insisted that their services were "as clearly due as those of any other class in the Confederacy."[11] Confederate authorities, however, were more concerned about finding means to utilize fully the vast reservoir of slave laborers. The Secretary of War frequently reminded President Jefferson Davis that "to command slaves . . . in anything like the number required for the many works of the government . . . compulsion in some form would be necessary." Seddon also pointed out: "There may be difficulties and embarrassments in enforcing the services of slaves, but they might be overcome on the principle of impressing them as property, or requiring contributions from their owners of certain quotas for public service, as has been done for works of public defense."[12]

Unfortunately, the first impressment act of March 1863 was inadequate, and Southern leaders considered more stringent measures. President Davis acknowledged the shortcomings of existing impressment laws in his message to Congress on December 7, 1863.[13] Consequently the 1863 law was supplemented by an amendatory act of February 17, 1864, which authorized a levy of 20,000 slaves throughout the Confederacy between the ages of eighteen and fifty, when conditions should require. Slaves were to be impressed, however, only if the supply of free Negroes failed to meet the needs of the War Department. If the owner had but one male bondsman between the ages of ten and fifty, that one was not to be taken without the owner's permission. Only one fifth of the male slaves were to be taken, and credit was to be given for slaves already impressed by the government. By September 1864 the War Secretary had issued a requisition for 14,500 slaves, of which Virginia was expected to furnish her quota of 2,500.

The second slave impressment act was not altogether successful, and within a few months a new levy was contemplated. President

Davis, in November, 1864, asked the Confederate Congress for additional legislation to employ forty thousand slaves.

IV

The Confederate Congress's second impressment act of February 17, 1864, was also designed to make all male free Negroes between the ages of eighteen and fifty liable "to service in war manufactories, in erecting defensive works, and in military hospitals." The act, moreover, required that they be taken in preference to the 20,000 slaves eligible to be impressed, and that such free Negroes should receive the same pay and subsistence as soldiers. The 1864 conscription act allowed the creation of the Bureau of Conscription to administer the drafting of persons. A bureaucracy of officers, medical examiners, and other agents was authorized to handle the task of enrolling or exempting white males between the ages of seventeen and fifty. The Bureau was also entrusted with the task of procuring Negroes, free and slave. In the spring of 1864 War Secretary Seddon instructed Brigadier General John S. Preston, Chief of the Bureau of Conscription, to bring into service the free Negroes authorized by the act of Congress.

Subsequently A. R. Lawton, the Quartermaster General, commented about the issuing of clothing and suggested that blankets, shoes, and woolen garments be provided by bureaus employing Negroes. Lawton stated that his department could provide some summer clothing and cotton pants, shirts, drawers, socks, and caps. In November 1864 a directive from the Quartermaster General's office ran:

> Each bureau will also provide such Negroes and all other employees in service with the necessary woolen shirts, jackets, and pants, and blankets, overcoats, and shoes. Cotton pants, shirts, drawers, socks, and caps will be provided by the Quartermaster Department on requisitions made quarterly. . . .[14]

Among the 27,771 free Negro males in Virginia, there were approximately 5,000 who were between the ages of eighteen and forty-five, and thus liable for military service. Well over 50 per cent, however, were already usefully employed in transportation, mining, and industrial pursuits as well as in government shops, depots, and yards. Also to be included were free Negroes working in arsenals, armories, salt works, niter works, and military hospitals. This helps to explain why the Assistant Adjutant General was informed by the Bureau of Conscription: "The orders for the enrollment and assignment of free blacks have been carried out as effectively as could be done under the circumstances." On September 19, 1864, the Bureau of Conscription reported:

Upon a general examination of the returns of the enrolling officers it is manifest that all the labor of this class which could well be has been withdrawn from the agricultural districts.

The Niter and Mining Bureau desires every one that can be found. Colonel Corley, Chief Quartermaster Army of Northern Virginia, calls for 500, and the Engineer Bureau makes a requisition for a large force on the line of the Richmond and Danville and the South Side Railroads. General Walker, commanding defenses on the Richmond and Danville Railroad, also calls for assistance from this class. The officers of the Quartermaster Department collecting forage in the Valley have received assistance, but are demanding more. Major J. G. Paxton, in charge of extensive operations for the Quartermaster's Department at Lynchburg and in the Piedmont counties, is asking for aid. All the demands are pressing and of the most vital importance, and the number required by the officers making the requisitions for them approximates, if does not exceed, the whole number of free Negroes within the military lines of the prescribed ages.[15]

There were, moreover, a number of free Negroes who either deserted or successfully managed to evade the enrolling officers. The Bureau of Conscription was informed that several free Negroes in Culpeper escaped conscription with the aid of their white friends. The matter was referred to Colonel J. C. Porter, enrolling officer of the Eighth District, with instructions to enroll the Culpeper Negroes. Such free persons were to be employed in saving the large crop of government forage and in obtaining fuel for the army.

The complete story of the impressment of free Negroes and their war experiences in Virginia can never be told, because the records were imperfectly kept, and no returns were sent from some sections of the state. Late in February 1864 the Bureau of Conscription reported the occupations of a large portion of the conscripts as listed in Table 1.2.

From February 1864 to March 1865, when the Conscription Bureau was abolished, no fewer than 1,818 free Negroes were enrolled, and of this number 45 were reported as deserters.[17] To meet the demands of the state's diversified war economy the versatility of its free colored population was exploited. A free Negro had to be just as much at home in the cornfield as in collecting forage; he had to be prepared not only to care for stock, act as a sawyer, repair a wagon, serve as a teamster or boatman, and procure raw materials, but even to furnish skilled and unskilled labor for the South's war industries and defensive works. To the Confederate States Navy at Richmond, for

Table 1.2 *Conscription Act of 1864: free Negroes enrolled, 1864–1865*[16]

Occupation	Number	Occupation	Number
Ambulance driver	2	Mason	48
Baker	9	Mechanic	31
Barber	23	Messenger	7
Carpenter	25	Miller	4
Coffin maker	2	Miner	1
Collier	1	Nurse	1
Cook	15	Ostler	1
Cooper	12	Packer	2
Depot hand	18	Painter	4
Drayman	3	Plaster	4
Engineer	2	Porter	7
Engine cleaner	12	Railroad hand	29
Engine hand	20	Sawyer	32
Farmer	175	Shearer	1
Farm hand	129	Shoemaker	61
Fireman (train)	24	Striker	6
Fisherman	17	Tanner	36
Gardner	1	Teamster	29
Grave digger	1	Tobacco hand	38
Groom	2	Tobacco factory	47
Hackman	2	Tobacconist	3
House servant	16	Wagoner	11
Huckster	4	Wagon maker	13
Laborer	440	Waiter	10
Lumber man	47	Wheelwright	14
Machinist	16	Wood house hand	2
		Total	1,464

example, the Bureau of Conscription assigned 83 Negroes to alleviate the scarcity of both skilled and ordinary labor for naval ordnance, naval works, shipyards, and depots. The Conscription Bureau also responded to the urgent appeals of Virginia railroads, ironworks, flour mills, niter works, tanneries, and mines. Although several hundred free Negroes were assigned to the aforementioned areas, the engineers, quartermaster, and ordnance consumed more than 70 per cent of the free Negro conscripts. Throughout 1864 there was a mounting need for the labor of free Negroes, and to meet such crises they were impressed, gathered, and turned over to the enrolling officers, usually located at camps of instruction. Then the conscripts were detailed to areas where their labor was needed (see Chapters 3, 4, 5).

V

Much of Virginia's war effort was effected by the legal machinery devised for the mobilization and the regulation of slave and free Negro labor. Although impressment by the state and the Confederate government prompted bitter criticism by slaveholders, it produced tangible and significant results. Negro labor, for example, became a key factor in the mechanism of Virginia's wartime economy. Mobilization of the state's colored manpower considerably enhanced Confederate fighting strength, as whites were freed to swell the Southern armies. Mobilization eventually made available a greater variety of foodstuffs and manufactured commodities for military and civilian needs.

Mobilization also attracted the attention of the North and the South. As early as October 1862 James S. Wadsworth stated the value of assembling Negro labor. As he accepted the Republican nomination for governor of New York, Wadsworth stated, "Six million whites, having had time to organize their government and arm their troops, fed and supported by the labor of 4,000,000 slaves, present the most formidable rebellion in recorded history." He added, "Strike from the rebellion the support which it derives from the unrequited toil of these slaves, and its foundations will be undermined."[18] Seven months later the Richmond *Examiner* asserted that the North had discovered from this war the value of the slave to the South as a military laborer, and "Lincoln's proclamation is designed to destroy this power in our hands."[19]

Once mobilized, Virginia was able to minimize, until the closing months of the war, the number of Negroes who were captured by

Federal raiding parties or who escaped into Union lines. No doubt, the presence of Lee's armies as well as Confederate patrols, at points accessible to Union lines, sealed off possible avenues of escape for the Negro.[20] After thirty-two months of warfare, in December 1863, J. M. Bennett, Auditor of Public Accounts, reported to the General Assembly of Virginia that the loss of slaves to the enemy by flight or seizure by Federal raiding parties was not as large as expected. Bennett indicated that the loss of slaves, based on tax returns, totaled less than 10 per cent (exclusive of West Virginia) of the slave population, or 31,551 slaves. The auditor's report also disclosed that in 1860 the proportion of slaves (exclusive of free Negroes) was 47 to every 100 whites, and by 1863 there were 71 slaves to every 100 white persons in the 78 counties and 5 cities included in his report to the Virginia lawmakers.

It would appear that Virginia was not faced with a serious breakdown of its holding power over the Negro noncombatants until the closing days of the war. Flight into Union lines, however, or seizure by Union troops, though seemingly less extensive than in other parts of the Confederacy, was a cause of concern. In countless ways, the war came closer to the Virginia Negro than to other Negroes within the South. Both of the war governors, John Letcher and William Smith, encouraged and supported Negro mobilization and war measures whereby the labor of Negroes contributed to the ability of the Confederacy to keep an army in the field. The Virginia Negro resided in what was not only the industrial heart of the South but also the major battleground of the Civil War. Armed conflict greatly increased the technological and military demand for his brawn and his

Table 1.3 *Loss of slaves from Virginia, 1861–1863*[21]

Year	Total in Counties	Total in Corporations	Total
1860	355,632	22,767	378,399
1863	331,537	15,311	346,848
Loss	30,250	7,456	37,706
Gain	6,155	0	6,155

skills. Virginia's coal mines, ironworks, lead-smelting works, nitriaries, harness shops, arsenals, naval yards, and machine shops offer unique examples of the state's efforts to match Negro manpower to the need for increased production. The many and diversified needs of the war involved the Virginia Negro in a correspondingly wide variety of tasks—procurement operations, processing of minerals, fabrication of the weapons of war, transportation of war materials by land and by river, and construction of fortifications and defensive works. Probably no other southern state offers a better example of the premium placed upon Negro manpower.

CHAPTER TWO

Quartermaster and Commissary Noncombatants

In describing the logistics of war, Karl von Clausewitz, the great Prussian military expert, remarked that "an army is like a tree. From the ground out of which it grows it draws its nourishment." This ground, in warring Virginia, was tilled by many thousands of Negroes, free and slave. Not the stereotype plantation darkies, these men were expert boatmen and teamsters and skilled craftsmen—butchers, curriers, bakers, coopers, wheelwrights, wagonmakers, blacksmiths, millers, boatmakers, ropemakers, shoemakers, mechanics, harnessmakers, and bricklayers. This Negro labor force was ever present in the multiple operations required by the Quartermaster and Commissary departments.[1]

There is no definitive study of the Confederate Quartermaster and Commissary. Infrequent historical publications are usually oriented toward a special problem of Southern subsistence and are of limited value in providing information pertaining to the structure of the services of supply within the South. Consequently, the war records of the Negro labor force, an incalculable addition to Confederate logistics, do not lend themselves to ready synthesis. Their story, however, will contribute to the understanding of the Confederacy's preparation to support her armies in the field.[2] The sprawling system of supply services required constant stockpiling of provisions at several depots throughout Virginia for transportation by trains, boats, or wagons to the combat zones. The details of providing Negro workers for these tasks were usually left for local commanders to work out with the various state and local officials. Subsequently, post and depot commanders throughout Virginia either employed or utilized local hiring agents to procure slaves and free blacks. This policy proved to be somewhat successful and was continued throughout the war. Quartermaster officers, however, were frequently forced to impress Negroes for public service on the ground "of exigencies imposed by the conflict."[3] Fighting forces in Virginia were supplied from a system of quartermaster posts or depots—general, advance, or temporary—scattered throughout the Tidewater, Piedmont, Valley, and southwestern Virginia. The Richmond and Lynchburg depots were the chief depositories for receiving, stockpiling, and delivering supplies. Richmond's logistical activities towered in contrast with those of other parts of the state. As headquarters of the Quartermaster Department, it was the point to which General Lee's armies submitted requisition. It was beset with the necessity of maintaining teamsters and boatmen for land and water transportation. And obviously, supply services in Richmond had to expand domestic production largely by Negro labor and by creating their own facilities—government shops, shoe factories, saw mills, boat construction yards, harness shops, bakeries, and clothing factories.[4]

II

Richmond's quartermaster officers could not have tackled the many problems of Confederate logistics if thousands of Negro laborers had not been available. Early in 1862 Major J. B. Harvie was put in charge of water transportation for the Richmond area. The Richmond wharves were essential to troop movements for hauling war materials and for the reshipment of tons of food, feed, and other cargoes gathered from various locations throughout the state. Vessels laden with supplies constantly plied the waters of the James, York, Rappahannock, Pamunkey, Appomattox, and North Anna rivers. Cargoes were deposited at the Richmond docks and subsequently transferred to several large warehouses for stockpiling. Several of these vessels were owned by the Quartermaster Department. During the course of the war, government vessels under the command of Harvie included at least 17 canal boats, 2 batteaux, and 2 towing barges. The crews of these 21 vessels consisted of 103 Negro boatmen (84 slaves and 19 free men). Such boatmen were employed at a monthly wage of $25 with clothing furnished by the government, or $33 a month without clothing. By the end of 1864 inflation had caused their salaries to increase to $75 per month.

In the fall of 1862 another vessel, the Confederate States Steamer *Logan*, was acquired by the Quartermaster Department. Among its 29 crew members were 19 Negroes—10 whip hands, 5 deck hands, 1 teamster, 1 cook, 1 cook's boy, and 1 cabin maid. At all of Richmond's wharves and boatyards several gangs of Negro stevedores were on hand to load and unload provisions, while many additional Negroes labored as sawyers, shipwrights, wagoners, boatmen, caulkers, blacksmiths, and carpenters. Two free Negroes, for example, John Gordon and George Sprills, and one slave, William, were hired as ship carpenters at $1,200 annually. Jim, a slave shipwright, was chiefly employed in mending, repairing, and caulking vessels. John T. Smith and Robert Fagan, free blacks, worked as blacksmiths.[5] Two free Negroes, Clem Young, a boatman from Richmond County, and John Gibson, a wagonmaker from Rockingham County, were detailed to Major Harvie by the Bureau of Conscription in the spring of 1864. Virginia's colored boatmen were described as among the best to be found in southern waters. T. C. De Leon felt obliged to record a colorful Civil War description of the Negro boatmen he observed in southern waters:

> A splendidly developed race are those Africans of the river boats, with shiny, black skins, through which the corded and tense muscles seem to be bursting, even in repose. Their only dress, as a general thing, is a pair of loose pantaloons, to which the more elegant add a fancy colored bandanna knotted about the head, with its wing-like ends flying in the wind; but shirts are a rarity in working hours and their absence shows a breadth of shoulder and depth of chest remarkable, when contrasted with the length and lank power in the nether limbs.[6]

Like Major Harvie, other Richmond quartermaster officers made effective use of Negro labor, free and slave. This was especially true of Major John C. Maynard, Assistant Quartermaster, who was in charge of receiving and delivering all supplies arriving at Richmond for the Quartermaster, Ordnance, Commissary, Engineer, Navy, and Medical departments. He was also in charge of warehouses and storage of surplus baggage belonging to the Army of Northern Virginia. Maynard's previous experience had taught him the value of a division of labor, and he organized his civilian staff accordingly, with a superintendent in charge of each of the five categories under his command.

The five categories were procurement of food and forage, land transportation, storage, fuel, and domestic production and repair. Each of the large colored labor groups within each category was placed under the direct supervision of one or more superintendents. In January 1863, for example, George B. West, superintendent of forage, employed over 280 Negroes (principally slaves) in the vicinity of Richmond.[7] P. A. Webster, the superintendent of forage warehouses, was responsible for stockpiling all forage delivered by the 160 Negro teamsters who were under the supervision of C. J. Hatcher. The teamsters' salaries ranged from $200 to $400 annually. Approximately 40 Negroes were kept on hand by Superintendent Webster to attend to the unloading of forage.[8] Apparently several hundred additional Negroes were employed in other Richmond warehouses and quartermaster installations. In May 1862, twenty were engaged in the storage of tobacco. During the hiring season in December 1862, Captain W. E. Warren reported that he hired 112 Negroes to work in the government warehouses in Richmond.[9] Between 1862 and 1865 the Quartermaster Department assigned to Major John H. Parkhill the additional duty of securing Negro help for the Confederate States Barracks, hostler headquarters, offices, and warehouses. These Negroes served in various capacities such as messengers, porters, and cooks. Sully Wright, a slave nurse, was hired by Major Parkhill to assist Dr. Lyon (assigned by the medical director) in giving medical attention to hired hands. Many of the colored employees were frequently called upon to work overtime and on weekends. It was not uncommon for money earned in such extra work to be paid directly to the slaves. In June 1864 Superintendent Webster included in his monthly payroll a figure of $639 to be paid to 32 Negroes for overtime work. During the same month, C. J. Hatcher submitted a voucher calling for $2,256 to be paid to 140 teamsters who put in extra time.[10]

Working closely with the local transportation superintendents were superintendents of government stables, who retained Negro farriers, blacksmiths, and strikers. Hatcher employed nine skilled slave blacksmiths to work in the blacksmith shops adjacent to the stables.[11] Each slave was hired by the year for $1,000, and much of his time was consumed in making horseshoes and nails.

Another Quartermaster responsibility was to provide fuel for government buildings and military commands. Both the government sawmill and woodyards required a large labor force of Negroes. Seven-

teen slaves were employed for work on the wood train, each receiving
$300 annually for loading and unloading wood fuel. The cut wood
was shipped to Richmond for stockpiling and future delivery by a
special crew of yard hands. One of the largest of the many government sawmills was located in Fluvanna County under the supervision
of H. H. George. Fifteen slave sawyers were regularly engaged in
felling trees and other cutting operations at salaries ranging from $300
to $600 yearly, but one highly skilled slave sawyer named John,
owned by John Buschett, was employed at $1,500 annually. Addi-
tional Negroes were on hand to haul cut timber to the wood train.[12]

Government repair and construction shops on the outskirts of
Richmond employed several skilled Negro craftsmen. Major R. P.
Archer was in command of one such shop located at Bacon's Quarter
Branch. There John H. Gentry superintended the work of almost
200 Negroes and 55 white employees. Major Archer's duties involved
the receipt of unserviceable field transportation, the construction and
repair of wagons, ambulances, and such equipment as harnesses, sad-
dles, bridles, and collars. He was also responsible for the purchase and
issuance of field transportation, the operation of shops for shoeing
horses and mules, and the manufacture of horseshoes and nails. An additional duty was to supervise the Confederate States Ambulance
Shop, an extensive ambulance works located on the docks 2½ miles
from Bacon's Quarter Branch. This shop worked closely with the
Petersburg Wagon Shop, commanded by Captain G. C. Reid, where
eight Negroes—seven blacksmiths and one wheelwright—were making wheels for the government. In reporting on the many activities
conducted under his command Major Archer wrote that he "serviced
in my stables and yards, at one time, as many as 2600 animals and
1500 wagons." The major also noted that his employees worked from
4:30 A.M. to 8:00 P.M.[13] There were eight trades in which the more
than a hundred skilled Negro laborers at Bacon's Quarter Branch
were engaged—harnessmaker, blacksmith, carpenter, wagonmaker,
painter, farrier, wheelwright, and bricklayer. Eighty-six additional
blacks were employed as hostlers, sawyers, shop assistants, stock
drivers, teamsters, and yard hands. Henry, a slave harnessmaker
owned by John M. Gregory, was hired at $1,200 annually. Four slave
blacksmiths—George, John, Jim, and Dick—also received $1,200
each, and five others—Jordan, Williams, Jackson, Henry, and Beverly—were each hired for an annual wage of $1,000. No fewer than

sixty-three blacksmiths and helpers were employed by Superintendent Gentry.[14] Sam, a slave boy, served as a messenger for Major Archer and the superintendent.

Like Bacon's Quarter Branch, Major Archer's Confederate States Ambulance Shop was engaged in extensive repair and construction of wagons and ambulances. Captain R. C. MacMurdo, who administered this shop, was responsible for the purchase of materials to repair and construct ambulances and for the manufacture of wagon spokes. D. C. McMinn, the shop superintendent, employed 32 white and 23 Negro skilled laborers. The spoke lathe, for example, was operated by a slave, Jack, whose owner, E. P. W. Apperson, was paid $2.50 daily for his services, and an additional $5.00 for the hire of Mat Black, a slave machinist. Wages varied between $2.50 and $5.00 for the services of Negro craftsmen, but most were paid $5.00 a day. Eleven of the 23 artisans were free Negroes—4 blacksmiths, 5 sawyers, 1 carpenter, and 1 ambulance painter; 12 were slaves—10 blacksmiths and 2 machinists.[15]

III

The Quartermaster Post at Lynchburg commanded by R. E. Colston, like the Richmond Quartermaster Headquarters, was a vital supply artery. As the main depot for the Army of Northern Virginia, it was the key to the inside lines of communication and supply which enabled Confederate troops to be moved from one line of defense to another, west, east, and north. Here were gathered and stockpiled quartermaster and commissary supplies from the rich productive territory lying between Lynchburg and Knoxville, Tennessee. A vast quantity of supplies were also secured from the productive lands tributary to the Virginia and Tennessee Railroad. Consequently, the Lynchburg depot remained the agricultural heart of Lee's armies. Yet, without the labor skills and brawn of free and slave Negroes employed by the Lynchburg and other depots scattered throughout the Piedmont, the Army of Northern Virginia would probably not have sustained its expenditure of energy.

Construction and repair at the Lynchburg depot was conducted through the post quartermaster, Captain E. McCormick. Although McCormick supervised three government shops—carpenter, wheelwright, and blacksmith—Superintendent C. H. Locker was in charge of shop personnel. The enormous amount of work to be done in the three government shops required more than three hundred white and Negro skilled laborers. For example, besides the usual post construction and repairs, cavalry horses were shod, defective harnesses, bridles, and collars were mended or replaced, and supply wagons and ambulances were repaired. The Table 2.1 lists the Negroes employed in the Lynchburg government shops as submitted to the Adjutant and the Inspector General Office. In reporting to the Adjutant and the Inspector General Office on these shop employees, Inspector A. C. Cunningham remarked:

These hands are fully employed and kept at their work industriously. The workmanship in every branch is very fine, and all materials economized, and worked up to the best advantage. Locker's men are well provided in every particular. Shoes of a much superior quality to any furnished the army are made for his employees. Clothes also have been furnished them by buying up material which had been thrown aside. . . . I would suggest that a surgeon and medical supplies be furnished as the Negroes . . . are good mechanics, and of great service, and their health is of grave importance. . . . The same would apply to . . . all Negroes under Major Paxton's charge.[16]

Table 2.1 *Negro employees in government shops, Lynchburg, Virginia, 1864–1865*

Occupation	Slaves	Free Negroes
Blacksmiths and strikers	145	3
Boatmakers	8	—
Boatmen	15	—
Wheelwrights and carpenters	16	1
Cooks	4	—
Laborers	30	—
Ropemakers	16	1
Shoemakers	18	1
Tanners	1	—
Teamsters	8	—
Totals	261	6

Fifty-five whites (detailed soldiers, conscripts, disabled men) worked systematically with the 266 blacks employed in the government shops. Superintendent Locker maintained a separate mess hall, kitchens, and living quarters for his Negro employees. Commissary supplies were obtained by trading cotton yarns and tobacco. Hides of every description were saved to make leather for shoes, bridles, harnesses, and collars.

Another significant Negro labor force worked for John R. Todd, who was in charge of the niter works at the Lynchburg post. In 1862 niter, obtained from the many niter beds located on the outskirts of town, was hauled to the post shops where other employees (principally Negroes) refined from 900 to 1,000 pounds per day.

Undoubtedly Major J. G. Paxton, Post Field Transportation Officer, engaged the services of the largest number of Negroes. Besides providing field transportation, two other major responsibilities of Major Paxton involved extensive forage and horse-procurement operations. Paxton was assisted by Captain D. L. Hopkins and two bonded agents, W. Coles and G. M. Bruce. Captain Hopkins provided forage for animals in the Army of Northern Virginia, plus cavalry and draft horses purchased or impressed for government use. Agent Coles was in charge of unserviceable military animals, while agent Bruce made periodic inspections to determine which animals had responded sufficiently to treatment to be returned to Lee's armies. Bruce also assisted in purchasing and impressing horses for the government. Paxton and his agents, during the last two years of the war, obtained 4,929 horses and mules in Virginia at an average price of $524.00.

On August 10, 1863, Colonel John R. Chambliss, Jr., commander of Lee's Cavalry Brigade, recommended "the establishment of a veterinary hospital in some locality secure from cavalry raids, convenient and accessible to the main railroad communications." He also suggested that Negroes be hired to attend to the horses and that sheds or coverings for the winter season be constructed.[17] Subsequently, a horse and mule infirmary was established in the Lynchburg region in October 1863. Most of the animals were not sent to this infirmary until they were worn out. Many developed glanders and had to be destroyed; others were simply too exhausted to recover. Major Paxton reported that from October 1863 to January 1865 he received 6,875 horses from the army, of which only 1,057 recovered. He added that 2,844 had died, 133 had been lost or rustled, 559 had been condemned and sold, 799 had been transferred to an infirmary farther south, and the remaining 1,483 were still unserviceable. Of the 2,855 mules received, 1,644 recovered, 575 died, and the remainder were still under treatment.[18]

Paxton claimed that 7,000 horses and 14,000 mules were required every fifteen months in Lee's army and neighboring posts for artillery and transportation. Under these conditions it was essential to supply sufficient labor to provide proper care for these animals. Walter Coles, in whose custody the animals were placed, employed 83 whites and 179 blacks (19 free, 160 slave) for this task. The slave-owners of surrounding counties were assured that those who furnished slaves to manage the Confederate stables would not be called upon to furnish slaves to work on fortifications. Over 60 slaves were supplied by citizens in Henry county in 1864, and their owners petitioned the governor to give them proper credit for their slaves.

Like providing care for almost 10,000 unserviceable animals, the procurement of forage demanded a large Negro labor force. Hired agents and impressment officers combed all the countryside within reach of the Lynchburg depot for Negro laborers. With some difficulty 90 Negroes were hired from Campbell County. Many more were secured from neighboring Roanoke, Montgomery, Bedford, Franklin, Floyd, and Bath counties. Finally, 244 Negroes, 44 whites, 39 horses, and 55 mules were engaged in the winter of 1864–1865 in collecting and baling forage throughout the Piedmont and Valley.[19] In each of the forage districts Captain McCormick divided the colored workers into two groups, one to collect and the other to bale forage. Additional Negro teamsters were hired from the various counties to haul forage to the Lynchburg post. Once the forage reached this point, Captain W. M. Jones was responsible for prompt shipment to the Army of Northern Virginia. Each Negro teamster from the Lynchburg post was issued a cap, pants, shirt, shoes, and private's uniform jacket.[20]

Apparently there were few, if any, departments in the vast Lynchburg post where Negro labor was not in great demand. Both Captain John Brannon, post tax-in-kind officer for the Seventh Congressional District, and Major John M. Galt, post commissary, required the services of many hundreds as teamsters, butchers, drovers, draymen, bakers, warehouse hands, and boatmen. At times the same was true of Captain F. Hutter, who was in charge of the shipment of all local and through freight by the different railroads serving Lynchburg. His assistants consisted of a transportation master, 2 clerks, a storekeeper, a wagonmaster, and 15 Negroes—12 teamsters, 2 laborers, and 1 messenger.[21] Yet, the most energetic efforts during the war years failed to obtain a sufficient supply of colored workers for the many needs of the post. It was not uncommon for Post Quartermaster McCormick to sign contracts with local citizens to employ their slaves to perform specific functions. In 1862, for example, William and Robert Scott contracted to have their slaves supply the post with wood.[22]

IV

Heavy reliance was also placed on Negro labor by other Piedmont quartermasters for extensive use in government shops, sawmills, freightyards, and boatyards. In 1863 the government shops at the Salem depot employed at least 21 slaves—9 shoemakers, 2 blacksmiths, 5 teamsters, and 1 hostler.[23] After inspecting the Burkeville depot, Colonel A. S. Cunningham notified the Quartermaster General that he "recommended a shifting engine be furnished Captain Waggoner as the time of his Negro laborers is very much taken up in shifting the [freight] cars from one track to the other." The colonel noted that such an engine would facilitate shipments of supplies to the Army of Northern Virginia.[24] The Burkeville depot was located at a key railroad terminal in Piedmont, Virginia, where essential war supplies were shipped over the Virginia and Tennessee Railroad to Lynchburg, and from there to the Burkeville depot. Similarly war supplies from North Carolina were hauled over the Piedmont Railroad to Danville, and then to Burkeville over the Richmond-Danville Railroad. From this point, rail deliveries were made to and from Richmond. Captain Waggoner employed Negroes to load and unload freight and to deliver supplies.

Like the Burkeville depot, the Clarksville depot was strategically located. In March 1864 Captain J. E. Haskins, post quartermaster, appealed to Governor Smith for authority to impress Negro boatmen and blacksmiths from Charlotte and Mecklenburg counties. The governor was informed that such Negro boatmen would be used on the Roanoke River and its tributaries in transporting government stores. Captain Haskins advertised in the Richmond *Examiner* for twenty Negro boatmen and promised that "persons hiring my Negroes for this work will be allowed credit for them if further impressment should be made by the government."[25] Several miles west of Clarksville was the Danville post, another important railroad junction. In 1863 almost 200 Negroes were employed in the repair and construction of wagons, in warehouses, in handling freight, and in forage operations. For example, 10 carpenters, 5 blacksmiths, 1 wheelwright, and 9 wood choppers worked in the government shops.[26] Captain H. Robertson was responsible for the procurement and delivery of forage, and was assisted by a large labor force of Negroes. One gang was engaged in collecting, another in stacking, and a third in baling forage. Once the forage had been baled, twenty-five Negro boatmen transported it by batteaux on the Dan and Staunton rivers. Fifty-two Negro teamsters were available to deliver the forage to Lee's armies or to the Danville post. Another gang of blacks was hired to handle all freight delivered by the Piedmont or Richmond-Danville railroads.[27]

Quartermaster operations were also quite extensive in the Shenandoah Valley—the "Valley District"—located between the Blue Ridge and Allegheny mountains. Few reliable facts are available on the extent of Negro involvement in the quartermaster depots of this productive area. In 1864 Captain T. H. Tutwiler, the post quartermaster of the Lexington depot, reported that he issued clothing to 38 Negroes working at the post—25 slaves and 13 free blacks. Among the 13 free blacks were 2 female cooks, Nell Hays and Mary Jones.[28]

Perhaps the largest labor force of Negroes gathered together in the Valley was at the Staunton depot. Many skilled workers were employed in the government wagon, blacksmith, and gun shops. In 1861 two slave harnessmakers, Jinks and Joe, worked in the gun shop.[29] The smith shop employed 39 slaves to make horseshoes and horseshoe nails. In February 1863 they manufactured 6,689 horseshoes and 31,588 horseshoe nails. A slave was paid an average of 5 cents for each ordinary shoe and as high as 8 cents for special shoes.[30] Another 44 slave blacksmiths labored in the wagon factory; and when not assisting in the repair or construction of wagons, they were expected to manufacture shoes and nails. For example, in June 1862 Captain R. Turk reported that they made 960 shoes and 29,885 nails.[31] There were also 23 slave teamsters employed to haul supplies.[32] In all, some 121 Negroes seem to have been employed at the Staunton post. At the Warrenton depot, a gateway into the Valley, the quartermaster operated a government stable commanded by Captain W. W. Weisinger, who was assigned 14 slaves—6 stock drivers, 3 hostlers, and 5 teamsters.[33]

Quartermaster warehouses in the western Piedmont were also stocked with provisions gathered from southwestern Virginia. The tons of provisions which moved daily from these remote western outposts were delivered largely by Negro teamsters and boatmen. It was no easy task to haul heavy loads over rugged mountain paths, bad roads, and swollen rivers and streams. The major quartermaster depots in southwest Virginia were found at Narrows New River and Central, Dublin, Abingdon, Wytheville, Marion, and Montgomery Springs. As with the Valley District there is insufficient information available to determine the number of blacks employed by each of these quartermaster offices. Major J. Green, commanding the Department of Southwest Virginia, retained 19 Negro teamsters and laborers to haul and store grain, wool, leather, and other provisions purchased or impressed by his agents.[34] From 1863 to 1865 Captain V. G. de l'Isle, post quartermaster of Narrows New River and Central depot, employed 29 Negroes—18 boatmen, 7 teamsters, 1 stable hand, and 3 warehouse hands.[35]

A few miles to the south other Negroes labored at the Abingdon and Dublin depots. At the Abingdon post, for example, 8 blacksmiths, 4 teamsters, and 5 depot hands (all Negro) were assisting Captain W. Rodefer.[36] In May 1864 Colonel G. B. Crittenden authorized the impressment of 9 slaves as drivers for six-horse, four-horse, and two-horse wagons. These and other impressed slaves also carried the wounded from the battlefield, loaded and unloaded freight cars, shifted grain, and so forth.[37] Two months later the Bureau of Conscription detailed 24 free blacks to the Abingdon post.[38] Apparently the Dublin depot employed at least 34 free blacks and 24 slaves as boatmen, teamsters, woodchoppers, and warehouse hands.[39] Similarly Captain J. R. Ward of the Wytheville depot made extensive use of Negro labor. In November 1864 the depot diverted its Negro manpower (10 free blacks and 42 slaves) to the collection and hauling of forage.[40] At the Montgomery Springs depot Captain E. Gibson was assisted by 20 Negroes—9 teamsters, 7 woodchoppers, 1 blacksmith, 1 stable hand, 1 cook and 1 messenger.[41]

Regardless of heavy rains, extremely cold weather, and bad roads, Negro teamsters penetrated into every inhabited part of Virginia, gathering food, forage, supplies, and equipment, and hauling these supplies to the nearest quartermaster or railroad depot. Once the supplies were stockpiled at the depots, the most important and immediate problem was to see that they reached the armies in the field. Here again, the Negro teamster served purposefully, driving the wagon supply trains of Lee's armies and the military posts in Virginia. Negro teamsters in Virginia alone numbered in the thousands. While exact figures cannot be verified, records show conclusively that hundreds of slaves were impressed in the field as teamsters, other hundreds were attached to regiments and brigades of the Army of Northern Virginia, and well over a thousand Negro teamsters were employed by Virginia quartermasters throughout the state.[42]

V

Like the quartermasters, the commissaries were hampered by a shortage of Negro manpower in their efforts to provide food and supplies. To feed Lee's armies Lucius B. Northrop, the commissary general, established several post commissaries throughout Virginia. Northrop also assigned commissary officers to military posts in the state. Eventually the Bureau of Subsistence in Richmond became the main supply depot for stockpiling provisions that were purchased or impressed by commissary agents and officers. Unfortunately, all general records of the Commissary General of Subsistence Office were destroyed in the Richmond fire of April 3, 1865, and only those of a few commissaries of subsistence serving with military commands are available. Virginia Negroes, free and slave, served the Commissary Department as butchers, bakers, cattle drivers, teamsters, boatmen, millers, and packers. The greatest number of Negroes, however, were employed in slaughterhouses, railroad depots, wharves, and military posts. For example, in 1862 and 1863 the Richmond meat and packing house employed fifty slaves.[43] Jacob and Chester, slave butchers, cut meat in the Richmond slaughterhouse, and Charles, Marshall, and George worked in the Confederate States Bakery.[44] The payrolls submitted by the commissaries stationed at military posts or depots such as Smithfield, Burkesville, Waverly, Lynchburg, Danville, and Charlottesville include the names of slaves and free blacks hired as porters, freight hands, drovers, and teamsters.[45] In November 1862 Captain R. H. Vaughan, a commissary officer stationed at Gordonsville, employed 9 Negroes at $20 a month per man.[46] Captain J. N. Crockett issued shirts, drawers, boots, and blankets to 18 Negro teamsters attached to the Division Commissary Train.[47] At the large Danville post, Captain T. S. Knox served as the post commissary. In September 1862 his Negro labor force numbered 30, of whom 24 were slaves. William and George, both slaves, served as messengers in the commissary office. When rations were furnished by the owner, a slave was paid $30 a month; otherwise the wages were $20 monthly. Three slaves, Tom, Joe, and Armistead, were employed in the issuing department of the commissary warehouses.[48] The functions of Negro teamsters attached to commissaries with military units were limited to trips to depots to procure provisions and to driving the supply wagons en route to combat. Normally 7 wagons were needed to provision 10,000 men for one day: 3 for bacon, 3 for flour, and 1 for miscellaneous stores. Beef traveled on the hoof, usually attended by Negro drovers. Likewise the commissary officers at military posts in the Valley employed Negro cattle drivers. For example, in 1862 Captain J. T. Stuart employed 14 slaves as cattle drivers, and Captain R. W. N. Noland, in the spring of 1863, hired 6 Negroes—5 slaves and 1 free.[49]

Both the Quartermaster and Commissary departments were conscious of the logistical importance of Negro manpower, and they competed effectively with other departments for their services. As the needs to increase the war output multiplied rapidly, both the Virginia and the Confederate governments made provisions for placing the black noncombatants at the disposal of the services of supply through military hire, impressment, and conscription. From February 1864 to March 1865 the Bureau of Conscription detailed 341 Negroes to the quartermasters scattered throughout Virginia. As in any undertaking which involves large numbers of persons, the Negroes who met the needs of supply will forever remain anonymous to posterity. Yet thousands and thousands of Negroes played a vital part in feeding, supplying, and sustaining Confederate combat forces in Virginia.

CHAPTER THREE

Naval and Ordnance Works

As Confederate war needs mounted, so did the urgency for Negro labor. Since the five hundred or more Negroes employed in Virginia's naval works were few compared to the multitude employed in other areas such as ordnance, niter mining, and iron works, the significance of their contribution to the war effort becomes a real question. The answer is to be sought in the importance of Virginia's naval ordnance works to the Confederacy and in the extent to which Negro dexterity and brawn proved indispensable in procuring materials and in matching the needs of naval ordnance. Coal, naval stores, and seasoned timber had to be assembled, while boilers, heavy plate iron, engines, rope, and many other materials which went into the construction of steamers and gunboats had to be fabricated.

On the eve of the Civil War a meaningful segment of Virginia's skilled labor force consisted of Negro machinists, shipwrights, carpenters, blacksmiths, coopers, and miners. Colored pilots, boatmen, fishermen, and stevedores likewise held an important place in the internal navigation of the state. One Negro, John Updike of Petersburg, owned sloops and schooners which included the *Jolly Sailor*, the *Two Brothers*, the *Janett*, and the *William and Mary*. Another Negro boatman, Richard Parsons of Campbell County, owned nine slaves and several small boats.[1] As shipbuilding, lumbering, iron forges, ropewalks, and naval stores increased in size and number, especially during the 1850's, the demand for free Negro and slave workers grew. Help was also needed for the blacksmith shop, the tannery, and the docks. The wide variety of occupational opportunities proved to be a valuable training school for Virginia blacks. By 1861 there were numerous colored people with a background in maritime technology who could augment the forces available for Confederate naval needs.

The Confederate Congress established a Navy Department by an act approved on February 21, 1861, and Stephen R. Mallory was named as its secretary. The Navy Department was organized into four bureaus: Ordnance and Hydrography, Orders and Details, Medicine and Surgery, and Provisions and Clothing. Of the four bureaus, Ordnance and Hydrography employed the largest number of Negroes. The records of the bureaus are fragmentary, and reports indicate that most were destroyed during their removal from Richmond to Charlotte, North Carolina, late in the war. Nevertheless, existing records conclusively establish the role of Virginia Negroes in helping to accomplish the gigantic task facing Ordnance and Hydrography.

Virginia's resources were largely in the raw and unmanufactured state: timber for ships stood in the forest, but had to be cut; iron ore and coal were available, but had to be mined; hemp required for rope had to be procured; and sufficient manpower had to be mustered to serve the many needs of naval ordnance shops and boatyards. By the fall of 1861 large gangs of blacks had been hired to assemble commodities: seasoned timber, tar, pitch, turpentine, lubricants, minerals, and niter.

Richmond, headquarters of the Navy Department, maintained five major naval installations: an ordnance work, a navy yard, and a naval station, laboratory, and academy. In 1862 the naval ordnance shop was manufacturing, repairing, and distributing ship parts and other necessities. Lieutenant J. D. Minor commanded the shop, and R. B. Wright, the shop superintendant, secured from local slaveholders a total of 36 slaves: 3 machinists, 8 carpenters, 4 boilermakers, 2 firemen, 8 blacksmiths, 3 molders, and 8 shop hands. Nat Jackson, Kingston Price, and Willis Scott, slave machinists, were hired at $4.00, $3.50, and $3.25, respectively, for each day's work. The hire for one slave boilermaker, John, was set at $2.00 per day, while the other three—Joe, Toby, and Henry—were hired out for $1.75 daily.[2] From Talbott & Son, the owners of a Richmond foundry, additional slave technicians were hired. This ordnance shop supplied nearly all the equipment for the gun vessels of the James River Squadron and also manufactured carriages for the heavy guns used in naval shore batteries.

Like the ordnance shop, the Richmond navy yard (Rocketts) employed both skilled and unskilled Negro workers. The workers were under the supervision of Lieutenant J. H. Parker. In writing about typical Confederate navy yards William N. Still, Jr., asserted that Naval Secretary Mallory took control of several privately owned boatyards in order to "construct or to equip vessels." Still portrayed such yards as "often no more than a small clear area on a beach, or the bank of a river, creek, or inlet, just deep enough for launching."[3] Inland river towns became important construction centers, particularly after the capture of Norfolk in the spring of 1862. According to Still, interior sites provided more security from attack, and the decision was made to locate naval facilities in the interior whenever possible. Hence, Richmond afforded an excellent site for a navy yard. In December 1862 the navy yard employed 87 blacks: 32 axemen, 11 sawyers, 2 cooks, 3 boat hands, 4 caulkers, 15 carpenters, 3 whitewashers, and 17 yard hands.[4] The available records disclose that a few of the naval officers from time to time hired their own slaves in the navy yards. Lieutenant R. Minor, for example, received a total of $3.00 a day for Randolph and Villy, first class axemen, and Lieutenant Parker was paid $3.75 daily for his two slaves, Charles and Davy. Nevertheless, there was always a labor shortage, and in December 1862 the Richmond *Whig* advertised for "150 able bodied Negro men, with axes to cut and hew timber near Richmond, for the Confederate States Navy Department."

Directly across from the Rocketts Navy Yard was the Richmond Naval Station which also used colored laborers. In 1863 James Meade, the master builder, supervised no fewer than 67 skilled Negro technicians—7 caulkers, 3 joiners, 19 carpenters, 1 sawyer, 2 bricklayers, 3 whitewashers, 26 blacksmiths and helpers, 1 fireman, and 5 machinists. The $7.00 daily hire paid to the owner of Joe Thomas, an exceptionally skilled slave blacksmith, made Joe one of the highest paid among the naval employees. The other blacksmiths averaged from $3.50 to $5.00 a day; the seven caulkers were hired for $4.50 daily; each owner of the three slave joiners—Isaac, William, and Joe—received $3.50 for a day's work. The remaining 55 workers brought the total number of Negroes employed at the Naval Station to 122.[5] When Confederate authorities finally took steps to effect a more satisfactory method of obtaining free Negro labor, the Richmond Naval Station and installations were able to secure additional help. In 1864 the Bureau of Conscription detailed 61 free conscripts for work in the naval ordnance shops and boatyard. Subsequently, 3 machinists— Henry Lewis, John Nickens, and Thomas Cole—as well as 5 blacksmiths and 17 laborers were assigned to the naval ordnance works.

An additional 36 free blacks were assigned to the naval station and Rocketts Navy Yard; these were 3 bodymakers, 1 cooper, 3 carpenters, 3 blacksmiths, 1 shoemaker, and 25 laborers. James Roberts, Thomas Smith, and James Woodson, skilled bodymakers, worked directly under the supervision of the master builder of the naval station.[6]

In Petersburg, some twenty-odd miles south of Richmond, the Navy operated two other facilities, a powder works and a ropewalk. In 1862 the powder works, operated by Chief Engineer T. A. Jackson, produced an excellent grade of powder, employed 17 whites as powdermen and wheelwrights, as well as 15 blacks in the capacities of powdermen, millwright, coal burners, oiler, carpenters, and driver.[7] Although its operations were limited, the ropewalk furnished cordage for gunboats, railroads, and the quartermaster. One of the slave technicians blended tar with cotton to make a substitute for hemp cordage.

Aside from the Petersburg and Richmond naval works, three important boatyards were located in the city of West Point, and Fluvanna and Powhatan counties. These interior yards, within a 45-mile radius of Richmond, offset somewhat the serious deficiencies in river gunboats. In 1862, the West Point yard employed twenty-one whites and forty-three blacks—sawyers, laborers and a cook. It also operated three smaller neighboring boatyards at Romancoke, Randolph Farm, and Indian Town which engaged respectively 34, 8, and 12 Negroes.[8] In Fluvanna County, Captain T. R. Rootes and a white foreman supervised a naval station which employed in 1863–1864 approximately 57 Negroes as teamsters, canal boat hands, blacksmiths, boat captains, and axemen. The two captains Isaac Howell, a free person, and Samuel George, a slave, were each paid $2.50; and two slave blacksmiths each received $3.59 daily.[9] The Keswick and Mosely Farm navy yards, located in Powhatan County, were also commanded by Captain Rootes. In 1862 the Keswick yard employed 47 Negroes —24 axemen, 2 cooks, 3 teamsters, 1 blacksmith, 13 laborers, and 4 boys. At the Mosely Farm yard Negro carpenters and shipwrights assisted in the construction of several Maury gunboats. At least 49 Negroes—axemen, carpenters, blacksmith, teamsters, cooks, boatmen, and barge hands—served at the Mosely yards.[10]

The Confederate Navy Department's hope for increased domestic production in naval essentials also included limited mining efforts in southwest Virginia. Only a small portion of the iron ore and coal used by the navy came from this remote mountain area. The ore bank at Purgatory Mountain was worked by two blacks and four whites under the direction of Henry Foreman. In 1864 Peter Wilson, foreman of the Stone Cave Gap naval coal mines in Botetourt County, was assisted by nine Negro colliers and nine whites.[11]

As in the naval coal mines operation, there were apparently very few Virginia Negroes hired to serve on Confederate vessels. During the months that the Confederacy controlled the Gosport Navy Yard, for example, Flag Officer French Forest ordered five Negroes to report for duty on the Receiving Frigate *Confederate States* (formerly the *United States*).[12] Perhaps the largest number served with the James River Squadron, but very few of its official records survive. Table 3.1 gives a sampling of Negroes who served in the maritime

Table 3.1 *Negro seamen in the James River Squadron*[13]

Name of vessel	Landsman	Cook	Deckhand	Fireman
Harriet Lane	6	1	—	—
Patrick Henry	3	—	—	—
West Point	3	—	—	—
Virginia	—	—	2	—
Paul Jones	—	—	4	8
Battery Buchanan	1	—	—	—
Totals	13	1	6	8

service. Slave craftsmen also engaged in maintaining and repairing the vessels of the James River Squadron. In May 1862 the gunboat *Hampton* was repaired by four slave carpenters—Shad, Jacob, Stephen, and Willis—at the shipyard near Norfolk.[14] The Richmond *Examiner* on January 27, 1863, advertised for two slave "lightermen" to serve on a large flat cargo vessel which operated on the James River from Drewry's Bluff to Richmond.

The sinew and craftsmanship of Virginia Negroes contributed much to Confederate naval ordnance and navy yards. They worked diligently procuring raw materials and fabricating naval essentials. Beset with a blockade which eventually sealed Virginia from the outside world, the state had to depend upon the maritime skills of its Negro population. Yet, the need for Negro labor by the Confederate ordnance was far greater than that of the Navy Department.

II

The Ordnance Bureau of the War Department, headed by Josiah Gorgas, was responsible for providing the Confederate armies with weapons and war materials.[15] As Chief of Ordnance, Gorgas worked with tremendous zeal to increase the Confederacy's pathetically small supply of available guns and munitions. During the first two years of the war the South produced only 10 per cent of its small-arms requirements and was forced largely to rely upon munitions seized from Federal arsenals or purchased in Europe. Nevertheless, continual expansion of the domestic manufacture of military stores and munitions led to the establishment of a variety of war industries within Virginia. A production arsenal, armory, supply depot, and laboratory were established in Richmond, and two important arsenals were located in Danville and Lynchburg. Iron, coal, lead, copper, and zinc works were operating in the Piedmont and southwestern sections of Virginia. There were small ordnance depots at Dublin, Lexington, Abingdon, and Staunton; a large harness shop was established in Clarksville. To offset the shortage of saltpeter (or niter), one of the essential ingredients (along with sulfur and charcoal) of gunpowder, the Confederate Congress in 1862 created the Niter and Mining Bureau. Virginia was rich enough in industrial raw materials, but unless these could be converted into finished products, the South's reliance on costly European goods would continue. While white manpower was occupied in holding the Union at bay, something had to be done to fulfill the enormous labor requirements of Confederate ordnance manufacture. Consequently, with wartime expansion of general manufacturing, black manpower was indispensable to the arms and munition industry which sprang up in Virginia.

Since there was no time for new production facilities to be built, ordnance officers had to manage with existing or makeshift accommodations in Richmond, Farmville, Danville, Lynchburg, and Clarksville. In June 1861 the Ordnance Bureau began operations in Richmond by taking possession of the large state armory and several tobacco factories, which were converted into arsenals and supply depots. It took over and operated the machinery of several iron mills in the city. By the end of 1862, Richmond's arsenals were turning out a modest supply of rifles, cartridges, gun carriages and caissons, small arms, and artillery ammunition. Not only was Richmond destined to become the arsenal of the Confederacy, but the Tredegar Iron Works was to make it the center of iron manufacturing in the South. The city also afforded convenient access to war materials for the largest concentration of troops in the Confederacy—the Army of Northern Virginia.

In the Richmond arsenal, armory, and laboratory the many and diversified labor needs of Confederate ordnance resulted in a correspondingly wide variety of tasks for Negro labor. Similarly, in ordnance works throughout Virginia, Negro labor was highly diversified. For example, Negro sawyers supplied unfinished lumber for rifles, crates, gun carriages, and caissons; coopers made staves, hoops, and headings for powder kegs; wheelwrights constructed hubs, spokes, and rims; and carpenters built boxes to house artillery shells. Negroes worked with leather as tanners, curriers, and harnessmakers. Of those working in the open-hearth furnaces, erecting blast furnaces, and labeling or painting boxes, there were puddlers, bricklayers, and painters. Of those refining raw materials there were hundreds cutting and charring wood, working in artificial niter beds, and smelting lead sulfide. There were other hundreds who served as packers, blacksmiths, teamsters, porters, boatmen, and ordnance depot hands. Countless other tasks had to be performed in order to procure, fabricate, and distribute ordnance stores. Moreover, throughout the war a large Negro labor force engaged in tasks which involved the preparation of raw materials for fabrication into needed commodities of war.

Since the records of the Richmond Ordnance Headquarters were destroyed, there is no way to determine the exact number of whites or blacks employed in the various ordnance works within the state. Reports to the Secretary of War by the Chief of Ordnance are misleading and inconclusive and frequently give only rough estimates of the total number of employees. For example, in November 1863 Gorgas informed the Secretary of War that the principal establishments in five southeastern states "employ 5,090 persons, of whom two-thirds are non-conscripts, disabled soldiers, boys, females, and slaves."[16] For the year 1864 Gorgas reported that "the number of Negroes on the rolls of the department . . . is 830, add to these, say 1,000, in the employ of contractors, of which there are no returns in this office, making 1,830 Negroes employed."[17] On December 31, 1864, the Chief of Ordnance wrote that "2,245 Negroes and 3,091 whites are required for the whole operations of this Bureau."[18] It should be noted, however, that frequently there were hundreds of Virginia blacks who labored under circumstances in which their names would not be carried on the rolls of ordnance depots and arsenals. For example, following the Battle of Bull Run on July 21, 1861, over a hundred Negroes were hired from slaveholders to collect and haul weapons from the Manassas battleground. In late July several Negro teamsters arrived at the Richmond armory and arsenal with more than fifty cannons (mostly rifled), and several hundred rifles, muskets, and other ordnance stores. After the Seven Days' Battle, June 26 to July 1, 1862, Negroes again were hired to collect and clean weapons. Subsequently, many wagonloads of weapons began rolling into Richmond from the nearby battlefields. The yield in guns, knives, howitzers, caissons, ammunition, and supply wagons was enormous. A Negro teamster had the fingers of his left hand blown off while attempting to pull a musket from underneath the load in his wagon. Even with the large quantity of ordnance stores collected from the field of combat there were still many military units which were woefully short of essential materials throughout 1862. Even these limited supplies, however, did help to provide time for holding out until production of arms and ammunition could get under way in Virginia.

Ordnance production centers in Virginia were Richmond, Petersburg, Lynchburg, Farmville, Danville, Staunton, and southwestern parts of the state. By November 1862 the Richmond arsenal was supplying most of the ammunition for the small arms and artillery of Lee's army. Chief of Ordnance Gorgas reported that the daily rate of ammunition production in this arsenal amounted to 60,000 rounds of small-arms ammunition, from 300 to 500 rounds of field ammunition, and a monthly production of 60,000 pounds of lead.[19]

The Richmond arsenal, armory, and laboratory, however, were to compete continually with each other as well as with the naval ordnance shops and the Tredegar Iron Works for Negro labor and raw materials. In the Richmond arsenal no fewer than 150 Negroes performed much of the hard work imposed by procurement, repair, fabrication, and transportation of ordnance materials. Aleck, a slave of S. B. Boyd, was employed to make alterations in small arms, while several other slaves worked as shop hands.[20] From time to time, shop or yard work resulted in injuries to the slaves, which were duly reported in the Richmond newspapers as were stories of the mistreatment of slaves working in government shops. In May 1863, for example, the Richmond *Whig* reported that a slave belonging to J. H. Grant was accidentally caught in the machinery gearing, and his right arm was wrenched off. Months later the *Whig* was critical of the actions of Captain R. Boyce, foreman of the smith shop, for the beating of a slave belonging to T. N. Jones. In August 1864 the Richmond press carried the story of the explosion of fifteen artillery shells as they were being unloaded from wagons by slave laborers. As one of the slaves tossed a shell to another, who was arranging them in piles, it hit the pile and exploded, killing five men and wounding several others. Another explosion occurred on November 23, 1864, at an ammunition storage depot where several Negro depot hands and teamsters were unloading thirty-pound Parrot shells. Three slaves were killed and many others were seriously injured, along with the superintendent of Negro hands W. B. Ingersoll. Virginia newspapers also carried advertisements requesting slave and free Negroes for work in ordnance shops. Owners of slaves for hire were requested to contact or write Lieutenant L. Zimmer at the office of the Richmond arsenal.[21]

Negro ordnance workers contributed significantly to the ability of the Confederacy to keep armies in the field. Guns and bullets had to be transported to infantry and cavalry divisions, and heavy cannons and shells into the hands of field and fort artillery units. Lieutenant J. McHenagh, in charge of transportation at the Richmond arsenal, engaged Negro teamsters to transport stores to the ordnance officers of the various commands of the Army of Northern Virginia. In October 1864, for example, Captain F. M. Colston, Assistant Chief of Ordnance of the Army of Northern Virginia, received ordnance stores and cannons. A slave, Tom Peters, was the driver of Colston's supply wagon. The captain was instructed to mount the heavy cannons on batteries located on the south side of the James River, along the approach to Richmond. Each of the Brooke-banded heavy guns weighed over ten tons, and several Negro laborers were required to install them beneath specially constructed carrying logs. In describing the Negro teamsters and their work in hauling the heavy guns Colston wrote, "Imagine about 30 mules in a team, with the Negro drivers all yelling and cracking their whips. It was like a charge of artillery."[22] When water transportation was necessary to deliver supplies from the arsenal, Lieutenant McHenagh had available five slave boat hands—William, John, Robert, Lee, and Edward—who were hired at annual wages ranging from $460 to $540.[23] Slaves were also used to pack and crate ordnance stores. At the arsenal's depot Captain J. Dinwiddie had nine slave packers. One slave packer, Daniel, was hired at $75 monthly, and the other eight were hired at $60 each per month. Two slaves, Philip and George Washington, served as messengers for the ordnance supply store and depot.[24] In September 1864 Captain Dinwiddie was asked to have the Bureau of Conscription detail Nelson Davis, a free Negro from Hanover County, to the Richmond arsenal shops. Davis was a skilled wheelwright and blacksmith whose services were urgently needed.[25]

Another occupation in which slaves were engaged was that of oilmakers. By melting down animal fats they produced lubricants for shop machinery; they also made lubricants from peanuts, fish, cotton seed, flax seed, and castor beans.[26] It is significant that for the first three months of 1864 the owners of 94 slaves employed in the Richmond arsenal received from the paymaster, Lieutenant Colonel W. LeRoy Brown, a total of $21,487.50. This figure, however, does not include the wages paid to other slaveowners or to free Negroes. The latter worked as boat hands, teamsters, packers, and shop and depot hands.

Not very far from the Richmond arsenal were the Confederate States Armory and the Central Laboratory, both engaged chiefly in the manufacture of small arms and munitions. The laboratory produced and tested cartridges, percussion caps, ammunition, gun carriages, canteens, and small arms. By 1863 its productivity (50,000 to 100,000 rounds of small-arms ammunition and 900 field artillery shells daily) reflected increased reliance upon the Confederacy's own manufactories. The Laboratory's Negro employees were sometimes impressed to work on fortifications, as in July 1864, when Colonel D. W. Parker secured fourteen persons to work at Richmond.[27] The Armory's white and colored employees were supervised by Mr. O. Porter. Although there is little documentary information about them, the local press did report on accidents or crimes in which Negro laborers at the Armory were involved. On December 31, 1864, the Chief of Ordnance informed the Secretary of War that 450 persons were employed at the Richmond Armory, but he failed to distinguish between white and Negro workers.[28] The few existing payrolls clearly portray the extensive use made of Negro labor. For example, Henry Eacho, a free Negro, was paid $4.25 per day to clean and alter small arms. Tom, Peter, and Mingo—slaves belonging to William Gray—were hired as bricklayers, and fourteen other slaves were employed as carpenters.[29] From time to time Colonel J. H. Burton, superintendent of armories, required Labor Foreman Porter to report on the labor skills of slaves employed in the armory. In 1862 a select group of shop slaves were classified by Porter as either first- or second-class workers. Of the 54 slaves Porter classified, 37 were represented as first-class workers and the rest—including 3 females, Minta, June, and Rosanna—as second-class workers.[30] On December 31, 1864, the labor foreman reported that illness prevented 24 slaves—18 males and 6 females—from working the entire month. The foreman noted that Mary and Easter had given birth, while Pauline was expecting within a few days.[31]

Ordnance production in Petersburg, Danville, and Lynchburg supplemented that of the Richmond area. In late August 1862, Gorgas received Congressional approval to purchase land in Petersburg for the erection of a lead-smelting works. By September Captain J. Morton had hired two slaves, Soloman and Peter, to assist in smelting lead from the Wytheville and Wythe lead mines. Once smelted, the lead was poured into bullet molds. Lead pellets were produced by pouring the molten lead into a container with a small hole in the bottom. This allowed the lead to form pellets as it dropped into a vat of water which was placed about three feet beneath the container. By the winter months the Petersburg lead works was capable of smelting a thousand pounds of lead a day.[32] Such lead was essential for cartridge production and was shipped by canal boat to the Richmond arsenals. The smelting and casting operations at the Petersburg Copper and Zinc Works also involved slave labor. Lieutenant H. F. Reardon, in command of this work, employed twenty-one persons, of whom five were slaves. Winfield, a slave blacksmith, was hired from E. O. Pegram, and the other slaves—Ned, Thomas, William, and Sam—assisted at various stages in the production of brass for ordnance purposes.[33]

Over 130 miles southwest of Petersburg was the Danville arsenal, commanded by Captain E. S. Hutter. At least twenty-one slaves assisted in the fabrication and transportation of ordnance stores.[34] On January 21, 1862, Belhartz Hall from Pittsylvania County secured a contract from the Danville arsenal to manufacture breach-loading carbines. In addition to employing his own slaves, Hall hired a slave blacksmith from Mart T. Shelton to work in the factory. Three other slave craftsmen were furnished by his partner C. D. Bennett. In November 1862 Hall wrote to the governor of Virginia seeking to have the slaves employed in his gun factory exempted from laboring on the Danville fortifications.[35] Hall told Governor Letcher, "These hands . . . are now experienced and efficient and therefore indispensable to us in carrying out our contract." At the Danville arsenal Captain Hutter made strenuous effects to retain sufficient laborers. In order to alleviate the labor shortage the Bureau of Conscription in July 1864 assigned eleven free blacks—two smiths and nine shop hands—to assist the depleted labor force.[36] In the Lynchburg arsenal, both slaves and free Negroes were employed to remove powder to railroad depots and canal boats. Captain G. T. Getty engaged slaves to work in the ordnance shops where small arms were repaired, cartridges produced, and field pieces—such as caissons from the Army of Northern Virginia—were brought in to be repaired. Another slave task was that of dyeing the cotton belts for cartridge boxes.[37]

The ordnance harness shop in Clarksville was engaged in extensive production of such leather products as bridles, collars, artillery harnesses, halters, saddle trees, and cap pouches. Captain J. Kane, in command, was assisted by Henry Pride, the shop superintendent. The employees averaged ten hours of work per day throughout the year. Although some leather was produced on the shop grounds, much of it was prepared by slave labor at local tanneries under contract to furnish leather for the Clarksville harness shop. Considerable skill and hard work were required for the conversion of hides into leather.

Tanning was essentially a series of procedures carried out by hand. The first stage required bark which a team of slaves would cut from trees and chop and grind into fine pieces. These were placed in a large vat of boiling water and allowed to soak for ten or more days. Meanwhile the hides were split lengthwise into two parts and stretched and hung from overhead beams so the membrane could be scraped away. The heavy hides were difficult to lift. The skin was scraped with a concave blade until the hide was clean and smooth, then soaked in lime water for several days until the hair would "slip." Then the hides were again worked over and rinsed several times, and the lime was removed from the skin tissues by bathing in a special hen-dung solution called "bate," which also softened the hides. After further rinsings the hides were put in the vat in which the bark had been soaking for several days, and they remained there until they were evenly colored. While soaking in the "tan-ooze" they had to be raised and lowered at least three times a day. An experienced tanner was essential to keep the "tan-ooze" at the proper strength and temperature. When the tanning was completed, Negro curriers dressed the leather.

Tanning yards were in the open air or only partially under a roof owing to the foul odor of the hides. Inclement weather added to the unpleasantness of the tanners' chores. Negro wagoners hauled the wood, hides, and other necessary items from the surrounding countryside to the harness shop, and delivered finished products to ordnance supply trains, river boats, and military commands. With only two slave wagoners—Walter and Jim—and four horses of his own, Captain Kane doubtless used the Negro teamsters supplied by the local quartermasters.

Like other commanders of ordnance shops, Captain Kane was continually plagued with labor shortages. Slaveowners demanded that the government furnish rations and clothing before they would hire out their slaves. In 1864 the captain informed the Richmond Ordnance Headquarters that "the lowest rate I can hire Negroes for without rations furnished is Sixty dollars per month. A No. 1 hand cannot be hired for less than seventy-five."[38]

The captain also appealed to the Bureau of Conscription to furnish free Negro laborers. In June 1864 he requested that Nat Epps and Henry Lester be detailed to assist in the procuring of lumber in Halifax County.[39] Several weeks later he wrote of the difficulty he experienced "in keeping the shops supplied with fire wood" and lamented that he was compelled to have wood cut by his Negro shop hands. At the same time he secured permission for the slaves employed in the harness shop to purchase brogan shoes. In November, Captain Kane submitted another urgent request to the Bureau of Conscription to detail John Moore, a free Negro currier, to the harness shop. Moore had been preparing hides for several years and was needed to assist in the production of leather.[40] The Clarksville harness shop employed several slave and free craftsmen; and Captain Kane was at times forced to pay them excessive wages in order to retain their services. This practice prompted a sharp comment from the Richmond Ordnance Headquarters, and the captain was instructed to explain his actions. On October 15, 1864, he wrote:

> Your communication relative to the pay of Negroes is at hand. I am satisfied you do not fully understand the class of free Negroes we have here when you say seventy to seventy-five dollars per month would be enough at Clarksville. We have been paying near these rates for laborers but the Negroes to whom I refer are almost altogether carpenters, blacksmiths, or blacksmith helpers, and selected as the best of that class of mechanics to be found in the neighborhood, some of them in fact superior workmen to many white men.
>
> We have one boy, although a slave, and whom we are now paying $182 per month who as a general workman is the best blacksmith in the shop; on piece work at home this boy excells in industry any of the workmen. If the rule is applied in this case we most certainly will lose one of the best hands; so will it be with the others, although compelled by the conscript law to remain where detailed; still they will desert to find employment with the Quartermaster. . . . Besides it is an impossibility for me to hire slaves without coming into competition with the public on the 1st day of January and hiring in the same terms.[41]

Less than three weeks later Captain Kane informed the Richmond office that he had employed two additional Negroes to assist P. A. Peterson in the leather shop.[42] In the blacksmith shop Armisted and John, both skilled blacksmiths, were hired at $1,500 and $1,200 per year, respectively, while their helpers—Peter, Braxton, and John—received $600 each annually. Bob, a slave fireman, was hired at $840 per year. At least eighteen slaves and twenty free blacks were employed by the Clarksville harness shop.[43]

III

The critical need for potassium nitrate (saltpeter or niter) in making gunpowder placed a premium on Negro manpower to increase domestic production of this material. The niter shortage resulted from a combination of the South's failure to accumulate ample stocks and the Union's blockade of Southern ports. Early efforts were made to supplement imports by working limestone caves in most of Kentucky and Tennessee, but during the spring campaigns of 1862 most of these caves fell into the hands of Northern armies. Faced with a domestic production of less than five hundred pounds a day, Confederate authorities moved to institute a large-scale program of niter production. The Confederate Congress on April 11, 1863, passed an act organizing a separate Niter and Mining Bureau under the Secretary of War. In addition to procuring saltpeter, coal, and the ores of iron, zinc, copper, and lead, it was charged with supervising the production of iron, lead, and brass. Sulfur was obtained by roasting iron pyrites, and charcoal by charring oak, birch, or willow wood. Major Isaac M. St. John was placed in charge of the Niter and Mining Bureau. His main activities in Virginia were the stimulation of both private and government production niter and a systematic exploration of the state for niter caves and deposits. Private producers were encouraged to utilize their slaves to work every available source of niter supply— limestone caves, nitrous earth under tobacco barns, old cellars, plus the construction of artificial niter beds.

Nitrate caves in the southwestern part of the state provided a fairly pure niter which could be refined for use in a short time, but supplies from this source were not fully adequate. Accordingly, Virginia had to resort to artificial niter beds, which took eighteen months or more to produce. Slave labor was used in preparing artificial niter beds throughout Virginia. Pits two feet deep and four feet wide of varying lengths were dug and filled with carcasses, animal refuse of all kinds, and decaying vegetable matter. This was mixed with old mortar, and as decomposition progressed, putrid water and waste liquids, collected from surrounding areas, were sprinkled over the beds. Stirring was necessary to expose fresh surfaces to air. After eighteen months the solution was scooped from the pits and placed in hoppers. After the water was drawn off, the impure niter was recovered and refined. Both Richmond and Petersburg were involved in the artificial production of niter, and by the end of 1864 the Richmond area stood first in the Confederacy, claiming 265,000 cubic feet of niter beds. It was through eight government caves in southwestern Virginia, however, that the War Department acquired most of its essential stock of niter.[44]

In July 1862 Major St. John remarked: "Our power to work these natural [cave] deposits is controlled by three conditions—labor, hostile interruption, and transportation." He also noted that the yield should have been much greater and explained that slaveowners were unwilling to send their Negroes far from home.[45] Nevertheless, both slaves and free Negroes were hired to procure and refine niter from the eight limestone caves operated by the Niter Bureau in Virginia. A productive cave was dry, and the floors and crevices contained at least five thousand cubic feet of nitrous earth, which was shoveled into iron pots. Potash, firewood, and easy access to water were essential to the production of the niter obtained from the natural deposits found in caves. When taken from the caves, the niter was unfit for immediate use. All the impurities which would prevent the necessary combination with other ingredients of gunpowder had to be removed. The niter was refined by a solution in an equal weight of boiling water. The solution was then filtered, cooled, and allowed to crystallize; the crystals were then collected in pans. After a second refining the water was expelled by fusion, and the refined niter, now a delicate white, was ready for future use.

From the fall of 1862 to the spring of 1865 Virginia's niter production increased significantly. Major St. John was able to produce at least two thousand pounds a day, and to this may be added the supply from four other Confederate states. But most of the gunpowder used by Lee's Army of Northern Virginia was manufactured within the state. To systematize the supervision of niter production in Virginia, Edmond Harrison was appointed Superintendent of Nitriaries, and Lieutenant H. F. Reardon served as disbursing officer in charge of contracts and payrolls. Of the ten niter and mining districts in the Confederacy five were located in Virginia (Districts Nos. 1, 2, 3, and 7 encompassed southwestern Virginia, and No. 4 included the Valley and Piedmont sections). The commanding officer of each district worked to assure an ample supply of niter, and by the fall of 1862, niter production in nitrate caves or by artificial means was well under way.[46] Although Negroes were employed in procurement operations in the government caves in southwestern Virginia, they were found in the largest numbers working in both government and private nitriaries located near urban areas such as Petersburg and Richmond. For example, beginning with the fall of 1862 George W. Trice hired out twenty-eight slaves—one blacksmith, and twenty-seven niter hands —to work in the Petersburg niter beds. In December 1862 Trice was paid $526.66 for their labor, but by January 1864 the pay had increased to $910 a month.[47] The same monthly increase of wages came about for the slaves hired by W. C. Rawlings and F. S. Anthony to work in Petersburg nitriaries. What is more important, however, is that the retention of such slaves resulted in the better training of workmen and increased production. In Richmond an all-Negro labor force of sixty-one hands worked in the niter beds.[48] By March 1864 the Niter and Mining Bureau advertised in the Richmond *Examiner* for four hundred slaves and free Negroes. Owners were offered $300 yearly plus board and clothing for each slave. Chief of Ordnance Gorgas notified the Secretary of War, "It will be indispensible that the efforts of the Niter and Mining Bureau be sustained, in order that home production may not be lessened. A certain force of white and black labor ought to be permanently assigned to this duty of procuring niter and sulphur, and the other operations of the Niter and Mining Bureau."[49] Gorgas reported that in southwestern Virginia primarily white labor was used because slaveowners refused to send their slaves to this remote and exposed frontier region. Yet, in February 1863 Smyth County officials reported that approximately 75 per cent of their men and boy slaves were employed in the manufacture of niter, salt, and iron under government contract. The county clerk expressed concern that such a large number were engaged to manufacture niter at the expense of their loss as agricultural laborers. Similar letters were sent to the Virginia governor from other officials in the southwestern counties of the state. Their complaint centered on the large number of slaves impressed to produce niter and to work in the many blast furnaces operating in their vicinity. Reports submitted in 1864 show that only forty-seven slaves and free Negroes, as compared to over six hundred whites, were engaged by the Niter and Mining Bureau to procure niter from domestic sources.[50] It is significant that such reports pertained only to hired Negroes and did not include impressed slaves. The difficulty in hiring slaves to labor in areas far from their owners may be seen with respect to the entire labor force employed in government niter works east of the Mississippi. In October 1864, for example, Major St. John reported that 52 whites and 581 Negroes were employed in nitriaries located near urban areas, compared with 1,836 whites and 823 Negroes employed in niter production in remote frontier nitrous-bearing caves.[51] Negro manpower made a contribution in assuring that the Confederate armies had an ample supply of powder to carry on an extended war.

Many Negroes worked for private contractors engaged in niter production, and their names were never carried on ordnance payrolls. Many others worked for the Niter and Mining Bureau in niter beds and government caves.

IV

In 1862 leadership in the processing of minerals also fell upon the Niter and Mining Bureau. The Virginia coal and iron industry became an integral part of the South's vastly accelerated war program. Fortunately for the region, the needs could be met merely by enlarging existing coal-mining operations and expanding production. Here as elsewhere in the Confederate war effort, Negro manpower was used in the procurement of coal, iron ore, lead sulfide ore, and limestone, as well as various organic products. Negro labor was also very valuable in subsequent stages of refinement and processing of ores and minerals into manufactured products such as iron and lead. To stimulate war production the Confederate Congress authorized the government to lend capital to new industries with contracts to produce war materials. Loans and subsidies were also granted to the operators of iron works and coal mines who needed capital to introduce improved machinery and mining applications in order to step up their production.

On the eve of the Civil War, coal mining was one of the major industries of Virginia. The state was in an excellent position to take advantage of coal markets both along the coast and inland, but the state never developed adequately the necessary canal and rail facilities to take advantage of the interior coal markets. Nevertheless, enormous quantities of coal from the Richmond and Tidewater fields were shipped to the eastern markets. Virginia was one of five states which produced in 1860 more than 400,000 tons of bituminous coal. The annual value of coal mined in Virginia increased from over $467,000 in 1850 to more than $798,000 in 1860. Of the 473,360 tons of coal which were mined in the state approximately 25 per cent came from the Richmond coalfield, where Negro labor was largely used. For example, in the two decades prior to the Civil War, the collieries of Chesterfield, Goochland, Henrico, and Powhatan counties had a combined labor force which totaled over 600 men. More than 90 per cent of these men were slaves and free blacks, and they mined annually over 100,000 tons of bituminous coal. The pits, with few exceptions, lay below the water level, and required extensive pumping of water. In 1860 the Clover Hill and Midlothian mines in Chester-field County employed no fewer than 350 blacks and produced nearly 86,000 tons of coal.[52] Consequently, at the opening of hostilities, Virginia had a sizable force of experienced Negro miners. The Richmond coalfield contained the only source of coal available to the Confederacy, although mines later established at Egypt, North Carolina, and Montevallo, Alabama, did furnish coal.

The coal mines of the Confederacy offer another interesting example of the effort to match Negro manpower to the need for increased war production. Probably most of the mining of coal was performed exclusively by Negro labor. Moreover, the only mining of any consequence in the Richmond coalfield occurred at the Midlothian and Clover Hill properties in Chesterfield County. However, the yield of coal pits in Henrico (Tuckahoe) and Goochland (Dover) counties was to increase significantly with the revival of abandoned coal pits by enterprising persons who held government contracts.

The Richmond coalfield crossed the James River on the west side of Richmond and extended in a north and south direction, with the Appomattox River as its southern terminal. It was approximately 30 miles long and 5 miles wide. One of the seams on the north side of the James River contained a bed of natural coke ranging in thickness from 5 to 6 feet. The Richmond field was within a few miles of railroads and navigable waters, and consisted of an area of 96,000 acres of coal measures, containing beds of coal ranging from 5 to 50 feet in thickness. In this narrow 30-mile belt the Midlothian and Clover Hill coal mines were located southeast of the James River, the Tuckahoe coal pits northeast, and the Dover coal pits northwest.

In the 1860's James McKillop, a coal man from Scotland, visited the Richmond coalfield and was extremely critical of the unnecessary hard labor performed by the Negro miners in order to reach and remove coal. McKillop stated that they "could be seen removing as high as 30 feet of cover to obtain 4 feet of coal; while the seam [coal beds] at the same time was finely exposed in the side of the hill, and could have been obtained with one-tenth of the labor by the ordinary process of 'drifting' [tunneling] on the seams." He also indicated that "in the Richmond coalfields numerous excavations of this kind are found along the out-crops of the seams; in some cases immense quan-

tities of earth have been removed to obtain a small quantity of coal."
McKillop noted the abuses of slave labor in the Civil War mining
operations and the primitive methods employed to procure coal.[53] In
this connection advertisements in the local press for additional Negro
laborers carefully pointed out that the mines were safe, the slaves well
treated, fed, clothed, and attended in sickness, and under the superin-
tendence of skilled mining agents. In December 1862 the Richmond
Examiner notified slaveowners that 150 slaves were required at the
coke and coal operations at Salle's Pit in Chesterfield County. The
announcement mentioned that "The best prices will be paid. . . . the
workings are shallow, dry, perfectly safe, and descended on foot, thus
affording desirable employment." Similar advertisements came from
the Clover Hill and Midlothian mines.

At the Midlothian mines there were several shafts, which varied
in depth from 150 to 700 feet. This was necessary in order to reach
the coal deposits, which usually averaged about 36 feet in thickness.
The Negro labor force, including coal-yard hands and top and bottom hands, consisted of about two hundred men and boys, both slave
and free. Each gang of laborers had a specific task to perform—remove dirt, dig coal, bore and blast rocks, fill and manage coal cars,
attend or sink shafts, sack bags of coal, construct or repair drifts or
passages. A contemporary, describing his visit to the Midlothian
mines, wrote:

> Each with a lighted lamp, sprang into a basket suspended by
> ropes over pulleys and framework, above a yawning abyss seven
> hundred and seventy-five feet deep. The signal was given—puff!
> puff! went the steam engine, and down, down, we went. . . . We
> came to the bottom with a bump. The underground Superinten-
> dent made his appearance. . . . Him we followed . . . through
> many a labyrinth, down many a ladder, and occasionally penetrat-
> ing to the end of a drift, where the men were at work shoveling
> coal into baskets . . . or boring for blasts.
>
> The drifts, or passages, are generally about sixteen feet wide, and
> ten feet high, with large pillars of coal intervening about sixty feet
> square. . . . Doors used in ventilation were often met with, through
> which we crawled. . . . The Midlothian mines employ Negroes.
> . . . I could not but almost envy their well developed muscular
> figures. The Negroes prefer this labor to any other, enjoy many

perquisites, and generally the labor of the week is performed in five days. . . .[54]

Not far from the Midlothian mines were the Clover Hill coal pits, which were located on Winterpock Creek. They consisted of three pits, known as Bright Hope, Raccoon, and Hall's. From these pits the Confederacy was supplied with a large portion of the coal it required during the first three years of the war. Like the Midlothian coal mines, the Clover Hill pits employed at least two hundred Negroes. A small steam engine attended by slave hands was used to raise coal and to drain the pits. The Tredegar Iron Works was perhaps the most important munitions work to obtain a major portion of its coal from these pits. A disastrous explosion occurred in the Raccoon Pits on April 15, 1863, which resulted in the instant deaths of sixteen slaves and the wounding of a number of others. The accident was caused by the ignition of gas in the pit where eighty Negroes were at work. Three of the fatally injured slaves were owned by the mining company.[55]

The Tuckahoe coal pits, located on the northeastern end of the Richmond coalfield, were within 1,200 yards of the James River Canal and about 12 miles above Richmond. As early as September 1863 the Richmond press reported that these pits were seeking to employ an additional seventy-five slaves.[56] The Virginia Iron Manufacturing Company, the Tredegar Iron Works, and the Belle Isle Rolling Mill were supplied with coal from these pits for smith's work and puddling and heating and for melting horseshoe, gun, and nail iron. Although these pits were not plagued with excessive water, they were troubled with gas and impurity content once shafts were sunk five hundred feet or more. Nevertheless, their more productive coal-bearing pits plus the Dover pits in Goochland County were acquired and operated by the Tredegar Iron Works in 1862. The company experienced considerable difficulty in hiring Negro miners, and in 1863 it was still advertising for slave hands for the Tuckahoe and Dover mines.

Although prospects for increased Confederate coal production brightened considerably throughout 1861, the scarcity of Negro manpower grew more severe with the passing of time. War, however, did bring about an expansion of mining activities; and the Richmond field production increased to over 200,000 tons annually, even under the most adverse of circumstances, such as periodic impressment of miners to labor on the Richmond fortifications, frequent loss of experienced slave miners to other war industries, and mounting reluctance of slaveowners to release sufficient slaves to labor in the Richmond coalfield.

V

Like the Richmond Colliery, the ironworks of the city became another mainstay of the Confederate war effort. As the center of southern manufacture, Richmond in 1860 had over 1,600 mechanics in four rolling mills, fourteen machine shops and foundries, a nail factory, six works for producing iron railing, two circular saw works, and fifty iron and metal works—a total investment of nearly 4 million dollars.[57] Yet these industries were grossly inadequate to meet the war needs of ordnance and rail transportation. Before the firing upon Fort Sumter the total output of pig iron in Virginia, the Carolinas, and Alabama was only 14,488 tons, and of this amount Virginia alone produced 11,646 tons.[58] Such production figures do not compare favorably with the total United States output of 987,559 tons of pig iron in 1860.

As before the war, hundreds of slaves and Negroes worked in Virginia industries, and they constituted a considerable industrial force. In the Virginia iron industry "the Negro slave was depended on not only for his muscle but for his skill," and by the 1850's he had become an important factor in the various processes of iron manufacture. Not only did he constitute the major part of the required labor in the Valley blast furnaces, but he worked side by side with the white skilled mechanic as puddler, heater, and roller.[59] He also mined iron ore and limestone, felled trees, made charcoal, assisted in blowing and tapping blast furnaces, drove wagons, and worked on canal boats.

Virginia manufacturers attempted to increase their skilled labor force by apprenticing slave boys in their many works. Under the direction of a white supervisor, several Negro boys were employed in the cooper shops to build kegs for spikes produced in the Tredegar Iron Works.[60] The thirty-five slaves, however, who were carefully trained for over a decade, comprised the most highly skilled Negro employees in the Tredegar plant. In referring to these slaves Joseph Reid Anderson remarked that "he owned a pick lot of men and boys whom he brought up to be puddlers, heaters, and rollers." He added that they were "as a choice set equal to any white hands who had ever worked for him."[61] Consequently, on the eve of the Civil War the Richmond iron industry had the nucleus of skilled and experienced Negro technicians to impart their skills to other Negroes introduced into less skilled positions such as smith's helpers, strikers, and foundry, forge, and mill hands. The less experienced Negroes could also work at the squeezer and puddle rolls and serve as shop hands in the machine shops.

Industrial Negro laborers, both free and slave, were to play an accelerated role in all operations of Virginia ironworks as the needs of the Confederate armies drastically reduced the number of white laborers. This was particularly true following the conversion to military production of Richmond's three most important plants—the Virginia Iron Manufacturing Company, the Old Dominion Iron and Nail Works, and the Tredegar Iron Works. Although the Tredegar Iron Works was to remain the industrial heart of the Confederacy, the Virginia Iron Manufacturing Company became a significant source for the supply of pig iron. After the beginning of hostilities, its Westham Furnace, located 5 miles outside Richmond, advertised for forty "able bodied Negro men to be employed in chopping wood and working at the Iron Furnace."[62] Late in 1862 this became a government furnace, and the Niter and Mining Bureau advertised in the Richmond press for "practical blast furnace hands, such as founders, helpers, and colliers."[63] Slaveowners were asked to contact Lieutenant J. Ellicott at the office of the Mining Bureau.

Throughout 1863 and 1864, almost one hundred slaves were engaged in the various stages of the production of pig iron. For example, sufficient raw materials had to be accumulated to allow the furnaces to be put in blast and kept in constant operation. Traditionally this hard work was performed by Negro manpower, both skilled and unskilled. As woodchoppers blacks were each expected to cut at least 1½ cords of wood per day. Those involved in mining operations worked in limestone quarries and ore banks. Negro miners were necessary to procure coal and wood to make charcoal. Boatmen and wagoners were responsible for the delivery of mineral ores to the blast furnaces. Those not engaged in the primary job of acquiring "stock" —iron ore, limestone, and coal—worked at the blast furnaces smelting pig iron. Five slaves, Robert, John, Berry, Ralph, and Bob, fed the fires at the Westham Furnace. The tapping and casting (making pigs) operations involved at least three slaves—Boswell, Harry, and Frank —who were the highest-paid slaves working at the blast furnaces. Another slave, Sam, was apparently employed to regulate air drafts or bellows at one of the furnaces. Once the molten metal was released from the furnaces, other slave furnace hands were responsible for its transportation to the casting beds, which were formed or shaped of sand. Harry and Bob, slave carpenters, worked throughout the plant;[64] and Jim Bubee, a free Negro, was employed as an engineer. Bubee apparently controlled the charging of one of the blast furnaces. Once the pig iron was smelted, Negro boatmen transported it to the Richmond ordnance depots for further delivery.

Both the government and private blast furnaces in the Valley of Virginia required considerable Negro manpower. During the war the pig-iron furnaces were largely tended by Negroes and superintended by a white foreman. However, the Engineer Bureau's demand for their labor to erect military defenses periodically reduced the work force throughout the war. Legislation enacted by the Virginia General Assembly in 1862 and 1863 gave the governor authority to impress Negroes for sixty days whenever fortifications demanded their labor. These acts, however, made no provisions for exemptions of those engaged in mining and manufacturing. Owners of ironworks with government contracts made frequent complaints to the governor concerning the impressment of their workers. As early as August 1861 W. C. Baker, who operated the Cape Blast Furnace in Hardy County, expressed concern that his slave hands and mules might be impressed.[65] In Patrick County the Barksdale and Stovall Iron Works refused to submit a list of the slaves in their employment to county authorities for fear that they might be impressed.[66] The superintendent of the Elizabeth furnace in Staunton complained to the local justices of the peace because over ten of his slaves were impressed.[67]

Finally, in January 1863 both the Engineer Bureau and Governor Letcher recommended that the Virginia lawmakers amend the law so as to permit the exemption of slaves engaged in mining and manufacturing pursuits. At the same time the Governor reported that in the Virginia penitentiary 298 convicts were employed in manufacturing and mechanical pursuits. Of this number 107 were slaves and free Negroes, and they were hired to the owners of blast furnaces engaged in the manufacture of pig iron for the Confederacy.[68] The following month Letcher issued a call for the impressment of slaves to labor on fortifications; the county authorities of Smyth County notified the Governor's office that over 75 per cent of their slaves were already engaged in the production of iron and salt peter under government contract and that such a draft would impair the agricultural needs of the county for slave laborers.[69] On December 31, 1864, Lieutenant Colonel R. Morton, acting Chief of Bureau, reported to the Chief of Ordnance that 841 whites and 941 blacks were engaged in the production of pig iron and its subsequent refinement.[70] Only a month before this report Colonel I. M. St. John had reported to Gorgas that of the 31 blast furnaces in Virginia 18 were still in full blast and 13 had been shut down for lack of labor and raw materials.[71] In Wythe County forty-three slaves—woodchoppers, wagoners, wood haulers, colliers, and teamsters—were secured to continue the operation of its blast furnaces after a like number of whites had been returned to the army.[72] Likewise in Buchanan County "an unexpected force of 10 Negro men and boys, a woman and a girl was sent from the California" blast furnace which had been temporarily shut down for repairs. At the same time nine free blacks from Richmond were sent by the Bureau of Conscription. O. J. Hennick, superintendent of the Buchanan works, notified the Mining Bureau that he had a limited supply of tools which forced him to release some of the colored employees. Referring to his recent additions, Hennick wrote, "The Negro force is composed of very good boys as far as I can judge."[73] Negotiations with private ironworks for contracts to supply iron and other metal products were carried on through St. John's office. The Niter and Mining Bureau eventually found itself more and more dependent upon these works for the production of pig iron. Table 3.2 lists employees engaged in pig iron production in southwestern Virginia in 1864. Following an inspection of these ironworks, Lieutenant Colonel Chandler recommended that the Niter and Mining Bureau replace forty white conscripts—employed as woodchoppers, colliers, and wood haulers—with a like number of slaves.[74]

VI

The industrial heart of the Confederacy was Richmond's Tredegar Iron Works. This greatest of all Southern factories consisted of five acres of buildings between the James River and the Kanawha Canal.

Along the canal at the east end of the plant stood the Armory rolling mill, with nine puddling furnaces and four heating furnaces for preparing pig and scrap iron for two trains of rolls, capable of producing 5,000 to 6,000 long tons of railroad and bar iron per year. Twelve tenements for housing the slave labor force stood west of the Armory, and beyond them stood the vast rolling mill, with its nine puddling and seven heating furnaces, and three trains of rolls. Adjoining the mill was the spike factory, a three-story structure containing spike machines, a cooper shop, and a pattern-storage attic. This factory, fed by spike rods directly from the rolling mill, could produce 15 tons of railroad and ship spikes per day. Directly south of these buildings stood the foundry, machine, and forge departments, each bordering on the James River. In the L-shaped gun foundry, skilled workmen melted specially manufactured gun iron in two large furnaces, prepared the flasks, and cast cannon ranging in size from small mountain howitzers weighing several hundred pounds to great 10-inch columbiads, coast-defense cannon weighing over 10 tons. In the neighboring gun mill the cannons were cut, bored, turned, and finished. A foundry for general iron work, a new brick car-wheel foundry, and a

Table 3.2 *Employees in iron manufacture, District No. 1*

Furnace or forge	County	Whites	Slaves
Wilkinson Forge	Carrol	5	2
Peach Batter Forge	Grayson	—	3
Barton Forge	Smyth	5	1
Marion Forge	Smyth	—	6
Marion Magnetic	Smyth	20	38
Quebeck Forge	Smyth	7	4
Staley Creek Forge	Smyth	5	1
Barren Springs	Smyth	—	1
Beauregard and Mt. Hope	Wythe	46	7
Cedar Run	Wythe	23	23
Graham Forge	Wythe	—	—
Grey Eagle	Wythe	8	38
Lockett's Forge	Wythe	9	2
Summerman's Forge	Wythe	12	2
Total		140	128

small brass foundry composed the rest of this department. Next to the gun mill was the machine shop, where car wheels were bored, axles turned, and numerous other similar jobs performed. To the west of the machine shops stood the locomotive shop, a sprawling three-story building, 150 feet long and 45 feet wide. Here was also to be found a large finishing shop and carpenter shop where freight cars and other items were constructed. The forge department, which formed the southern boundary of the plant, consisted of several buildings which ran along the river bank. The boiler shop, which was 180 feet in length, had twenty-five fires and a number of large tilt hammers. Powered by water drawn from the canal, the forges and rolling mills consumed annually some 12,000 long tons of pig iron, over 16,000 tons of bituminous coal, and 1,500 tons of anthracite coal and required 150,000 fire brick, as well as smaller amounts of copper, wood, and other raw materials. The facilities of the Tredegar Iron Works could produce every conceivable type of finished iron product.[75]

As the "mother" arsenal of the South, Tredegar plants fashioned much of the machinery for other new-founded arsenals. Moreover, from its doors poured forth the diversified tools and weapons of industrialized warfare—heavy ordnance, plating for ironclads, bar, sheet, and railroad irons, shells, torpedoes, and nearly eleven hundred cannon employed by Confederate forces on field and sea. This remarkable establishment was owned by Joseph Reid Anderson, a West Point graduate and brigadier general in the Confederate Army, who after less than a year's service was drafted back to operate his vital war establishment. At the peak of its productivity, the Tredegar Iron Works employed over 1,200 Negroes, free and slave, and 1,200 whites.

Negro manpower enabled this plant to fulfill vital contracts with the various bureaus of the War Department. Negroes worked in the Tredegar foundries, rolling mills, spike factory, machine shops, forges, gun mill, tannery, coal mines, and blast furnaces. This vast colored labor force was concentrated in four major areas—the Richmond plant; the coal pits located in Chesterfield, Henrico, and Goochland counties; the tannery works; and the Valley blast furnaces. Their pattern of employment, however, makes it difficult to estimate the total number of Negro employees during any single month or year. For example, many blacks were discharged after working for only a few days, weeks, or even months. Their dismissal was prompted by shortages of materials and by lulls during the business season. Subsequent needs for their labor resulted in re-employment for brief periods. This hiring practice occurred periodically throughout the war. Such part-time laborers numbered from five to six hundred blacks, and they must not be confused with the full-time Negro employees who ultimately numbered over a thousand.

There were glaring inconsistencies in monthly payrolls of the number of full-time employees. This may be explained partially by incomplete records and also by the fact that slaveowners were paid not only by the month, but quarterly, semiannually, and annually. Consequently, the names of slave employees who qualified for annual payments would appear less frequently on monthly payrolls. Similarly, the names of skilled slave workers owned either by Anderson, his partners, or the Tredegar plant frequently did not appear on company payrolls. Shop payrolls usually indicated only the amount paid to Anderson, Tanner, Archer, and others for the services of their slaves.

Tredegar's Richmond plant was paramount among the four major areas engaging skilled and unskilled laborers. Its expansion and conversion to military production made it increasingly dependent on Negro manpower, especially during the final two years of the war. In the various shops Negroes, free and slave, were engaged in highly skilled tasks previously performed almost exclusively by white technicians. Slave technicians were perhaps most noticeable in the company's rolling mills. Some thirty-two puddlers, heaters, and squeezers were the key slave workers.[76] Their skills were acquired by long years of prewar experience, and they worked alongside Irish puddlers, Welsh heaters, and English rollers. A large force of Irish, Germans, and Negroes, free and slave, formed the bulk of Tredegar's unskilled and semiskilled working population.

To process bar iron from pig iron both brawn and keen perception were required. The high carbon content coupled with the presence of silicon, sulfur, phosphorus, and manganese in the pig iron made the metal too brittle for bending, forging, and rolling. Puddlers performed the first step designed to remove the impurities by feeding specially constructed furnaces with pig iron. Generally each furnace was manned by two puddlers and charged with 600 pounds of pig iron. In less than two hours the metal became molten and the puddlers stirred or thoroughly agitated the white-hot mass, gradually accumulating on the end of long rods (rabbles) heavy, pasty balls. The spongelike mass of iron saturated with slag was divided into two or three pasty balls weighing 200 to 300 pounds each. When it was determined that they had reached the proper consistency, the iron balls were removed from the furnace by mill hands. Each ball was strengthened by pounding with a tilt hammer and then passed on to the squeezer and puddle rolls. These machines were manipulated by both whites and slaves—one machine to squeeze the pasty ball and to eject the surplus slag, and the other to roll or pass the metal ball back and forth until it emerged as a rough, flat section called a "muck bar," free from impurities. After cooling, the muck bar was sheared to short lengths and then turned over to the heaters. A skilled heater could judge when the reheated iron was ready to be fed into the rollers for the best results. Rollers took the mass of metal and rolled it on a finishing mill, producing either billets (iron bars), slabs (flat plate iron), or blooms (usually 4 feet by 6 feet and rectangular in shape).[77] In September 1861 Jay, a slave roller, was paid $18.00 "for rolling four days at the plate rolls."[78] By January 1862 forty-eight slaves and one free Negro were employed in the rolling mills.[79] Anderson and Company gave the slaveowners bonds which stipulated that their slaves would be fed, clothed, and housed during the year. As the war dragged on, more and more Negroes were needed to replace white artisans who left the plant or were drafted into the army.

Skilled Negro technicians were first introduced into the Tredegar machine shops in March 1862, when twelve slaves reported—among them Abner, William, Arthur, George, Lindsay, and Henry. At least two of them operated punch machines. Second-class machinists received $2.50 per day and shop hands were hired for $200 and $250 annually. By December the number of slave workers had increased to fourteen, and about thirty served in the machine shops in 1863 and 1864.[80] During this same period twenty-six slaves worked in the spike factory, the new armory mill, and the fire-brick plant.[81]

At the Tredegar gun mill shop, slave grinders and core makers were engaged in the production of munitions.[82] However, next to the rolling mills, the largest number of Negro craftsmen were employed in the blacksmith shops. In August 1861 Anderson informed H. W. Dunkley of Clarksville, "We would employ your smith and striker for the balance of the year. If they are good men we will allow you $1.25 per day for the smith and $1.00 per day for the striker."[83] Beginning with fewer than 10 slave blacksmiths and strikers in June

1861, the 180-foot-long blacksmith shop within seven months had increased its Negro labor force to 46 workers—blacksmiths, helpers, strikers, and laborers.[84] By the opening of 1863 the smith shop had engaged 47 slave blacksmiths and strikers.[85] Throughout 1864 the shop's 25 fires and tilt hammers were manned by 91 workers—27 whites, 52 slaves, including blacksmiths, strikers, and helpers, and 12 free blacks.[86] Another 19 slaves were engaged as smith shop laborers.

The loss of slaves to other shops sometimes occurred at the Richmond plant. One of the forge strikers, Henry Fox, a free boy, "left the works on the plea of being sick" and secured employment in the engine shops at the Richmond and Danville Railroad. Anderson wrote the superintendent of the railroad company and requested that they return the boy to his plant.[87] The forge blacksmiths were called upon to perform a wide variety of special jobs. Morris, the slave of J. F. Tanner, was engaged to make almost 1,300 odd-sized horseshoes for draft and artillery horses,[88] while another slave, Aaron, received $50 for repairing and making bellows.[89] Many slaves like Aaron took advantage of the opportunity to earn extra money for themselves by doing piecework during their spare time. Owners were also anxious to increase the money paid to them for their slaves. When D. Griggs of Petersburg attempted to secure a salary increase for his slave Morris, Anderson informed him that the rate of hire he paid for Morris plus the food and clothing he provided made "his pay exceed that of any white man in the shop with him."[90]

Work for slaves at the Tredegar foundries was always arduous, but the exigencies of wartime production were much more demanding on their skills and brawn than peacetime industrial work. The foundries depended on Negro workers for tasks which ranged from highly technical to unskilled positions—from casting cannons to their delivery to wharfs and freight depots, from grinders and core makers to procurers of minerals, and from finishing shops to scrap-iron piles. Ed Taylor, a slave belonging to the owner of the Tredegar Iron Works, "hammered out the iron bands used to strengthen Tredegar Parrott and Brook guns."[91] Anderson was paid $1,000 a year for the hire of this slave; yet he was only one of over sixty highly skilled slave craftsmen acquired by the Anderson company. By 1863 Ed Taylor was permitted to earn for himself $6.00 a day, plus $3.00 for each band he hammered out during the six or seven days of each month that he was not required to work for the company. In January 1864, when he shared in a general pay raise that boosted his wages to $7.50 per day and $6.00 per band, Taylor earned $127.50 in overtime.[92] During the war sixty or sixty-five Negroes performed a variety of tasks in the foundries. Approximately ten worked at the two large furnaces melting gun iron or assisting in the preparation of molds in flasks to cast cannons. A Negro engineer operated the steam engine at one of the foundries.[93] John assisted in the weighing of iron,[94] while Guy, Cox, and Thomas, slave boatmen, were responsible for beating tons of iron rails, sheet iron, rivets, and ordnance stores.[95] In December 1861 some of the foundry hands were engaged in laying a spur rail line into the foundry yards.[96] In January 1862 Isaac and Hy were sent to the fire-brick factory to assist in making bricks for the foundry and rolling-mill furnaces.[97] Five slave bricklayers received overtime pay for repairing the furnaces at the gun foundry.[98] Three female slaves—Rhoda, Clara, and Cynthia—were apparently employed as cooks for the foundry hands.[99] Anderson hired his nine slave boys, who were especially trained for foundry work and received $19.00 per month for each one.[100] The increased cost of clothing was reflected by the $33,357 which the company was forced to pay for garments furnished to foundry slaves between September and December 1864.[101]

The cost of labor employed in the Richmond plant increased rapidly. In August 1861 Anderson hired skilled and unskilled slave labor at $1.25 and 75¢ per day, and by December he was forced to pay $2.25 and $1.00 per day. As the need for laborers increased Anderson wrote to the owner of Graham Forge in Wythe County concerning the hire of some of his slave craftsmen.[102] In the early fall of 1864 the Bureau of Conscription detailed twenty-two free blacks to work at the Tredegar works.[103] In October the War Department requested information concerning the pay scale for mechanics working at the Richmond plant. Anderson replied that he employed 400 whites and 200 Negroes, but that he never classified mechanics. He pointed out that he usually paid $3.50 per job and that he recently had adopted a new pay scale whereby heaters were raised from $3.25 to $4.00 and rollers from $2.00 to $2.50. He also indicated that the fee paid for molding an 8-pound or 24-pound shell was increased from 14 cents to 28 cents and from 25 cents to 50 cents, respectively. For skilled, semiskilled, and ordinary forge and foundry hands the pay scale ranged from $5.00 to $2.25 per day.[104]

The story of those Negro wagoners, boatmen, and cartmen who loaded, transported, and unloaded the multitude of finished products which continually poured from the doors of Tredegar's rolling mills and foundries is a striking example of the incalculable importance of Negro labor to the Confederacy. From the early months of the war they were responsible for the entire burden of transporting heavy ordnance and other products to the Richmond railroad depots and docks, to ordnance and naval shops, and to river batteries and defensive works. During the first year of the war 200 eight-inch, 150 ten-inch, and 120 fifteen-inch columbiads were hauled to the proving grounds and placed on skids for testing or actual firing. The ten-inch columbiads and smooth-bore coast-defense cannon weighed approximately 15,000 pounds; and both backbreaking and skilled labor were involved in throwing up sand banks, rigging, and placing the heavy guns on skids. After firing, the guns had to be remounted on gun carriages and carry logs and returned to the gun foundries for repairs or alterations. Generally the hauling of a ten-inch columbiad required sixteen mules, four drives, and twelve hands. As many as thirty slaves from the Tredegar works were necessary to load the many cannons, guns, carriages, ammunition, caissons, and other heavy ordnance on trains at the five railroad depots in Richmond. Twenty slave cart drivers hauled shell, shrapnel, shot, and other smaller ordnance stores

Table 3.3 *Items transported by Negro labor at the Tredegar Iron Works, 1861–1865*[105]

8- and 10-inch columbiads	Mortar shells (8- and 10-inch)
Brooke rifled guns (7-inch, 8-inch)	boilers
12-, 24-, 30-, 32-, 42-pounder siege and parrot guns	10-foot propellers
	gunboat engines
9-inch Bellona guns	bellows
8-inch siege howitzers	1500 feet (2-inch plank) for redoubts
9-inch Dahlgrens	24- and 30-inch train wheels
Parrot rifled cannons	tanks for gunboats (iron plate)
8-inch gun carriages	sheet iron and rivets
caissons	heavy plate iron
howitzers	iron rails
7- and 8-inch shells	nails, spikes, bolts, axles, wheels

and munitions to the Confederate States Laboratory, arsenals, gunboats, batteries (Drewry's Bluff and Chaffin's Bluff), and ordnance depots. As the Union Army marched on Richmond in 1864, Tredegar's black and white labor force had constructed virtually all the Confederate cannon (heavy and field), caissons, and carriages, had rolled the heavy plate iron for the *Merrimac* and other ironclads, and was supplying the government shops with materials from the machine shops, rolling mills, and foundries. Fortunately, as labor shortages mounted with expanded production, Anderson was able to either purchase or hire skilled slave craftsmen to work at the Richmond plant.

Deeply interwoven with the success of the Richmond plant were the local coalfields which provided the fuel to feed the furnaces. The Midlothian and the Clover Hill mines in Chesterfield County were the two largest pits in the area. Midlothian coal was relatively free of the sulfur which is so undesirable in the working of bar iron and steel by forge and hammer. Consequently, these mines furnished much of the coal used for smith's work, for melting gun iron, and for puddling and heating in the rolling mills. The Clover Hill mines were located in the Appomattox River basin near Petersburg. A spur rail line linked the mines to a wharf near City Point at the confluence of the Appomattox and James rivers. During the war coal was shipped by boat to the Tredegar works.[107] In the fall of 1862 Tredegar owners acquired the coal pits in Goochland (Dover mines) and Henrico (Tuckahoe mines) counties. Anderson and Company signed a five-year contract with the War Department (effective January 1, 1863) to furnish the government "all the coal we may raise over and above what is necessary for these works."[108] A government loan of $200,000 enabled the Tredegar management to purchase the Dover pits for $90,000 in October 1862. This property contained 1,100 acres and had 15 shafts (deepest 400 feet). The land also had an excellent farm which permitted the growing of food for the miners and employees at the Richmond plant. The James River and Kanawha Canal provided a direct link with the Tredegar works.

The Tuckahoe pits, which were leased for five years by Anderson and Company, were located 12 miles above Richmond. This property contained 250 acres and was only 3 miles from the canal. It also had several shafts, including one over 200 feet deep. In February 1863 Anderson notified the Secretary of War that recently installed pumps were drawing the water out of the old pits and slaves were engaged in sinking a new shaft at Dover. He added that he had acquired a part of the Tuckahoe coal mines which would require a considerable capital outlay "to open the main body of the coal, by erecting the necessary pumps and other machinery to draw the water out of the inclave or slope which penetrates over 1,000 feet, and thence by drifting to the principal seam."[109] Anderson was confident that he would have a surplus of 20,000 tons per year that he could turn over to the government. The Dover and Tuckahoe coal pits were gaseous, however, and they were plagued by inundations and by impurities of sulfur.

Throughout 1863 and 1864 the newspapers of the state advertised for Negroes to work in the Tredegar coal mines. In January 1863 Anderson notified E. R. West, a hiring agent from Petersburg, that he

Table 3.4 *Skilled slaves purchased by the Tredegar Iron Works 1862–1865*[106]

Name	Purchased from	Price
1862		
Alfred	John B. Davis	$ 1,450
Willis, Dick, John	Mary N. Skinner	$ 3,000
Robert	C. Warwick	$ 1,950
1863		
Henry	H. Fisher	$ 1,250
Coleman	J. Jacobs	$ 1,400
Randolph	J. Jacobs	$ 1,400
Daniel	W. Anderson	$ 800
William	C. G. Morris	$ 1,700
Allen, Chester, Robert	J. L. Maycee	$ 2,700
Kiziah	Mrs. Keeling	$ 1,000
Monroe, Turner	Burton and Arnold	$ 4,210
Thomas, Peachy, and Child	C. Warwick	$ 5,000
Jaspir	R. P. Blount	$ 2,500
Tom	M. C. Morson	$ 3,000
Sam	W. L. Salmon	$ 3,000
Two slaves	J. S. Atlee	$ 4,210
1864		
Colbert	J. W. Burch	$ 4,000
Toney	L. Wilson	$ 2,060
Israel	B. F. Childrey	$ 3,500
Morris	W. L. Salmon	$ 4,600
Edom	Mrs. Hutchinson	$ 4,500
1865		
Leroy, Henderson, George, Alfred	H. W. Bernard	$12,000

was willing to employ ordinary pit hands for $250 annually plus food and clothing.[110] A slave boy, Isaac, was secured by Colonel W. W. Forbes to haul lumber to the mines. Isaac was well acquainted with

Goochland County and was permitted to determine for himself "how far he will travel each day, and where he will stay at night" while hauling lumber. John Steele, the foreman of the Dover pits, was instructed to supply Isaac "with money to pay his expenses, and that of the oxen."[111] By February of 1863 the Dover and the Tuckahoe pits employed sixty-nine Negroes as blacksmiths, strikers, carpenters, top and bottom hands, and yard hands.[112] These Negroes provided the coal so badly needed by the rolling mills and foundry furnaces.

After expanding coal production by reopening old mines, building mining machinery, and hiring Negro workers, the Tredegar ironmaster purchased his own tanneries to provide footwear for his employees. Large quantities of leather were required also for machine belting and harnesses. In the fall of 1862, one tannery was established in Fincastle and another one in Buckingham County.[113] The Fincastle tannery was anxious for the return of an experienced slave boy, Joe, a tanner belonging to Captain Carper who had been impressed to labor on fortifications. In January 1863 the tannery superintendent reported that "the business is suffering now for want of him [Joe] as I have not been able to secure another of any experience at the business price of $120." Anderson was also informed that seven slave tanners had been hired for the tannery. The following month Anderson was again notified that "especially do we want the tanner" belonging to Captain Carper.[114]

In February 1864 Mr. Pitzer offered to sell his tannery in Covington for $5,000. The purchase price included 400 acres of mountain land, 2,000 pounds of leather, the right to occupy the premises until October, and a guarantee to "work without charge all the hides furnished him," providing Anderson provided one tanner.[115] In April the Tredegar works purchased the tannery, and a few weeks later Anderson hired a slave harnessmaker from Pattonsburg.[116] The tannery slaves performed a variety of tasks such as collecting bark, skinning animals, cleaning hides, tending vats, dressing leather, and converting the hooves of animals into glue for use on gun carriages. The shoe and harness shop at the Cloverdale furnace was also manned by slave workers.[117]

Besides mining coal and tanning leather, Anderson had to smelt his own pig iron in primitive blast furnaces located in the Valley of Virginia. At the beginning of the war the Tredegar plant was almost entirely dependent on the Valley's blast furnaces for pig iron, and by the fall of 1861, the plant's stockpiles were nearly exhausted. At this time a large percentage of the pig iron shipped from Virginia blast furnaces was diverted for speculation on the open market, while only small lots were delivered to the Richmond plant. Faced with a severe shortage of raw materials, the Secretaries of the War and Navy Departments were informed of the production difficulties facing Anderson and Company and the dire need to increase pig-iron supplies. On April 29, 1862, the Tredegar owners signed a contract whereby they agreed to produce a large proportion of the iron required to meet their production quotas. To facilitate this the War and Navy Departments advanced the Tredegar Iron Works $300,000 to be invested in the purchase and maintenance of blast furnaces. On May 1, 1862, the Tredegar management purchased four furnaces and their equipment—the Catawba, Cloverdale, and Grace furnaces in Botetourt County, and the Australia furnace in Alleghany County. On September 22, 1862, an additional $200,000 was advanced and six more furnaces were acquired. The Rebecca and Jane furnaces in Botetourt County were purchased, while the Glenwood furnace in Rockbridge County, and the Colombia, Fort, and Caroline furnaces in Shenandoah County were leased. Thus, by January 1863 the Tredegar plant controlled ten blast furnaces designed to promote the production of pig iron.[118] The acquisition of these blast furnaces increased the company's Negro labor force almost fivefold.

Negro manpower was essential for mining iron ore and limestone, for felling trees to be converted into charcoal, for smelting pig iron, and for boating the iron metal to the Richmond plant. The preparations involved in getting a furnace into operation were elaborate and extensive and required much physical labor. Stacks had to be rebuilt, worn-out machinery replaced, cylinders and pipes fabricated, and water wheels and bellows repaired. Over five hundred horses and mules and numerous wagons were acquired to haul raw materials and provisions. Only the Australia and Fort furnaces were steam powered, or "hot blast," and the Tredegar management decided to convert both the Grace and Glenwood furnaces to hot blast so that they could operate when the streams froze in the winter or went dry in the summer.

Furnace superintendents had to be hired to direct the Negro labor force and to sustain a steady output from the furnaces. Francis T. Glasgow was appointed to control the five furnaces in Botetourt and the two in neighboring Rockbridge and Alleghany counties. The high level of production demanded by both government and private orders required tremendous amounts of the best gun and rail iron that could be produced. Slight variations in the method of manufacture or in the fuel, fluxes, and ore used could produce unsafe metal. Because of the importance of having a suitable pig iron, Glasgow's major responsibility was to provide a stockpile of proven gun metal. Cheaper grades, however, were suitable for foundry operations and for rolling mill work.

By October 1861 the Tredegar management saw that their fate lay in the valleys and mountains, where the pig-iron furnaces were operated largely by Negro labor.[119] Tredegar production had risen to a point demanding 15,000 tons of pig iron and 75,000 tons of coal a year.[120] The hard work entailed in preparing to put a furnace in blast was performed by Negroes—charcoal makers, quarrymen, bricklayers, colliers, miners, blacksmiths, teamsters, boatmen, woodchoppers, and carpenters.

Large quantities of wood had to be cut for conversion into charcoal. One acre of wood had to chopped down every day to supply the average blast furnace, which produced a little over 1 ton of pig iron per day. Ore and limestone had to be mined, and labor in ore banks and limestone pits was hard. Ore-bank hands had to dig shafts to get to the main seam of ore. Explosives were used to loosen the ore, which was dug out with pickaxes and hauled to the surface by means of buckets. The limestone also had to be mined. At the quarry it was broken into uniform small lumps, screened, and washed. Great care was taken to remove all clay, which is a disturbing element in blast furnace operation. Unfortunately, the mineral deposits and the forest surrounding the blast furnace properties were practically exhausted as a result of having been worked continuously for over two decades, and raw materials had to be procured at a considerable distance away from the stacks. Teamsters, wagons, and draft animals had to haul these essentials over dirt roads that became impassable during rainy periods. Ore, limestone, and wood were stockpiled near the furnaces.

Charcoal is produced by heating wood at a very high temperature in the absence of air. To do this, the logs in about 30 cords of wood were cut into convenient lengths and piled closely together in a large heap. The interstices were filled with the smaller branches, and the pile was covered with a damping material and set on fire. Care was taken to admit only sufficient air to consume the gaseous products of the wood and maintain a high temperature without needlessly consuming the carbon. When, after about six days, only carbon and salts remained, the heap was allowed to cool.[121] Usually each cord in the pile produced about 40 bushels of charcoal. The charcoal was usually made by Negro colliers. In January 1863 Anderson notified A. R. Blakey, the owner of a slave who directed the production of charcoal at the Australia furnace, that he was well satisfied with Beverly's performance and indicated a desire to rehire the skilled slave artisan. Anderson wrote, "It is very important that Beverly shall return to the furnace . . . and in the present condition of the country every ton of metal is important."[122]

As soon as adequate stocks of ore, limestone, and charcoal were accumulated at the stack, the blast began. The process consisted simply of blowing air on a mixture of iron ore, limestone, and charcoal in a furnace to make the charcoal burn hot enough to form a molten metal, mixed with slag (impurities). Water power was necessary for the turning of a water wheel which actuated the bellow of the furnace. Rushing streams of air aided in creating and maintaining the high temperature necessary to melt the metal. The labor of approximately a hundred men was required to put a furnace in blast and keep it operating successfully. The process of "blowing in" was begun by completely filling the furnace with charcoal, which was allowed to burn to the bottom of the bosh. This took several days. When the fire reached the base of the furnace, workmen refilled the stack with charcoal, and the fire climbed back to the top. The furnace hands then fed charcoal, ore, and limestone into the furnace, and bellows (blowers) which were actuated by a water wheel or steam engine, sent blasts of air through the bosh. The limestone served as a purifying agent or purge. As a sort of refuse carrier (flux), it combined with the impurities liberated in the furnace and formed a liquid slag (waste). Because the slag was lighter than iron, it floated on the molten metal; it was removed by tapping the slag hole. Once blown in, the furnace was worked day and night until the blast was completed. When in the judgment of the founder the iron was ready to be tapped, the molten metal was released (tapping doors) from inside the furnace into gutters where it flowed into sand molds to the pigs— molds forming slabs of pig iron, as it was called.[123] A furnace was generally tapped at least twice a day. It was hoped with all ten furnaces in blast that 8,000 to 10,000 tons of pig iron a year could be delivered to the Richmond forges and foundries.

When the furnace was in blast, the Negro workers toiled constantly —replenishing stockpiles, feeding the furnaces, repairing molds, removing pigs, and so forth. Anderson notified F. T. Glasgow, "We think you had better recommend to all in charge as much modification in the management of the hands as may be compatible with our interest. Negroes expect much indulgence now, and whenever we can do so, it may be best to concede something as it may aid hereafter."[124] He also informed Glasgow that he had recently hired two slave blacksmiths, three strikers, and one carpenter to be utilized at the blast furnaces.[125] Daniel, "a very trusty old Negro accustomed all his life to blast furnaces," was purchased for $800.[126] Roam, Moses, Dick, Charles, and Thomas, slave ploughboys, were hired to work on the farms located on blast furnace properties.[127] Only Negro laborers were employed at the Tredegar forges in Augusta County. Such slave and free Negro craftsmen were engaged in making blooms (finished iron bars) for the government. Corporal Brooks, a white technician, supervised the work at the Augusta forge. In 1864 Anderson wrote to the Secretary of War asking to have Corporal John D. Brooks detailed permanently to the forge.[128] He also negotiated with Henry C. Page of Nelson County to furnish eleven slaves to chop wood for the Mt. Torry furnace. At each of the mountain blast furnaces the cooking was performed by females, usually slave wives. Anderson permitted some slaves to bring their families with them, or he granted to them permission to visit their families at least once a year. He also encouraged slaves to earn extra money by laboring at the furnaces during their free time.

While Negro labor and water, iron ore, timber, and limestone were all essential to the successful operation of the Tredegar blast furnaces, still the precious pig iron had to be delivered to the main plant in Richmond. Fortunately, mountain streams and creeks and the James River provided means of transport to the doors of the Tredegar foundries and rolling mills, where pig iron was converted into rails, cannons, and plate iron.

Shipment of pig iron to Richmond from the widely scattered Valley blast furnaces involved three distinct operations which required about 130 Negroes—58 boatmen for small boats, 47 canalboat crewmen, and 25 teamsters. First, the metal was removed from the pigs (molds) and loaded on wagons for transportation to the banks of swiftly flowing mountain streams and rivers. Six mules were used for hauling, and they were hitched in pairs as the tongue, middle, and lead teams. The teamster often saddled the left-tongue animal; but when the load was extra heavy, he walked beside this mule and controlled the team with a single jerk line attached to the bridle of the left lead mule. The teamster was apparently alone on his trips to deliver the metal to the boatmen.

Second, the Negro boatmen loaded the iron on their small craft for delivery to Buchanan. The fleet of small craft served the furnaces in Alleghany, Augusta, Rockbridge, and Botetourt counties, and the risks involved in navigating the treacherous waters tested the skill of the boatmen. William Brackens, a free Negro, was in charge of the Tredegar small-boat fleet. His arrest and impressment in the summer of 1863 to labor on fortifications seriously impaired production in the Richmond plant. Gun iron and pig metal, sorely needed for cannons and gunboat plates, was piling up on the banks of mountain streams while Brackens, the only boatman who could direct the navigation down Craig Creek and Cow Pasture River, was heaving dirt on Virginia fortifications. Alarmed, Glasgow wrote Anderson that Brackens "is the best waterman that we have . . . he is experienced

Table 3.5 *Blast furnace hands, statistics and logistics for December 1864*[129]

Furnace	Negroes	Whites	Animals	Corn	Hay	County
Mt. Torry	55	20	40	1996 bu	58,240 lb	Augusta
Australia	53	29	38	2113 bu	55,632 lb	Alleghany
Catawba	90	38	72	3510 bu	105,405 lb	Botetourt
Clover Dale	105	30	76	3636 bu	111,264 lb	Botetourt
Glenwood	99	17	53	2760 bu	77,592 lb	Rockbridge
Rebecca	71	34	60	2958 bu	87,840 lb	Botetourt
Grace	78	29	62	2812 bu	90,760 lb	Botetourt
Boats						
8 canal boats	47	9	—	—	—	—
6 small boats	58	9	28	1487 bu	41,192 lb	Botetourt
Total	656	215	429	21,273 bu	627,728 lb	

headman and there are none such to be had here now." Anderson wrote the Secretary of the Navy that Brackens's "boats bring down to Buchanan the Grace metal intended for guns and the Lucy Selina

iron for gunboat plates. . . . No one else understands the small tributary streams by which the metal is brought down by boat." Anderson's protests to the War Department and the Engineer Bureau finally
secured Brackens's release in July 1864, and the Negro navigator
returned to serve for the balance of the war.[130]

Finally, upon reaching the town of Buchanan the small boats unloaded the iron at the Tredegar company wharf, whence it was
transferred to an old lumberhouse that served as a shipping point to
Richmond. Buchanan was the terminus of the James River and Kanawha Canal, and at this point a fleet of nine large Tredegar canal boats,
with an average capacity of 40 tons each, could transport the metal
195 miles to the Richmond plant in a week or ten days. From ten to
twenty Negroes were employed in Buchanan to store the iron deposited at the wharf and to dredge out the mud around the docks.[131] As
the iron was loaded on the canalboats, it was weighed by the Negro
crewmen and readied for transportation. Each boat was pulled by
four mules led by a slave as whip driver. A white captain commanded
each of the mule-drawn vessels.

Inadequate canal service forced Anderson into acquiring his fleet of
nine large canalboats as well as the many small craft which plied the
mountain streams. The ship captains received daily instructions to
pick up and deliver various items during their trips up and down the
canal. In February 1864, for example, the boat *Catawba* was ordered
to "proceed to New Canton and bring down an engine and boiler,
leaving the boiler at Dover and bringing the engine to Richmond.
Then drop back to mountain mill and take on timber for Richmond.
If not enough timber to make a load, then complete your load by
taking on brick at Beaver Dam, and leave same at Dover. After
discharging what you have for Dover, then take in coal sufficient at
Dover to complete your load for Richmond."[133] The boat *F. T.
Glasgow* transported 37 boiler plates, 16 railroad axles, 27 kegs of
spikes, 12 bars of iron, and 17 steel springs to be forwarded by the
Virginia and Tennessee Railroad west to Mobile, Alabama.[134]
Throughout the war the Tredegar canalboats hauled tons of food,
heavy plate iron, timber, coal, cattle, iron bars, engines, guns, forage,
and other freight up and down the canal. Anderson and Company
indicated the scope of their needs for Negro manpower in the many
advertisements placed in Virginia newspapers between 1862 and 1865.
During this period the number of hands requested increased from five

Table 3.6 *The Tredegar canal fleet*

Name of boat	Captain	Negro Crewmen
Tredegar	E. D. Pettit	Bob Gray (free)
		Isaac Banks
		Wesley
		Henry
		Cook
F. T. Glasgow	J. R. Williams	Stephen Moore
		Kyle
		Branch
		Robert
		Ned Cooper (free)
		Ned Staples (free)
Rebecca	W. G. Johnson	Joshua
		Edmond
		Henry
		Aaron Dunn
Clover Dale	R. S. Shepard	Joshua Henly (free)
		Davy
		James
		Peter
		Joe
		Joe
Catawba	L. B. Baird	Phil
		Ambrose
		Wilson
		George
		William
Grace	W. Allen	Thomas Heath (free)
		Ben Allen
		Chesterfield
		Rowland
Goldleaf	S. Crowe	Wm. Motley
		Phil Cousins (free)
		Eli Spierlock (free)
		A. Spierlock (free)
Imogene	E. J. Lane	George Kent
		Bagwill
		Pleasant
		Andrew (big)
		Andrew (little)
Fawn	W. R. Johnson	Jim
		Armistead
		Charles

hundred to one thousand able-bodied Negro men and boys. Hiring agents were sent into eastern and southside Virginia, into the Piedmont counties, and out into the mountainous regions. Such agents were promised employment as overseers if they secured thirty or more hands, and subsequent freedom from the army, as the law exempted one overseer for every twenty slaves. The agents appealed to the patriotism as well as the self-interest of slaveowners. Anderson wrote to his agents and informed them of their grave responsibilities to secure adequate Negro laborers.

In retrospect, the mountain blast furnaces, as they belched smoke and fire into the sky, dominated the industrial scene of the Valley. Industrial Negro labor was an indispensable factor as the Tredegar Iron Works wrestled to fulfill vital war contracts with the various bureaus of the War Department. The realistic war practices of this industrial plant were based, from the very outset of the war, on the full and extensive use of black manpower—skilled and unskilled—in the procurement, transportation, and fabrication of raw materials and the delivery of finished products to Confederate fighting forces, southern railroads, smaller industrial plants, and various branches of the War Department such as ordnance, quartermaster, engineer, and the navy.

CHAPTER FOUR

Transportation Laborers

Canal companies and railroads afford an excellent example of the extensive war demands placed upon Negro labor. Yet Virginia's vital transportation industries, handicapped in their efforts to procure sufficient Negro manpower, were forced to compete for laborers with others—the various bureaus of the War Department, planters, local hiring agents, and private industries. Consequently, to expedite the rapid movement of troops and military supplies, presidents of transportation companies frequently had to appeal to state officials to impress black workers.

Growing concern over the limitations of river navigation for the shipment of freight by batteaux prompted the shifting of cargoes to the James River and Kanawha Canal Company. Canalboats westbound from Richmond or Lynchburg could transport military supplies and goods five to ten times as large as batteaux could carry. Such westbound boats were loaded with a variety of manufactured items and merchandise. Subsequently, canalboats eastbound from the Valley carried wheat, corn, and other farm products, iron ore and other mining products, and lumber. Faster, however, and capable of carrying heavier loads, Virginia railroads were eventually able to divert the bulk of canal trade to their lines. The state's war transportation industries utilized tens of thousands of Negro laborers. They poled the batteaux, dug and maintained the canals, and repaired the railroads.

As the sky darkened over Virginia in May 1861, the James River and Kanawha Canal Company employed 455 persons, of whom the great majority were Negroes. To facilitate proper supervision, operation, and maintenance of the canal, the company split the canal into two divisions: the first extended west from Richmond to Lynchburg, a distance of 136 miles; the second, extended 60 miles farther west to Buchanan. For each division there was a superintendent of repairs who in turn divided his section into three subdivisions for the purpose of maintenance and ordinary repairs, such as ditching, riprapping, dressing the towpath, keeping embankments in order, and so forth. E. L. Chinn, superintendent of the first division, had a labor force of 28 whites and 136 slaves; J. H. Harris, superintendent of the second division, employed 12 whites and 109 slaves.[1]

The war significance of the James River and Kanawha Canal Company mounted as this waterway was used increasingly to transport troops and matériel, as well as food, forage, and other products which were gathered throughout the Piedmont and the Valley. The ante-bellum commerce—which extended along the James River from Richmond to Lynchburg, and on which the trade of the canal depended for profit—was to diminish rapidly. Such commercial traffic would be replaced largely by the Tredegar and the government canalboats which plied the waterway. The canal's growing importance as an avenue for military supplies, coupled with the lack of revenue to keep the waterway in good navigable condition, necessitated government assistance. Accordingly, in response to a request by Confederate officials, the General Assembly of Virginia on March 28, 1862, authorized a grant of $200,000 to keep the canal open from Richmond to Buchanan, a distance of 196 miles.[2] Meanwhile the first ten months of war had reduced greatly the company's skilled labor force. White technicians had responded to the governor's call for volunteers for the defense of the state, while slave artisans were periodically drafted to labor on fortifications. Superintendent E. L. Chinn, in charge of the first division, reported to President Ellis that "16 of our best mechanics and quarrymen exchanged the jack plane and drill for the musket." Chinn also complained that several of his slave mechanics had been impressed to labor on defense works.[3] Consequently, the fortunes of war had left behind approximately 50 whites and 281 slaves to maintain the canal's mechanical structures.

Beginning at Richmond, one of the most important works of the waterway was the Richmond dock, which reached for one mile along the north side of the James River. It consisted of a series of locks and basins extending from the main basin of the canal to the upper end of the dock. The ship lock, built of granite, was 185 feet long between the gates and 35 feet wide, had a lift of 15 feet, and would pass vessels of 500 tons.[5] The James River and Kanawha Canal was 30 feet wide at the bottom, 50 feet wide at the waterline, and 5 feet deep. The tow path was 12 feet wide, and the berm bank 8 feet. The locks were 100 feet long between the gates and 15 feet wide in the chamber. The total lockage from Richmond to Buchanan embraced 90 lift locks, having a total lift of 728 feet.[6] There remains, therefore, the question of the war responsibilities of the waterway's industrial Negro labor force.

During the early weeks of the war, President Thomas H. Ellis said in his annual report to the Board of Directors that full justice had not always been done to the Negro employees whose business it was to keep the line in repair. "On every case of emergency," Ellis stated, "the overseers and the hands under them have hastened to the scene of danger or disaster, and worked with considerable zeal, good will and efficiency." As the records show, Negro labor was essential to the maintenance and operation of the canal. Drillers, quarrymen, and stone cutters quarried and prepared the granite for construction purposes. Masons built retaining walls and repaired all masonry works such as dams, locks, bridges, abutments, and culverts. Boatmen transported granite and timber; sectional squads, when not engaged in replacing cribs (as a breakwater) and in dredging operations, were ditching, riprapping, raising embankments, mending breaches, and smoothing the surface of the towpath along the south side of the canal. Dock hands assisted in working the ship lock and towing

Table 4.1 *Slave occupations in the James River and Kanawha Canal Company*[4]

Occupation	Number	Occupation	Number
Messenger	1	Masons	4
Working ship lock	5	Mason helpers	26
Cooks	18	Patrollers	4
Carpenters	13	Painters	2
Blacksmiths	6	Quarrymen	8
Drillers (stone)	5	Quarrymen helpers	35
Driller helpers	7	Ferrymen	1
Boatmen	13	Dredgeboat hands	36
Laborers	93	Stonecutters	6
		Total	283

vessels. Carpenters kept in repair the huge wooden lock gates, the wharfing along the docks, and the bridges over the canal. When not engaged in ordinary repairs, the carpenters were framing timber, building houseboats, and doing other essential work at the canal. Blacksmiths fabricated and mended all kinds of metal pieces, and sharpened masonry tools.

In September 1861 the chief engineer reported that the slaves were completing the new dam at Joshua Falls and repairing canal damage inflicted by the heavy rains.[7] The following month the superintendent of the first division indicated that he had a labor force consisting of "one master mason, one foreman mason, 6 journeymen masons, 20 quarrymen, 3 blacksmiths, 3 master carpenters, 22 journeymen carpenters, 4 overseers, one supply agent, and 88 employed as boatmen, laborers, cooks, etc., in all 149; of whom 40 white men and 109 were slaves."[8] In describing the work they performed Chinn noted:

> The carpenters repaired Tye river and Joshua falls dam; framed and raised the superstructure of 10 bridges; framed and put in 11 pairs lock gates, and made repairs to many others; built 6 new lock houses, 1 carpenters' lighter and 2 mud flats; repaired 3 house boats, 3 dredge boats and 6 mud flats. They made repairs to the chamber locks; put in frame and head gates . . . besides doing many other jobs. . . .[9]

The divisional superintendent also reported that the slaves "under the charge of the master mason and foreman mason quarried and prepared a large quantity of granite for building purposes." They also pulled down "and rebuilt 6 bridge abutments, and repaired 7 others; built retaining walls and long wings at the lower end of the combined locks at the head of the Tye river pond." In completing his report to the company president, Chinn stated that the slaves built "the masonry of a forebay for supplying water power to the east wing of the state Armory" in Richmond.[10]

The report of the superintendent of the second division was equally illuminating. Superintendent Harris reported that "the force of Negroes (61) hired by the year for the repairs of this division . . . consist of 49 common laborers, 5 cooks, 5 carpenters, and two smiths, and an average force of 5 whites as carpenters." Harris divided the 61 blacks and 5 whites into five squads—three of common laborers and two of carpenters. The heavy rains and floods required an extraordinary amount of repairs, especially to the towpath. He indicated that the three dredging machines were almost constantly engaged in dredging and that the slaves were at work restoring embankments.[11] There were, however, so many landslides along the towpath and so many breaches in the dams that the labor force was not adequate to make the necessary repairs. Consequently, the company advertised in the Virginia press for additional slave hands.[12] The carpenters, in addition to making ordinary repairs, such as walling and riprapping, built four bridges and a carpenter's shop, installed four sets of new lock gates, strengthened the abutments of dams, and replaced cribs to sustain the embankments.[13]

Immediately after passage of the Subsidy Act of March 28, 1862, the company sent agents to hire more Negroes for the waterway. A survey of the entire canal line indicated that a much larger labor force was required to restore the waterway to the best possible condition. Confederate authorities empowered the chief engineer of the company to impress slaves and teams along the canal. The company was also permitted to purchase, at government prices, carts, shovels, picks, wheelbarrows, and other implements from government stores or agencies. Another government concession enabled the company management to advertise for five hundred Negroes, to be hired at the expense of the Confederate government, for work on the canal near Lynchburg. The Richmond *Examiner* requested that "persons having slaves to hire for the residue of the year, or for a shorter period" contact William P. Mumford, the secretary of the James River and Kanawha Canal Company.[14] Such measures did not suffice, however, and at no time did the canal have sufficient Negro labor to keep it in complete repair. Between 1863 and the fall of 1864, nearly all of the foremen and white mechanics had been drafted into the army. The detailing of 27 free blacks, by the Bureau of Conscription, to assist in making repairs was of limited value to the waterway.[15] The shortage of black manpower and the loss of white employees proved to be disastrous to the company. Finally in March 1865, a force of Union cavalry was engaged in the destruction of the canal to within 30 miles of Richmond. One cannot fail to be impressed with the significant wartime contribution of skilled and unskilled Negro labor to the James River and Kanawha Canal Company. During the final thirty months of the Civil War Negroes composed over 85 per cent of the labor force engaged in the maintenance of the waterway. Although the canal was of great assistance to the Confederacy it was constantly plagued with labor shortages. When compared with the equipment

and labor problems facing the Virginia railroads, however, the difficulties of the James River and Kanawha Company paled into significance.

II

Another essential war industry, the railroads, have already received
the careful attention of the historian.[16] The importance of the railroads of the Confederacy is also meaningful in terms of the Negro
labor force largely responsible for maintaining old lines and building
new rail lines which were intended to close the glaring gap in Confederate transportation. "At a time like this," said Governor Letcher of
Virginia, "nothing is more important than the preservation of our
railroads, and keeping them in safe running order." The governor
added, "The breaking of a bar of iron, may cause serious delay, unless
the means are at hand to replace it. A delay of a few hours, in the
transportation of troops or supplies for their subsistence, or ordnance
stores, may bring defeat to our arms, and even the success of our
cause."[17] Negroes, free and slave, performed the hard and menial tasks
associated with routine maintenance of Virginia's railroads. Yet a
surprisingly large number filled positions that required dexterity and
carried responsibility. For example, in company car shops there were
Negro boilermakers, blacksmiths, finishing carpenters, and other
skilled mechanics. Brakemen on passenger and freight trains were
usually Negroes, and the colored fireman was a prominent feature of
the Southern railway scene. Negro personnel often manned compli-
cated construction equipment and repaired and built bridges. At
wood stations, strong ebony arms filled the tenders of passing trains;
they laid tracks, repaired roadbeds, cut and hewed crossties, pumped
water, erected trestles, and they loaded and unloaded freight at the
many depots.

The railroad system of Virginia, though incomplete, was called
upon to transport troops as well as ordnance, commissary, and quar-
termaster supplies. Moreover, Lee's armies were often located at
points that were not very far from their main channels of delivery.
Four major railroads served the troops in the Valley and western
Virginia—the Virginia Central, the Virginia and Tennessee, the
Southside, and the Richmond and Danville. Likewise, troops below
Petersburg were dependent upon the Petersburg and Weldon, and the

Norfolk and Petersburg. Army operations in the Peninsula were supported by the Richmond, Fredericksburg and Potomac; the Richmond-Petersburg; and the Richmond and York. During the early months of the war the Orange and Alexandria and the Manassas Gap railroad lines served troops in northern Virginia and the Piedmont. Negro manpower was committed to the maintenance and repair of these roads throughout the war. In fact, so sensitive was the governor to their importance that he remarked, "If these roads are permitted to go down, the operations of our army in the field must be seriously embarrassed, if indeed they are not utterly and hopelessly paralyzed."[18]

Virginia railroads were much like other Southern railroads, in lacking tracks of uniform gauge. The two most common gauges used in Virginia were 4 feet 8½ inches and 5 feet. The usual rail was made in rolled wrought-iron T sections, varying in length from 18 to 24 feet and weighing from 35 to 65 pounds per yard.[19] Virginia railroad operators refused to join tracks with competitors at terminal points— even where they were using the same gauge—and they would not permit their rolling stock to pass onto the rails of another line, with the result that much transshipment of freight was required. Many railroads had their own maintenance shops. Such shops could generally build certain needed equipment, which sometimes included passenger coaches, baggage cars, flatcars, boxcars, and dump cars.

From 1861 to 1865, continuous maintenance was necessary to keep open and in usable condition the four important railroad lines serving army operations in the Piedmont, the Valley, and western Virginia. These lines also made it possible to transport industrial goods and to tap the food-producing regions of the Carolinas, Georgia, and Tennessee. The first and longest of the four railroads was the Virginia Central, whose 25 engines covered some 206 miles of track, terminating in Richmond. This railroad transported essential supplies for Lee's army, demonstrating that a single line could carry in one day what would take five days for 1,000 wagons and 5,000 horses to deliver. The Virginia Central moved 50,393 tons of freight in 1861.[20]

For administrative purposes this line was divided into areas—the Richmond depot, the station depots, the train and machine shops, and road departments. In 1861 W. G. Richardson, the roadmaster, superintended all repairs. He had a road labor force of 9 whites and 168 slaves.[21] Besides this road-repair gang, there were an additional 100 Negroes who made up the Virginia Central's black labor force in the fall of 1861. The Richmond depot had 25 slaves and 19 whites; there were 24 slaves and 26 white agents at the various stations; 39 Negroes and 38 whites worked as firemen and brakemen; and there were 12 Negroes (including one boilermaker) and 60 whites who worked in the machine department fabricating or repairing company equipment. Many other slaves were worked under separate contract between owner and employer to handle the loading and unloading of freight. By 1862 the Virginia Central employed 321 Negroes: 223 in the road department and 68 in the machinery and train departments, and the various stations engaged 30.[22] More than 100 slaves were working on the track between Hanover Junction and Gordonsville in July when the roadmaster received orders transferring them to assist the master road carpenter in the rebuilding of the South Anna bridge. The following month 30 Negroes were seized and carried off by Federal troops during a raid at Frederick Hall.[23] The roadmaster required a large labor force of slaves to clear the forest, drain marshes, erect way stations, depots, bridges, trestles, and maintenance shops. About fifteen slaves worked the gravel trains which provided ballasting material (broken stone or gravel used in making roadbeds solid). Many others were necessary for the grading and construction of roadbeds. No detail of a roadbed required more attention than proper drainage. Both the cutting and embankment had to be free of defects; stumps, stones, brush, and other obstructions which might interfere had to be cleared. Drainage was best achieved by raising the roadbed above the reach of the water. The open, porous character of good ballasting material permitted falling water to pass off freely. The ballasting had to give good support for the crossties (sleepers) and prevent them from moving laterally. Sleepers were made by squaring off two parallel sides on each tie; one to set firmly on the ballasting, the other to support the rail. With ample fastening to a firm, level base, the track was smooth and the trains ran accordingly.

In 1863 the Virginia Central faced a crisis caused by a combination of increased traffic, acute labor shortages, mounting repairs, and a deterioration of its equipment. Early in the year General Lee, as the result of prodding by the company president, urged the Secretary of War to divert one hundred slaves from fortification work for sixty days to repair the rail lines. "There was no other way," asserted Lee, "to prevent the road from failing the army at the very time it would be needed most."[24] During this period the line was hauling from

Richmond at least half of the supplies for the Army of Northern Virginia at Hanover Junction. In April, Lee again notified the Secretary of War, "We cannot retain our position unless the railroads can afford sufficient transportation."[25] Lee attempted to show that the railroads, especially the Virginia Central, were as much a part of the system of public defense as fortifications. The Secretary, however, felt that the 200 odd slaves employed by the company were ample to perform the necessary repairs. Nevertheless, the governor of Virginia was informed during the summer months that the company required an additional 260 Negroes: 90 men to cut and hew crossties, 60 to keep the company in wood, 100 to accumulate surplus, and 10 in the machine shops as smiths and helpers.[26] The company president pointed out to the governor that "formerly all our supplies of timber and fuel for engines were obtained by contract, but now, to a great extent, the company has to procure crossties and wood with its own labor."[27] The governor appealed to the General Assembly for appropriate legislation to aid railroads in securing additional Negro laborers. To relieve its labor shortages in the early fall of 1863, the Virginia Central purchased 35 slaves for $83,484.[28] In October 1863 the Virginia legislature authorized the governor to impress slaves to work on the Virginia Central lines. Finally in December 1864 the governor proposed that the legislature enact a law to impress free Negroes to labor exclusively on the various railroad lines in the state. Governor John Letcher pointed out that "many of the free Negroes are mechanics, and mechanical labor is indispensable to keep up the railroads." In 1864 the Virginia Central had 23 Negro workers at the Richmond depot, 41 at wayside stations, 63 firemen and brakemen, 15 machine-shop technicians, and 141 road hands.[29] An additional 153 Negroes detailed by the Bureau of Conscription during the fall of 1864, in response to an urgent request by company officials, increased the Negro labor force to almost 300 workers. They struggled to maintain the road and insure the transportation of troops and commodities.

The second important railroad serving Confederate troops in the Valley was the Virginia and Tennessee, whose 80 miles of track in southwestern Virginia ran from Bristol to Lynchburg, a strategic supply base. This road, Virginia's most direct link with the West, provided access to a flow of supplies from east Tennessee. Of additional significance, the South's principal source of salt was located at

Saltville, on a spur of the Virginia and Tennessee. Like other Virginia railroads, the line's principal labor force consisted of slaves owned by the company or hired by the year. Over five hundred Negro section hands maintained the way and structures, took care of wreck or flood emergencies, and repaired war damage inflicted by Union raiding parties. Although this was a normal part of railroad maintenance, such work involved a great deal of heavy labor: replacement of burned and rotted timber structures, erection of temporary trestles to substitute for destroyed bridges, and straightening and re-laying bent iron rails. As weather and heavy wear continued their deleterious effects, maintenance of railroad tracks required the constant attention of large crews.

In December 1861 the Richmond *Daily Examiner* informed slave-owners that the Virginia and Tennessee "wishes to hire, for the ensuing year, to work on the repairs of their road and in their shops, the following described slaves: 400 laborers, 50 train hands, 33 carpenters, and 20 blacksmiths and strikers." The following month the Richmond *Examiner* carried a similar advertisement stating that "Bonds, payable quarterly, will be given for their hires." In November 1862 the general superintendent at Lynchburg was seeking to employ 500 Negroes as depot and track hands, woodchoppers, brakemen, carpenters, and blacksmiths. Owners were promised that their slaves "will be amply supplied with good provisions and good clothing suitable to the season, and will be well taken care of." By 1864 the Virginia and Tennessee employed 650 slaves at an annual cost of $877,500. The company estimated that an equal number in 1865 would cost $2,000,000.[30] Throughout the war at least six Negro brakemen (passenger and freight trains) were killed in falls from moving trains.[31] By 1865 the Virginia and Tennessee had transported more than 475,000 tons of freight and over 500,000 troops.[32]

The third essential railroad having access to the Valley joined the Virginia and Tennessee as it terminated at Lynchburg. The Southside Railroad, another broad-guage (5 feet) line, provided through traffic from Lynchburg to Petersburg. As the Southside line wandered eastward to Petersburg, it tapped the food-producing regions of the state. It furnished the Confederacy with a vital interior line for the defense of Richmond and the transportation of troops and supplies. It also engaged a large force of Negro employees. In November 1861 H. D. Bird, the superintendent, had a labor force of 304 Negroes and

74 whites. Several colored carpenters were engaged in repairing the wharves at City Point, and others were constructing a new carpenter shop. Many section hands were repairing the Farmville and Lynchburg bridges and laying rails.[33] The Southside depended on local contractors employing Negro labor to supply wood for fuel, and this cordwood was stacked at intervals along the line. The line utilized its own laborers, however, to cut and hew crossties and to procure lumber. Chestnut, locust, or other hardwoods, from trees cut along the right-of-way, were used to make the ties.[34] Throughout the war one of the gravest problems facing the company was the impressment of its slaves for work on fortifications. In the winter of 1862 the sheriff of Appomattox County notified the governor that Southside officials refused to release slaves "upon the grounds that they are already at work for the government."[35] In February 1863, Petersburg officials were directed by the governor to release fourteen slaves employed by the Southside railroad who were impressed to work on defensive structures. The governor noted that it was "impossible to carry on the transportation of the State and Confederate Governments if the railroads are interfered with and their laborers taken from them."[36]

Additional attempts were made by local officials to seize the company's Negro laborers. To seek relief from this practice the presidents of the Southside and Petersburg railroads jointly with the president of the Petersburg Iron Works drafted a letter to the governor of the state. They pointed out that "the railroads do a large amount of army transportation both of troops and materials of war, and therefore the work of our Negroes on the railroads is in our opinion as important as it can be on the fortifications. This is also the case with the iron works —they are making shot and shell and doing other work for the government." The governor replied, "There can be no reason why capital in this form should not contribute its fair proportion to the public defense. . . . Nor is the fact that they have only the amount of labor they need an argument of force, that is precisely the case it may be presumed of every farmer engaged in cultivation."[37] Regardless of the many complaints pertaining to the impressment of Negroes who worked for the Southside Railroad, the newly elected governor of Virginia was not inclined to be as sympathetic as his predecessor. By 1863 over 400 slaves toiled on the Southside lines, and in 1864 the company was advertising for additional slave laborers to repair mounting damages. The superintendent notified the company president, "We had two freshets, or rather rain storms which injured the road very badly in some places; several culverts and portions of some high embankments were washed away." The superintendent also noted that the bridges were in good shape and that the carpenters had built new passenger cars and repaired many others. They also made repairs to the houses occupied by Negroes hired by the company. The road crews had installed 15,000 new sills along the line.[38] For the Southside line, Negro manpower served as a reservoir from which it drew its war labor force. The only line with which it came in physical contact was the Richmond and Danville, also a broad-gauge (5 feet) line, which ran from Richmond to Danville and intersected the Southside at Burkeville, some 53 miles southwest of Richmond.

The Richmond and Danville was the fourth major line that was essential to army operations in the Piedmont and southwestern Virginia. Angling in a southwesterly direction from the Confederate capital, it ran 140 miles through an agricultural region and ended abruptly near the North Carolina border. By 1864 it was of strategic importance, as Lee's main line was unprepared to assume the burden of heavy and constant transportation of war materials. Temporary stations and freight houses scattered along its right-of-way had to be replaced with permanent structures. Approximately 48 miles of track consisted of badly worn "flatbar" or "strap" rail laid on wooden stringers. Over 75 per cent of such rail, however, lay south and west of Burkeville, which received considerably less traffic than that to the northeast, where both freight and passengers bound for the capital had to transfer from the Southside line. Increased war traffic resulted in the rapid deterioration of the strap rail. Consequently, it became the immediate responsibility of most of the 250 company slaves to replace the strap rail with heavy rail supplied by the Confederacy.[39] In December 1861 Lewis E. Harvie, president of the company, reported that "the general condition of the road has been improved and is now in a situation to meet the demands of the government."[40] Charles G. Talcott, the superintendent, indicated that both roadbeds and tracks, as well as bridges and culverts, had been repaired at a cost of approximately $90,000 for materials and over $105,000 for working expenses. At stations and on sections and trains at an average cost of $102.37 per annum each, the line employed 283 slaves. The 14 Negro brakemen were paid 90 cents a day, while the 13 Negro firemen received $1.00 a day.[41]

By way of comparison, the Richmond and Danville provides an excellent picture of a railroad struggling to become self-sufficient. To stockpile sufficient crossties and bridge timber, the company employed slave labor in the operation of its sawmill and hauled in logs with its own teams and wagons. The company went so far as to purchase, slaughter, and cure its own beef and bacon. By 1862 the Richmond and Danville line employed 328 free Negroes and slaves—30 firemen and brakemen, 15 blacksmiths and helpers, 13 shop laborers, and 270 section and depot hands.[42] Other Negroes working on this line were slaves owned by persons with contracts to supply fuel or other provisions. A. J. Johnson of Clover, Virginia, operated a sawmill which employed slave labor. Johnson had a contract to supply lumber used to repair flat-bar track west of Burkeville.[43] The company purchased an additional 71 slaves in 1862, making a total of 221 owned by the railroad line. As the war progressed the company increasingly sought to hire slaves by offering their owners more than either the government or industry was willing to pay. By the end of 1863, 223 slaves were employed "at shops and depot sections and trains, at an average cost of $159.88 each." An additional 75 slaves were engaged as woodcutters, carpenters, shop hands, and freight handlers at an average salary of $50.00 per month.[44] Many of the skilled Negro workers labored at the recently acquired foundry which supplied the road with iron and brass castings. Most of the grease and lubricants used by the company were manufactured in the Manchester and North Side shops. These two shops also constructed and repaired all of the line's freight and passenger cars.[45] In late December 1864 Charles G. Talcott, superintendent of the railroad, advertised in Virginia newspapers for "1000 slaves to work on the Richmond and Danville, and 300 slaves to work on the Piedmont railroad."[46] Slaveowners were urged "to apply to any agent of the roads along the line or at the offices of the Richmond and Danville."[47] Among the 700-odd slaves employed in 1864, there were 22 firemen, 29 brakemen, 36 cleaners, 2 coach maids, and 51 machine-shop employees.

The Piedmont Railroad, a subsidiary line of the Richmond and Danville, ultimately provided an important link for the transportation of food and supplies.[48] Of special concern to both military and government officials was the military necessity of closing the 40-mile gap between Danville, Virginia, and Greensboro, North Carolina. This could be accomplished by building a new line (the Piedmont) to connect the southern terminal of the Richmond and Danville with the North Carolina Railroad at Greensboro. By May 1862 the details for construction of the line had been approved by both state and Confederate officials. On June 13 the president and the chief engineer of the Danville line were authorized to employ three divisional superintendents, 1,500 slaves, and the requisite number of overseers. Hiring agents were sent out to procure Negro labor, but they were unable to secure a sufficient force, at the allotted $12 per month. In July this figure was increased to $15, plus rations and medical attention. The railroad president was allowed $400,000 for the purchase of 400 slaves, but reported to the board of directors that he "was compelled to exceed the price authorized to the extent of $141 for each slave purchased."[49] Private contractors were also engaged to use slave labor to complete portions of the line. By December 1862 the 800 Negroes engaged in building the line were insufficient, and the chief engineer recommended that "a requisition be made upon the contractor to supply the additional labor according to the contract."[50]

In the meantime, to procure needed railroad iron, a large crew of slaves was employed to remove the tracks of the Seaboard and Roanoke line, east of Franklin. As the scarcity of railroad iron mounted, the track was torn up on the short York River line. From time to time in order to increase the force of Negroes employed by the company, the salary paid for Negro labor was advanced until it reached $22 per month for each adult and $15 per month for each boy.[51] Throughout 1863, hundreds of slaves were engaged in clearing the route of the line to a minimum width of 80 feet. Felled timber was used for crossties on the road. Negroes erected piers and abutments for bridges and other timber structures along the line. Several crews of woodchoppers and sawyers worked the green timber for framing purposes. Eventually the War Department intervened to insist that the construction force should number at least 2,500 Negroes. Virginia legislators authorized the impressment of as many Negroes as were necessary to finish the road within the state borders.[52] The governor requested information as to "whether the slaves ordered have been assigned to labor on the extension" into North Carolina.[53] In February 1864

President Davis applied to the governor of Virginia for several hundred slaves to work on the Piedmont line. Pittsylvania County was requested to provide 300 slaves, and the governor asked county authorities for information on the number of slaves to be impressed in Danville in order not to take too many from the county.[54] Finally the new Piedmont line was opened for service during the latter part of May 1864, but a difference of gauge in the line (not 5 feet) required a transshipment of goods at Danville. As a result of shortages in labor and materials, instead of completing the line within six months, as could have been done, the task took more than two years. Yet it was imperative that Danville be connected with Greensboro for strategic purposes.

From the beginning of the war Lee's major concern was logistics. For the transporting of troops and supplies as well as internal lines of communication, he was primarily dependent upon Virginia's four major railroads. There was the Virginia Central, which ran north of the capital for a few miles and then wandered westerly to provide an important link with the productive Shenandoah Valley. Next, running southwesterly from Richmond was the Richmond and Danville, which tapped the food-producing regions of western North Carolina. And finally, from Petersburg the Southside Railroad extended west to Lynchburg, which was also the terminal city for the state's fourth major railroad, the Virginia and Tennessee, and received from it a flow of war materials from the eastern section of Tennessee. It is highly significant that in each of the four roads, maintenance or operation of tracks, switches, turntables, water tanks, wood tenders, and trestle works was dependent upon the brawn and dexterity of Negro manpower. Likewise, Negro brakemen, blacksmiths, firemen, and mechanics were essential to the operation and upkeep of locomotives. This same pattern is clearly reflected in other Virginia railroads throughout the war.

For example, skilled and unskilled Negro labor (free and slave) was essential to the maintenance of passenger and freight trains, tracks, and timber structures of both the Richmond and Petersburg and the Petersburg railroads. No problem facing both railroads caused more worry and anxiety than that of shortages of rolling stock and Negro labor. Without Negro manpower Virginia lacked the means to repair and maintain her railroads. For both Petersburg lines the extraordinary demands of the war called for the frequent restoration of roadbeds and replacement of trackage. The advance, shifting, or retreat of armies, the transportation of forage and food supplies, and the hauling of coal, munitions, and heavy ordnance—all inflicted heavy damage upon the lines. Inability to replace rail and equipment increased maintenance problems and necessitated the employment of many more laborers than would have been needed had there been a sufficiency of these commodities. Furthermore, throughout the war the two Petersburg lines served as interior lines of defense and communication.

With roots that penetrated the seacoast of the Carolinas, the Petersburg Railroad was regarded as the most efficient of all the lines which carried supplies to Lee's army. In 1861 W. T. Joynes, president of the 65-mile line, reported that the company shop had built about twenty cars, including one for passengers.[55] During this period the company employed about 121 Negroes. By February 1862 the line employed 66 whites and 150 Negroes, free and slave. Included in the company's colored labor force were 20 firemen, blacksmiths, and engine hands whose wages averaged $113 yearly; 7 carshop mechanics, averaging $134 yearly; 9 carpenters employed to repair bridges and depots, averaging $160 yearly; and 13 free Negro firemen and train hands, each one averaging $19 per month; and 101 section hands, averaging $118 yearly.[56] The total of 191 Negroes employed by the road in 1863 was increased to 265 the following year. This increase was prompted by the need to resolve the great wear and tear of the

Table 4.2 *Negro employees of the Petersburg Railroad, 1864*[57]

Occupation	Number	Wages
Machine shop	35	$ 2.50 daily
Car shop	24	2.50 daily
Painters	6	2.75 daily
Train hands	10	35.00 monthly
Firemen	10	35.00 monthly
Depot	14	1.25 daily
Tracklayers	7	2.00 daily
Laborers	127	10.00 monthly
Carpenters	17	2.25 daily
Sawmill	15	2.00 daily
Total	265	

line resulting from its constant use. Repeated maintenance by slave section hands was necessary in order to keep it in operation. Fortunately both state and Confederate officials were aware of the prominent role of the line and its growing influence upon military operations. Their success in enlarging the Negro labor force helped materially in sustaining the transportation of war supplies and equipment. Past experience had shown that damaged or rotted rails, roadbeds, ties, bridges, and wooden trestles could be replaced at great speed when a sufficient force of slaves was detailed for the task. Consequently, rapid and constant maintenance of trackage was a normal part of the heavy work required of the large Negro labor force employed by the Petersburg Railroad.

The importance of the railroad operations of the Petersburg Railroad was somewhat matched by that of the Richmond and Petersburg Railroad Company. Its 22-mile stretch of line provided an essential link between the two industrial and rail urban centers in the state. Until the spring of 1862, when ballasting was deemed necessary, its roadbed and track were typical of Virginia roads: the ties were placed upon bare ground and laid with minimum preparation. Such a procedure resulted in the need for constant maintenance and made the line exceedingly vulnerable to weather conditions. During the summer of 1861, for example, a large crew of slave section hands was engaged in cutting and hewing crossties to replace 7,000 unballasted ties which were decaying.[58] By the fall of 1861 the line employed 120 Negroes, including brakemen and firemen as well as those working in the company shops, depots, and road department.[59] While coupling cars at the Clover Hill station, a slave hired from H. B. Holmes was crushed and killed. A slave brakeman was also killed as he fell between the cars.[60] There was no significant increase in the line's labor force in 1862; but in December, E. H. Gill, the superintendent, advertised in the Richmond and Petersburg newspapers for 100 Negroes to "work upon the repairs and in the shops and depots as carpenters blacksmiths, train hands, wood choppers, and laborers."[61] Like other railroads, the company was faced with the impressment of their Negro laborers. In February 1863 C. Ellis, president of the road, informed the governor that "if these Negroes could possibly be spared without stopping our transportation to and from Petersburg, or if I could hire Negroes as substitutes I would not hesitate cheerfully to provide our quota, but these hands are absolutely necessary to load and unload our trains at Petersburg."[62] In order to offset the damage done to the road and equipment the superintendent again advertised for 100 slaves—6 carpenters, 6 blacksmiths, 6 strikers, 12 train hands, 10 woodchoppers, and 60 able-bodied laborers.[63] Additional slave labor was necessary to repair the great damage caused by rain as it eroded portions of the track and inflicted damage on roadbeds and embankments. W. B. Ransom, master machinist of the machine shop, placed an advertisement in the Richmond press for four Negroes to clean engines.[64] Even though it was extremely difficult to replace damaged parts and equipment, the company's 22 miles of track appears to have had ample labor to keep it in fair shape for wartime traffic, although at intervals heavy repairs were required. President Ellis, in reporting to the Board of Directors, stated that "since the 1st of April, 1861, to the 31st of March, 1864, there has passed over this road more than one million of persons, and upward of 250,000 tons of freight."[66]

The two Richmond roads leading northward to Fredericksburg and eastward to the York River were of much less importance than the two Petersburg lines. Both the Richmond, Fredericksburg and Potomac, and the Richmond and York River railroad companies were severely crippled by wartime wear and tear on railroad equipment and raids by Federal forces. Yet both roads were involved in Confederate successes in Virginia campaigns, by transporting men and materials to gray-clad armies. Every mile of their track was laid in what was battle area at some time or other during the war. From the summer of 1864 the Richmond and York River line was almost

Table 4.3 *Negro employees, Richmond and Petersburg Railroad, 1864*[65]

Place	Number
Richmond depot	22
Richmond shops	23
Manchester shops	9
Petersburg depot	9
Clover Hill station	4
Firemen and train hands	22
Material and gravel trains	20
Woodchoppers and teamsters	8
Section men on repair of road	36
Total	153

completely torn up and its trackage used on the new Piedmont line and others.

The Richmond and York River Railroad ran from the capital 38 miles eastward to West Point, where the Mattapony and Pamunkey rivers join to form the York. This line was militarily important during the Peninsula campaign in the spring of 1862. It was directly in the path of Federal advance, and a heavy gun was mounted on a flatcar for use on the road. The gun, a rifled 32-pounder, was used with good effect at the Battle of Savage Station on June 29, 1862. Unfortunately both Federal and Confederate troops were engaged in the destruction of the line at various points. Subsequently the capital suffered from the loss of this line which had been transporting food and provisions. As the last of McClellan's soldiers left the area, however, slave laborers were promptly dispatched to repair damages. The war experiences of this railroad were marked by constant Federal raids, labor shortages, accidents, and equipment problems and the removal of its track for other lines.

Incessant rain and poorly constructed roadbeds were responsible for a freak accident in July 1861. As a train approached within 5 miles of West Point a bank gave way, causing the engine, tender, and one of the coaches to be thrown from the track and down the embankment. A slave fireman, belonging to Dr. Braxton of New Kent, was caught between the tender and engine and was killed.[67] Throughout the war, the line's Negro labor force apparently remained at less than 50 workers. In September 1862 the company employed 41 slaves—31 section hands, 6 firemen and train hands, and 4 depot and carshop

Table 4.4 *Negro employees of the Richmond, Fredericksburg and Potomac, 1861–1863*[71]

Place	1861	1862	1863
Machine shop, Richmond	3	3	2
Blacksmith shop, Richmond	4	6	6
Carpenter shop, Richmond	1	4	4
Firemen, cleaners, train hands	20	20	23
Richmond depot	10	10	17
Way stations	21	21	20
Repairs on road	54	56	61
Total	113	120	133

workers.[68] Alexander Dudley, president of the company, reported that only $13,402 was spent for repairs of trackage and roadbed. He also indicated that the line had transported Negroes to work on fortifications on the Peninsula during April.[69] To relieve its labor shortage the company invested $46,105 in the purchase of over 40 slaves.[70] For the most part, however, the line was unable to keep its track in repair, and after the winter of 1863, its military significance rapidly declined.

In 1861 the eleven locomotives of the Richmond, Fredericksburg and Potomac line—pulled 134 cars of various types over a 75-mile track which terminated upon an arm of the Potomac called Aquia Creek. Peter V. Daniel, Jr., the president, struggled throughout the war to keep the line operating, with only moderate success. The superintendent of transportation and upkeep, Samuel Ruth, was eventually replaced by William Bragg. Superintendent Ruth reported that repair expenses for the year 1861 amounted to $16,477. In 1864 this figure increased to over $133,000.[72] Depot expenses, including the hire of colored hands, rose from $13,655 in 1861, to $98,887 in 1864. Ruth noted that slaveowners demanded increased payment for the hire of their slaves, and that Federal raiders carried off a number of Negroes and destroyed railroad equipment and track. He also remarked that conscription had reduced drastically the white labor supply. Although labor costs steadily increased, the retention of skilled and unskilled Negro labor was absolutely essential to the existence of the line. It is significant that 120 slaves and free Negroes employed by the

Table 4.5 *Negro employees of Virginia railroads, 1861–1864*

Railroad	1861	1862	1863	1864
Virginia and Tennessee	564	711	714	722
Virginia Central	268	321	308	284
Richmond and Danville	283	328	477	700
Southside	204	370	439	439
Petersburg	121	150	191	265
Richmond and Petersburg	120	127	119	153
Richmond, Fredericksburg, and Potomac	113	120	133	133
Richmond and York River	24	41	—	—
Norfolk and Petersburg	54	28	—	—
Orange and Alexandria	148	151	109	—

company in 1862 also worked under Negro foremen as machine hands or members of section gangs.[73] Some of the slaves were owned by the company, but the majority were hired on a monthly or annual basis from slaveowners along the right-of-way. To add to the company's problem of maintenance, their slaves were periodically impressed for labor on fortifications. Indeed, the Negro labor force of the R. F. & P. Railroad Company played no little part in the vital war service of the 75-mile line.

It would perhaps be claiming too much to say that Negro manpower, the sinew of the war effort behind the scenes, provided Virginia with the means of continuing the uneven contest. Yet it is impossible not to conclude that had Virginia's transportation arteries been deprived of Negro brawn and dexterity, the Virginia war effort would have been severely and seriously hampered.

Illustrations

Plate 1. Negro Teamsters, 1864. The Confederate Quartermaster Department employed thousands of blacks as teamsters for transporting war supplies to Lee's armies. As the war progressed, Southern generals relied more and more on the services of black teamsters. [Brady Collection, Library of Congress.]

Plate 2. Negro Workers on a Pontoon Bridge. Both Union and Confederate armies made much use of improvised bridges to speed troop movements. For this bridge at Belle Plain Landing, as for most other bridges, black labor did the construction and repair work. [Brady Collection, Library of Congress.]

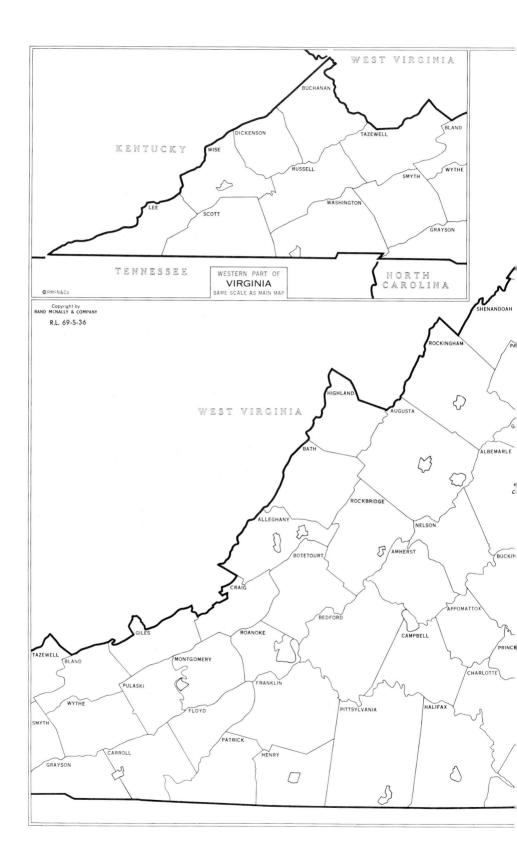

WEST VIRGINIA

BUCHANAN

DICKENSON

TAZEWELL

BLAND

KENTUCKY

WISE

RUSSELL

SMYTH

WYTHE

LEE

SCOTT

WASHINGTON

GRAYSON

TENNESSEE

WESTERN PART OF
VIRGINIA
SAME SCALE AS MAIN MAP

NORTH
CAROLINA

© R M©N&Co.

SHENANDOAH

ROCKINGHAM

HIGHLAND

WEST VIRGINIA

AUGUSTA

BATH

ALBEMARLE

ROCKBRIDGE

ALLEGHANY

NELSON

BOTETOURT

AMHERST

BUCKIN

CRAIG

APPOMATTOX

BEDFORD

GILES

ROANOKE

CAMPBELL

PRINC

TAZEWELL

BLAND

MONTGOMERY

CHARLOTTE

PULASKI

FRANKLIN

WYTHE

PITTSYLVANIA

HALIFAX

SMYTH

FLOYD

PATRICK

CARROLL

HENRY

GRAYSON

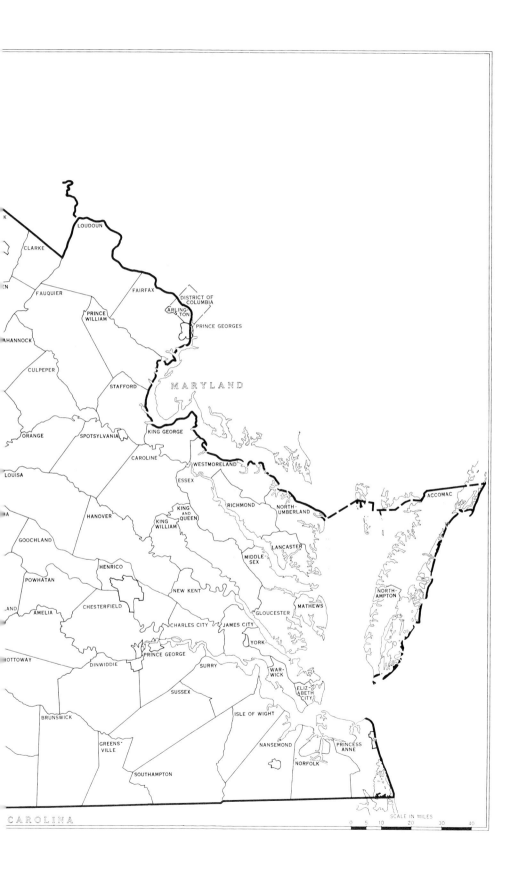

K

LOUDOUN

CLARKE

FAUQUIER

FAIRFAX

DISTRICT OF
COLUMBIA

ARLING-
TON

PRINCE GEORGES

PRINCE
WILLIAM

AHANNOCK

CULPEPER

STAFFORD

M A R Y L A N D

ORANGE

SPOTSYLVANIA

KING GEORGE

LOUISA

CAROLINE

WESTMORELAND

ESSEX

ACCOMAC

RICHMOND

NORTH-
UMBERLAND

HANOVER

KING
AND
QUEEN

KING
WILLIAM

GOOCHLAND

LANCASTER

MIDDLE-
SEX

HENRICO

POWHATAN

NORTH-
AMPTON

NEW KENT

AND

AMELIA

CHESTERFIELD

GLOUCESTER

MATHEWS

CHARLES CITY

JAMES CITY

YORK

OTTOWAY

DINWIDDIE

PRINCE GEORGE

SURRY

WAR-
WICK

SUSSEX

ELIZ-
ABETH
CITY

BRUNSWICK

ISLE OF WIGHT

GREENS-
VILLE

NANSEMOND

PRINCESS
ANNE

SOUTHAMPTON

NORFOLK

CAROLINA

SCALE IN MILES

0   5   10   20   30   40

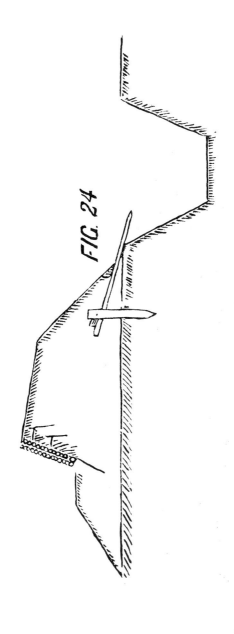

FIG. 24

Plate 3. Profile of a typical entrenchment with parapet (at left) ditch, and glacis. The sketch is from a standard manual of army engineering, Mahan's *Treatise on Field Fortification*, 1848.

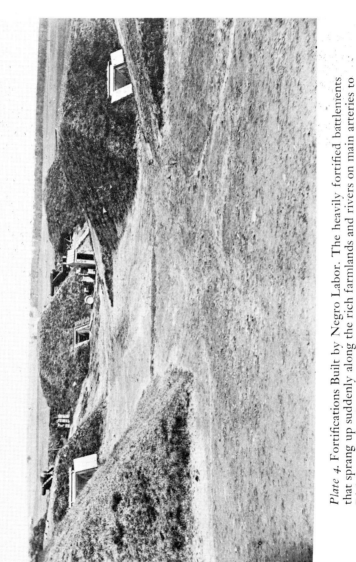

Plate 4. Fortifications Built by Negro Labor. The heavily fortifed battlements that sprang up suddenly along the rich farmlands and rivers on main arteries to Richmond were largely emergency work of black laborers. This is Fort Darling at Drury's Bluff along the James River. [Brady Collection, Library of Congress.]

Plate 5. Negro Railroad Workers Repairing the Track. Thousands of black men labored assiduously to keep the railroads of the Confederacy in operation. These men are repairing damage done in the Battle of Stones River near Murfreesboro, Tennessee, in 1864. [Brady Collection, Library of Congress.]

CHAPTER FIVE

Negroes in Confederate Hospitals

A nurse, a cook, and a laundress—three forgotten Negroes. Together they played a vital part in lightening the burden of caring for the sick and wounded in the Confederate armies. They numbered in the thousands—males, females, slaves, and free Negroes. Their services are obviously not the whole of Confederate medical history, but they served a cause, performed a job, and played an active role, doing no more and no less than others. Many performed their tasks ably, and many were unfit for their jobs. Viewed in the long historical perspective of a century, Virginia Negroes were full partners in the South's heroic efforts to care for the diseased and wounded soldiers.[1]

During the siege of Richmond in May 1862 an urgent message from the commandant of Chimborazo Hospital, the largest military hospital in the Confederate States, added a new dimension to Confederate medical history. Surgeon James B. McCaw informed Surgeon General Samuel P. Moore that "it will be utterly impossible to continue to operate Chimborazo without the 256 Negro nurses and cooks employed to take care of nearly 4,000 sick and wounded." Such a message was typical and was essentially an integral part of yesterday's factual history of Virginia's military hospitals. Today's mythological history pursues new lines, diverting historical attention to other significant phases of the Confederacy's medical organization.[2] Nevertheless, from the outset of the war, the Negro was indispensable in helping to resolve the mounting problem of establishing and staffing sufficient military hospitals in Virginia to treat the many casualties.[3] Virginia reacted calmly to the staffing of military hospitals with Negroes, free and slave, and this was a measure of the mood of the time. Their availability to serve undoubtedly alienated soldiers and others from performing this very important work. The Confederate Medical Corps readily trained Negro recruits, males and females, to become efficient as hospital attendants under the supervision of white personnel—matrons, assistant matrons, and ward matrons, stewards, and surgeons.[4]

In the opening weeks of the war there was a rapid growth in the number of Negro nurses. Yet, in such a well-studied area as the American Civil War, the legacy of Negro personnel in military hospitals has escaped comprehensive examination. It must be granted that the alarming increase of Confederate sick and wounded, the need to release soldiers serving as nurses, and the critical shortage of nurses, all accelerated the trend to utilize Negroes in this capacity.[5] Consequently, on August 21, 1861, the Confederate Congress authorized the employment "of nurses and cooks, other than enlisted men, or volunteers, the persons so employed being subject to military control."[6] To hire the necessary hospital attendants, $130,000 was appropriated. Thereupon steps were taken to halt the practice of drawing nurses from among the thinning fighting forces. In mid-December Thomas H. Williams, medical director of the Army of the Potomac (later the Army of Northern Virginia), took steps to enforce General Order No. 13 which directed surgeons in charge of general hospitals "to hire civilians and Negroes as nurses instead of detailed enlisted men." Post commandants were authorized to impress free Negroes into the service, if necessary, and all soldiers acting as nurses were ordered to be returned to their respective commands. By February 1862 mounting legislative sentiment favored the securing of additional Negroes as nurses, and the Committee on Military Affairs was instructed "to inquire into the propriety of employing slaves as nurses."[7]

II

In no other Southern city were so many Negroes employed in the Medical Corps congregated as in Richmond, the South's chief hospital center. This was especially true of the six large hospital encampments in or near the capital. The most notable of these, opened in the fall of 1861, was Chimborazo Hospital, commanded by Dr. James B. McCaw. Built by slave labor on an elevated plateau overlooking the James River, its forty acres contained 105 buildings.[8] Morley and Cornelius, slave welldiggers employed by Chimborazo, apparently helped dig five deep wells which were watered by three good springs. Chimborazo's sewerage disposal system was drained into a convenient gully. A brewery which produced four hundred kegs of brew was located on the southeast corner of the property beside one of the springs. Slave carpenters from the tobacco factories made bedsteads, tables, partitions, and other needed furniture. They built a guard house, bakery, soaphouses, and icehouses.

Dr. McCaw organized his vast institution to be self-sustaining. Large boilers obtained from tobacco factories were used by Negro cooks for soup making. A few boilers were set aside, however, to make soap from surplus kitchen grease and lye. Early in 1862, fifty-five Negro cooks and bakers were scattered throughout the hospital's five soaphouses, many kitchens, and the large bakery which produced between 7,000 and 10,000 loaves of bread each day.[9] Slaves were employed to attend the dairy, icehouses, farm, and herd of almost two hundred cows and four hundred goats.[10] The stock pastured on neighboring farms, including Tree Hill owned by Franklin Stearn. The hospital's trading canal boat, the *Chimborazo*, commanded by Captain Lawrence Lottier, had a crew consisting of eight slaves and a free Negro, Horatio Harris. On the James River and Kanawha Canal this vessel plied between Richmond and Lynchburg, bartering cotton, yarn, shoes, and other items to obtain fresh vegetables, food, and provisions for hospital inmates. John, the slave of Captain Lottier, and Tom Pryer, the slave of T. W. Scott, were boatmen. The duties of the other seven Negro "scalingers" apparently involved bartering with farmers for eggs, fruits, and vegetables, which they carefully weighed before making an exchange for dry goods.[11]

Throughout the war Chimborazo treated more than 77,000 patients, returning more than 70,000 of this number to their respective commands or to their homes. From its opening day, the institution's nurses, cooks, and laundresses were predominantly Negro, and this situation continued until the end of the war. In the spring of 1862 Chimborazo employed 332 nurses—76 soldiers and 256 Negroes.

The duties and responsibilities of Chimborazo's Negro nurses were about the same as those of nurses in other Virginia military hospitals. As a regular routine they were expected to bathe all patients as soon after admission as their conditions would permit. In order to keep a patient clean and comfortable there was daily sponging of the face and neck, chest and arms, and legs and feet. One nurse to every ten patients was the proportion recommended by the Medical Department. Nurses were expected to bring to the ward and distribute to the patients the daily rations and the medicines prescribed by the doctor. The nurses were required to change the straw in the bed sacks at least once a month, and the beds had to be well beaten and thoroughly aired daily. Scouring the floor space occupied by the beds under one's care was also a responsibility of the nurse.[12]

Many of the disabled veterans employed as nurses were physically unable to lift the sick, sit up at night, carry out the beds to be aired, scour the floors, or perform the many tasks required in military hospitals. For this reason they, along with female slave nurses, were less desirable than able-bodied male Negro nurses. Nevertheless, it is not uncommon to find both female slaves and disabled soldiers listed on hospital muster rolls. Table 5.1 permits a comparison of Chimborazo Hospital personnel. Eighty-five of the 166 detailed soldiers (see Table 5.1) served as guards, ward masters, and stewards, while the remaining 81 were engaged as nurses. There were fewer than 10 female slaves working as nurses or cooks. For example, among the 264 Negro nurses, there were 4 females. Emily and Jennie, both slaves, worked in Division No. 2 along with Candis, a free Negro. Emalene, owned by Surgeon Woodward, was assigned to Division No. 5. The 4 female cooks were hired at salaries which ranged from $180 to $240 annually. It is significant that 36 Negro boys were employed as nurses and 3 were hired as cooks. Their wages ranged from $60 to $300. Four slaves—George, Ben, Reuben, and Thompson—were hired as bakers, their owners receiving between $240 and $300 for each one.[14]

Table 5.1 *Employees at Chimborazo Hospital, January 1, 1863*[13]

	Whites			Negroes		
Division	Detailed soldiers	Matrons	Nurses	Cooks	Bakers	Laundresses
1	25	6	53	13	—	—
2	44	5	45	19	—	—
3	36	6	60	8	4	—
4	28	5	45	9	—	—
5	33	3	61	5	—	—
Totals	166	25	264	54	4	123

If the number of slave nurses owned by physicians is evidence that they had some nursing training, then Chimborazo was indeed fortunate. In 1863 the hospital's muster roles listed 15 medical doctors eligible to receive $7,000 for the services of 35 slave nurses. For example, Dr. G. E. Alsop was paid $2,040 for the hire of his 9 slave nurses. Dr. P. F. Brown of Accomac was paid for his 3 slave nurses, as was Dr. E. H. Smith who owned 6 slave nurses. The remaining 12 physicians, who owned from 1 to 3 nurses, also collected the money they were due for their hire.[15] In 1864 the hospital's commandant owned 2 slave nurses—Hannibal, who was employed in Division No. 3, and Bob, who worked in Division No. 2.

Slave hiring became an extremely important vehicle for securing needed personnel for Chimborazo Hospital. Owners were able to hire out their slaves for annual payments, including food and clothing, averaging from 20 to 30 per cent of their value. To supply these needs "agents" worked closely with Dr. McCaw. The muster roles of the hospital disclose the names of many agents in the Richmond area, including Clopton and Lyne, P. M. Tabb and Son, Turpin and Yarbrough, and E. D. Eacho. One agent, James H. Grant, supplied over 50 slave nurses and cooks.

Nevertheless, in November 1862 McCaw notified the Surgeon General that "the difficulty of getting Negroes is increasing daily, and I apprehend great trouble in getting the number (not less than 250) required for this hospital for the coming year." He then requested permission to hire Negroes by the year rather than by the month.[16] His request was favorably received, and within a few weeks newspapers throughout the state advertised that Chimborazo seeks "to hire, for the year, 250 men, women, and boys (over 12 years of age), as cooks and nurses."[17] Slaveowners responded promptly to this advertisement. C. W. Hubbell of Richmond wrote that he had three Negroes to hire, "one a first rate cook and two boys, 18 years of age." He cautioned that he would hire them by the month "if you have no cases of smallpox, and will return them if such should be the case."[18] C. J. Hancock of Chesterfield wrote, "I have some boys to hire between the ages of fifteen and twenty years." Medical Director William A. Carrington sent a note to McCaw which read, "This will be carried to Chimborazo by Albert a servant of William Sanford" of Orange Court House. The note requested that the slave be hired in one of the divisions.[19] Many other slaveowners notified the hospital commandant of their willingness to hire out their slaves. In 1863 they were paid $60,000 in Chimborazo alone for the services of their chattel.

Later records which show the cost of slave hire as the war went on clearly reflect the inflation of Confederate currency. In 1863 slave nurses and cooks were hired at the hospital for an annual wage of $180 to $240, plus food and clothing; in 1864, from $300 to $400; and in 1865, from $400 to $500 yearly.[20] On January 5, 1864, Dr. McCaw informed a slaveowner, "I will take your servant Richard at $400 and rations, but you to furnish clothing."

Another problem facing McCaw was the periodic drain of his employees to labor on fortifications or to be transferred to neighboring military hospitals. The latter was usually the case prior to and after major military campaigns, such as the campaigns of the Peninsula, Fredericksburg, and Cole Harbor and the siege of Petersburg. For example, in May 1864 Medical Director Carrington notified McCaw: "I desire to open a receiving hospital at the Old Fair Ground Barrack. To do so I will require 45 ward masters and nurses." Carrington asked McCaw to transfer as "many of these attendants as you can spare."[21] Scott, a slave carpenter, was sent to assist in the laying of floors and the building of partitions in the various wards. The hospital's slaves were also sent to labor on defensive works at Drewry's Bluff, designed to repulse the Union naval advance up the James River in 1862 and 1864. In October 1864 McCaw, in response to an urgent request by the Engineer Bureau to the Medical Department, sent only a small portion of the hospital's slaves to Drewry's Bluff to labor on fortifications. McCaw explained that the number of wounded being received made it impossible for him to release others. He, along with other hospital commandants, requested that the slaves not be detained for more than a few days.[22]

During the winter of 1864 the problem of securing fuel to heat military hospitals was very grave. Chimborazo patients were collected into as few wards as possible to conserve fuel. Over 280 fires were necessary to heat the kitchens, laundry, offices, wards, and other hospital buildings. Lieutenant Colonel John Saunders, a hospital inspector, reported: "From my observation in passing through the wards, I must say they were entirely too cold for the persons in health much less for sick and wounded."[23] Saunders found that similar conditions existed in the other large hospital encampments. Thereupon an investigation disclosed that contracts made by the Quartermaster Department with private contractors to supply wood for hospitals were unfulfilled "due to the great difficulties of securing the necessary labor."[24]

Hence, in January 1865 Medical Director Carrington informed Major J. C. Maynard of the Quartermaster Department: "I have directed 40 Negroes, ten each from Chimborazo, Howard's Grove, Winder, and Jackson hospitals be sent to your office tomorrow." They were "to cut wood for hospitals for fifteen days." The major reported that each Negro was expected to cut an average of 1 ½ cords daily, which would amount to 60 cords a day.[25]

McCaw was faced with another call for the services of his slaves when an attempt was made to impress some to labor on the Richmond fortifications. This caused a controversy which involved Henrico County officials. The medical director informed county authorities that any order for Chimborazo's Negro employees to perform other duties must come from the War Department, and he denied them the right to impress the hospital's personnel. Carrington assured McCaw that none of the Henrico County slaves employed by the hospital would be molested by the sheriff and requested that McCaw furnish the Engineer Bureau with a list of all able-bodied male slaves between the ages of eighteen and fifty.[26]

Outstanding among the sources of the commandant's ill-feeling over the reduction of his Negro workers was the knowledge that it hampered the efficient operation of his hospital and in general lowered morale. Dr. McCaw was extremely perceptive as to the Negroes' needs for well-being and happiness. Chimborazo's Negroes looked forward to the Christmas holiday; but their services were needed, and they were usually paid extra pocket money for doing "Christmas work." In 1862 W. E. Toombs, the hospital steward, reported that an average of 25 slaves in the first division received extra money for holiday work. Surgeon General Moore on December 27, 1864, officially notified all surgeons in charge of military hospitals that they were authorized to "pay hired slaves one dollar per diem during Christmas week, using the hospital fund for that purpose."[27]

Like Chimborazo, Winder Hospital was a large hospital compound into which many of the sick and wounded were concentrated. It is not altogether clear, however, how many Negroes were employed there, because the hospital records were destroyed in the Richmond fire at the end of the war. Located on Cary Street in the western outskirts of Richmond, Winder was established in 1862, with a capacity of 4,800 beds. Dr. Alexander G. Lane administered the five divisions, which included 98 buildings. In 1863 a tent division was added to care for 700 patients, and the following year a seventh and final division was constructed. Winder's 125 acres contained numerous natural springs, deep wells, a dairy, an icehouse, a bakery, a cookhouse, and warehouses. The hospital also owned twenty cows and had several large gardens, bathhouses, barracks, Negro quarters, and recreational facilities. The hospital's two canal boats made regular trips up and down the James River and Kanawha Canal for provisions.

Little is known about the many Negroes employed by Winder Hospital, but some facts may be pieced together. In February 1863 this institution employed 510 persons, of whom approximately 55 per cent were Negroes. A year later this figure had dropped to 486, and within two months the staff was again further reduced to 352 employees.[28] The few existing records disclose that 83 Negroes were employed in the second division. Harry, one of the 30 slave nurses, was owned by Surgeon John Chambliss who was in command of this division.[29] Winder was perhaps the only military hospital in the Richmond environs where the records indicate that for brief periods the majority of nurses consisted of detailed and disabled soldiers. For example, on September 11, 1864, only Winder's fifth division had a Negro majority, while in the second and third divisions the ratio was respectively 19 whites to 18 blacks and 24 whites to 23 blacks. In the first, fourth, and sixth divisions, Negro nurses averaged 45.7 per cent of the total number of nurses.[30]

The winter of 1864 was characterized by a steady decline of inmates confined to the hospital. Some were discharged, but the majority were transferred to other hospitals in Richmond. In November, Surgeon Lane was ordered to close the hospital's sixth division, leaving 85 Negro nurses to care for inmates. The next month only 577 patients were reported, and orders came to reduce Winder's divisions to two. Of the 38 colored nurses retained, seven were females; the twelve white attendants consisted of three stewards, three matrons, and six detailed soldiers.[31] Throughout 1865 Winder's facilities were used largely for emergencies only. However, of the facts Winder's Hospital records brought to light perhaps none was more surprising than the evidence that a company of Negro soldiers from both Winder and Jackson was actually engaged in combat during the defense of Richmond in March 1865. In commenting on the behavior of the hospital's Negro troops under fire commander Scott reported:

> I ordered my battalion form the 1st, 2nd, 3rd, and 4th divisions of Jackson Hospital to the front on Saturday night. . . . My men acted with the utmost promptness and good will. I had the pleasure in turning over to Dr. Major Chambliss a portion of my Negro Company to be attatched to his command. Allow me to state, sir, that they behaved in an extraordinary suitable manner. I would respectively ask that Major Chambliss be particularly noticed for the manner which he handled that very important element about to be inaugurated in our service.[32]

Meanwhile a Confederate veteran in recalling his experiences as a patient in Winder Hospital wrote that a few days after his arrival "Erysipelas developed in my wound, and four Negroes carried me on my cot across the field to the Erysipelas Camp." Former veteran J. B. Roden added that he did not have a change of clean clothing and somehow managed to lay claim to a bundle of clothes recently washed by a Negro laundress.[33]

Although a paucity of facts hampers the study of Winder's Negro personnel, a clearer story can be told about the colored employees of Howard's Grove. This hospital compound was established in June 1862 on a popular picnic-recreation area on the Mechanicsville Turnpike, one mile from Richmond. At first Howard's Grove Hospital was an encampment of tents, but eventually wooden buildings were constructed. During the smallpox epidemics from 1862 to 1864, one of the hospital's three divisions was set aside for victims of the disease. Commanded by Surgeon T. M. Palmer, each division had its own kitchen, in which food was prepared for patients. The hospital's capacity for 659 patients in December 1862 was expanded within a few months to accommodate 1,800. Among the 62 buildings were a bakery, laundry, storehouse, barracks, and Negro quarters.

The question of the number of Negro attendants employed by this institution is somewhat confusing and misleading. Upon close scrutiny two enlightening facts appear. First, the hospital had a permanent staff of Negroes serving as nurses, cooks, laundresses, and so forth. Second, there were also many other Negroes who served in the same capacities but not on a permanent basis. The temporary Negroes were dealt with variously. Sometimes they were transferred for short periods to other hospitals or government agencies. They were periodically released and subject to recall, and some were either permanently relocated in other hospitals or discharged. This helps to explain the sudden rise or drop of Negro personnel on the muster rolls at Howard's Grove. Another explanation arises from the military campaigns waged during the spring and the summer months. As Confederate wounded crowded the hospital beyond its usual capacity, additional Negroes had to be hired temporarily. Similarly, a reduction in the number of hospital inmates occasionally resulted in the temporary closing of some military hospitals.

In the early months of 1864 Surgeon General Moore notified Medical Director Carrington that Winder and Howard's Grove patients were to be transferred to Jackson and Chimborazo hospitals, because the former two were to be closed temporarily. Apparently this move was designed to conserve fuel because of critical shortages of wood. Arrangements were made, however, to retain some Negroes at both Winder and Howard's Grove, to transfer others, and to release several to the Engineer Bureau, with the understanding that they would be returned when their services were again required.

General orders, directives from commanding officers, and the correspondence of the medical director with the military hospitals in and around Richmond also disclose the transitory nature of the employment not only of many Negro hospital personnel, but also of many disabled and detailed soldiers. On December 7, 1864, Surgeon Palmer was directed to "take charge of and place on your muster role seven Negro women . . . hired by the year, at General hospital N. 4." The next day the commandant of Howard's Grove again received a similar order which involved the transfer of two slaves from the same hospital.[34]

Many details about Howard's Grove Negro employees can never be known, since extant records provide little more than fragmentary information. Duty rosters, ward rolls, and morning reports for 1863 indicate that 140 colored nurses were employed by the first and second divisions and that 29.6 per cent of this number were females.[35] These figures appear to correspond to the information and figures given to the medical director in May 1863 to justify the request for an additional 25 nurses. Surgeon C. D. Rice, who was in charge of the second division, indicated that the 77 colored nurses were far below the quota necessary to care for patients in his division.[36] Eventually extra nurses were employed for short periods which averaged from three to nine months, as the number of patients confined to the hospital declined during the winter months. As the Battle of the Wilderness opened the military campaigns of 1864, the need of Negro nurses increased. For example, in June the first division alone employed 25 soldiers as nurses, in addition to 118 Negro nurses—93 males and 25 females. The typical duty roster for a hospital ward contained the names of the ward master, the assistant ward master (detailed or disabled soldiers), and the colored nurses. In the making up of duty rosters for the first division's eighteen wards the general ward master usually assigned Negroes in pairs. For example, Ruffin and Corbin were assigned to Ward A; Samuel and Angeline to Ward D; Enoch, Lizzie, and Emma to Ward O; and Willis and Davis to Ward R.[38] In order to assure adequate care for sick and wounded soldiers, monthly rosters were posted which listed the names of the nurses, designating whether they were assigned to day or to night duty. One such roster posted during the Battle of New Market and Bermuda Hundred contained the names of 36 Negroes assigned to night duty.[39] Apparently an increase in war casualties made it necessary to assign an additional 24 colored nurses to night duty—9 females and 15 males.[40]

As the siege of Petersburg and Richmond took place, the daily morning reports for July 1864 disclose that between 58 and 70 Negro nurses, in the first division, were on hand to take care of wounded soldiers.[41] The monthly reports of attendants employed at Howard's

Table 5.2. *Employees at Howard's Grove Hospital, September 1864*[37]

Division	Detailed nurses	Nurses	Negro cooks	Negro laundresses
1	18	87	19	16
2	6	56	17	25
3	4	27	10	10
Totals	28	170	46	51

Grove show that whites in the first division constituted approximately 11 per cent of the nursing force, while they constituted less than 8 per cent in the second division.[42] Statistics, unfortunately, are sketchy on the number of nurses owned by physicians. In 1863 Dr. V. P. Jones hired out his five slave nurses—Mary, Emaline, Cynthia, Harriet, and George—for which he was paid at the rate of $2,400 per year. Other doctors who made available at least one slave to the hospital were Surgeons Wallace, Burwell, and Talbot.[43]

The demands upon Negro personnel in Howard's Grove's third division were much greater. A white flag flying over its buildings indicated that it was a smallpox hospital. As Virginia's first wartime epidemic reached its full fury in the early fall of 1862, the medical corps widened the duties of Negro hospital personnel to include the care of the many smallpox victims. Other Negro nurses were transferred from both divisions of the hospital as the number of cases increased. The Richmond *Examiner* reported that "City Hospital . . . crowded to its utmost capacity . . . obtained from Surgeon General Moore three of the wards of Howard's Grove."[44] The news release also pointed out that Negroes employed by the city who became infected with the disease would be admitted to Howard's Grove, a physician's certificate being necessary.[45] A second epidemic during the winter of 1863–1864 found medical authorities again making extensive use of Negro hospital personnel. In December 1863 Surgeon C. D. Rice dispatched a request to Surgeon Temple: "You will furnish a list of all colored attendants in your division who have had the variola or varioloid."[46] H. M. Pettit, steward of the first division, immediately informed Surgeon Rice that six Negroes—Bob, Lockie, Edith, Octavia, Judy, and Raney—were in this category.[47] Similarly S. H. Touries, steward of the second division, ordered four slave nurses—Fannie, Maria, Francis, and Robert—to report to the surgeon in charge of the smallpox hospital.[48] The extra Negro personnel was reflected in the morning report of attendants assigned to care for the physical needs of smallpox victims. The steward of the smallpox hospital, P. M. Spencer, reported that on December 22, 1863, the number of attendants on duty numbered twenty-seven (Table 5.3). The medical officer on duty, Surgeon George M. Lane, reported that "the smallpox wards were visited at 9 & 2 & 7 o'clock."[50] He also stated that they were in good condition and that the attendants were performing satisfactorily their respective duties—the application of ointment on sores, the frequent changes of gowns and linens, the sponging of inmates, the preparation of and feeding of liquid diets, and the washing of apparel. The number of colored nurses increased threefold as the epidemic reached its peak in the capital city, and over 70 Negroes were assigned to Howard's Grove hospital smallpox wards. By July 1864 the crisis had passed and 28 of the 30 nurses listed on the morning reports were Negroes. Other colored personnel included 10 cooks and 11 laundresses. During the siege of Petersburg in 1864 the third division was restored to its normal operations, namely, the care of sick and wounded Confederate soldiers.

Unquestionably there was much drudgery and hard work for those assigned to hospitals. Occasionally, small Negro boys were discharged for being physically incapable of rendering efficient service. Such was the case for Ned, Robert, and Ben, hired from Clopton and Lyne. Small boys were also employed or brought by a few hospital inmates to provide for their physical needs. This practice sometimes created problems for the hospital. For example, five patients were notified that their boys—Tom, Albert, George, John, and Wallace—were subject to hospital regulations, and, as such, were expected to perform other duties in the hospital.[51] Although nursing, cooking, and washing patient's clothes constituted the bulk of the work performed by Negro personnel, other duties were performed by a few. Such was the case of Alex, who worked in the dispensary; Albert, in the steward's office; Henry, in the medical purveyor's office; James, a free boy, who drove the hospital wagon; Taswell, the baker; and John, in the hospital commandant's office.[52] Other demands placed upon Negro attendants were reflected in orders from the Surgeon General's office. For example, Surgeon General Moore required "frequent whitewashing of the wards and the removal of the contents of bed sacks; the former twice or thrice yearly, the latter at least once each month."[53] He also insisted that "all bedding is to be aired frequently,

Table 5.3. *Smallpox hospital attendants, Howard's Grove, 1863*[49]

Matrons	2	Nurses, Negro	7
Clerks	1	Cooks, Negro	3
Ward masters	3	Laundresses, Negro	6
Nurses, white	5		

and two clean sheets will be kept upon each bed." The floors of the many wards were to be cleaned by "dry scrubbing with sand."[54]

Hospital requisitions also disclose the type of work performed by

Negro attendants. On March 2, 1863, one such requisition called for sufficient lime for 16 workers to complete the whitewashing of hospital wards. Two months later Surgeon Rice ordered 35,000 pounds of straw to fill the bed sacks of the second division. In June a request was submitted for two mules necessary to pull the ambulance wagon used "to transfer sick and wounded on furlough to railroads." Logan and Ben, both slaves, were employed as ambulance drivers for the hospital.[55] Perhaps the most unpleasant task the hospital's Negro employees were called upon to perform was that of laboring on fortifications in the Richmond environs—Drewry's Bluff, eight miles below the city, and the Richmond lines. Confederate engineers called for their service in the spring and fall of 1862 and 1864, when Union armies threatened the capital. On April 15, 1864, Medical Director Carrington asked Surgeon T. M. Palmer to "please report the number of Negroes sent to work on fortifications."[56] Again in October several Negroes from the hospital were dispatched, for twenty days, to assist in obstructing the James River and in the erection of earthworks at Drewry's Bluff.

Employment conditions were naturally better in Howard's Grove than in other hospital centers throughout the state, for it was near staff headquarters. It had the advantage of better facilities, and frequent inspections by the Surgeon General's office prompted the hospital stewards to supervise the Negro employees closely.

The chief surgeon of Howard's Grove expressed concern about the need for cleanliness in the Negro quarters. Each division's general ward master was ordered to make periodic checks to see that the Negroes' quarters were kept clean and "if necessary whitewashed." In October 1863 "the filthy condition of the privy used by the Negroes . . . near the stable" was brought to the attention of the hospital commandant. An order was issued that "the head surgeon of the 1st division will have the privy scoured on every Monday, and the head surgeon of the 2nd division on every Friday." This directive was referred by the hospital steward to the general ward master with a notation that it was to be strictly enforced.[57] Because of the aforementioned advantages, this institution compared favorably with Jackson Hospital in size, general facilities, and overall care of its patients.

Jackson Hospital, opened in the summer of 1863, was a large encampment located about two miles from the Confederate Capital. Surgeon Francis W. Hancock, who directed the Jackson establishment, proved to be a capable administrator. An official of the United States Sanitary Commission reporting on the hospital's condition at the close of the war asserted that "Jackson Hospital, as established and conducted by the rebels, was excellent; in some respects, few military hospitals of our own surpass it." The official also remarked, "It was excellent . . . in its administration; in its thorough policing; in the exceeding cleanliness of its bedding."[58]

From the day the hospital opened, its nurses, cooks, and laundresses were predominantly Negro. The hospital had four divisions, each under the charge of a surgeon, which were supervised by a senior surgeon. Its many wooden buildings could accommodate 2,500 patients. By January 9, 1865, over 19,000 inmates had been admitted into the hospital; 885 deaths were reported.

For the eleven months after August 1863 the heavy casualties caused by four sanguinary battles—Gettysburg, the Wilderness Campaign, Spotsylvania Court House, and Cold Harbor—created a hospital emergency in Virginia and a need for additional Negro nurses. Almost 5,000 wounded men were received into the Richmond hospitals between May 6 and May 20, 1864. F. W. Hancock, surgeon in charge of the Jackson Hospital, superintended the reception of wounded from the Army of Northern Virginia. Dr. Hancock, his colored aides, and the Richmond Ambulance Committee attended to the disabled. Like other Richmond hospitals, Jackson was crowded beyond its normal capacity for several weeks. On May 18 and May 20, 1864, Medical Director Carrington reported that "the hospitals then open were insufficient." Again on May 24 Carrington reported almost 18,000 sick and wounded in Virginia hospitals. In 1864 the medical officers in charge of hospitals near areas threatened by Federal forces received orders from Carrington to send as many Negro attendants as could be spared.

A year earlier, an effort to staff the newly opened Jackson Hospital with Negro attendants caused Carrington to dispatch a similar request. Between July and November 1863 the hospital managed to hire 133 Negroes—105 nurses, 17 cooks, and 11 laundresses.[59] As the hiring season for 1864 opened, several agents and slaveowners furnished the hospital with 128 slaves, each at an annual cost of $300 and clothing. In May 1864 an additional 84 Negroes were employed temporarily to care for the wounded admitted after the battles of the Wilderness and Spotsylvania. The following month another 41 colored nurses were employed to care for casualties from the Battle of Cold Harbor. By the autumn of 1864 the overcrowded conditions in Richmond's hospitals ceased. Over 100 Negro attendants employed at Jackson during the crisis were released and transferred to Confederate engineers. Thereafter the number of Negro employees at Jackson remained relatively unchanged until the collapse of the Confederacy. Following an inspection report of January 9, 1865, Colonel John J. Saunders, Inspector of Hospitals, reported that the 188 Negro attendants and the other employees at Jackson Hospital "are kept on hand ready to open in case of a battle taking place."[61]

Shortly after their arrival at Jackson Hospital some surgeons sent for their slaves to be employed as hospital attendants. Forty-nine of the slave nurses—27 females and 22 males—were owned by 18 physicians.[62] Of the 14 slave nurses owned by Surgeon B. Burrell, 11 were females and 3 were males. Similarly, 9 of Dr. J. S. Wellford's 13 slave nurses were females. Other physicians and well-known Virginians hired out their slaves to the hospital as attendants. For example, Sarah and Eliza, who worked as laundresses, were owned by the hospital's commandant, Dr. Francis W. Hancock. General George Edward Pickett owned a female nurse, Louisa, for whom he received $25 per month. Friday, a nurse in the third division, was owned by General R. S. Ewell. During 1863 and 1864, Judge J. A. Meredith hired out 10 slaves—8 males and 2 females—to the hospital. One of them, Milsetta,

Table 5.4. *Jackson Hospital attendants, December 1864*[60]

Negro		White	
Female nurses	27	Chief matrons	10
Male nurses	135	Assistant matrons	10
Cooks	36	Ward matrons	32
Laundresses	41	Clerks	1
	239	Messengers	1
		Ward masters	1
		Nurses	1
		Druggists	1
			57

was released for two months, however, in August 1864, to give birth to her child. A further glimpse into the activities of the colored employees shows that three free Negroes—Joe Ford, Joe Allen, and

Robert Adams—served on the ambulance train. A crew of 13 slaves was hired to whitewash the various buildings.[63] Other Negroes were scattered throughout the hospital's offices, mess halls, gardens, bath-houses, and baggage rooms.

Stuart Hospital did not have the bed capacity of its larger sister institutions. The movement of Negro attendants into this hospital followed the opening of the spring campaigns of 1864. The buildings constituting this encampment were originally the quarters for the City Battalion or City Guard. On June 2, 1864, these quarters were converted into a hospital, named for General J. E. B. Stuart. Surgeon R. A. Lewis was placed in charge of the 16 buildings, 8 surgeons, and 106 employees—63 Negroes and 43 whites.[64] The hospital could accommodate more than five hundred patients. During the first six months of its existence, 1,855 patients were admitted for treatment of gun wounds and sickness. By December 1864 only 147 inmates were still hospitalized. Consequently, the count of both white and Negro employees was subject to considerable fluctuation. During the winter months of 1864–1865, for example, Medical Director Carrington in-formed surgeon Lewis, "There are too many attendants at the Hospi-tal under your charge . . . . you will therefore get rid of all Negroes not actually required."[65] On February 17, 1864, Carrington wrote to the surgeons in charge of Jackson, Winder, Chimborazo, and How-ard's Grove: "There are also twenty-three experienced and well recommended Negro attendants at Stuart Hospital, hired by the year, who are not needed. If you want any of them . . . send tomorrow morning . . . and select them." Carrington notified the surgeons that "There are also ten white female . . . matrons" available. Surgeon Fisher was then directed to "turn over to Mr. Gustavus Lesnore, agent for Major Maynard, Q. M.," 9 Negro slaves to work as wood cutters for the hospitals. Still another directive ordered 16 Negroes—11 males and 5 females—to report "to Surgeon J. B. Reed in charge of General Hospital No. 22 for assignment." A final memorandum, sent on February 18, 1865, directed surgeon Fisher to send all the "super-numerary hired attendants" to Winder Hospital.[66]

Like Stuart, Louisiana Hospital was one of the smallest hospital encampments in the Richmond area, having a capacity of fewer than 200 beds. Yet it remained in operation from the very beginning of the war. Its brick buildings had formerly housed a Baptist college, and a large garden attached to the hospital provided the patients with a

bountiful supply of fresh vegetables. Surgeon W. C. Nichols, officer
in charge, was assisted by a staff of 5 doctors, 3 stewards, and 2 ward
masters. The inmates were rendered exceptionally skilled in nursing
by the "Catholic Sisterhoods" who were perhaps the only really
trained nurses in the South. Negroes and disabled white males, however, were also used as nurses to care for the sick and wounded. In
1864 the hospital employed 8 slave nurses and 6 white nurses, as well
as 5 slave cooks and 5 female laundresses.[67]

Richmond's hospital encampments were buttressed by 28 general
hospitals located in or near the city. Hundreds of Negro nurses were
also to be found working in these military hospitals. By January 1864,
however, the number of the hospitals in operation had been reduced
to six—Nos. 1, 4, 9, 13, 21, and 24. It is impossible even to approxi-
mate the total number of Negroes—nurses, cooks, laundresses, and
other hospital workers—employed in these general hospitals, either
throughout the war or in any one specific year. Even an approxima-
tion would exclude hundreds whose period of employment was limited to only a few weeks when hospitals became overcrowded and
their services were needed. But it is significant that no military hospital picture in the Confederate capital would be complete without
their presence. This is especially true of General Hospitals No. 9 and
No. 24.

General Hospital No. 24, also called Moore Hospital, was established in the summer of 1861, under the direction of Dr. Otis F.
Manson. This institution had room for 120 patients and usually employed about 30 attendants. In June 1862 its Negro attendants numbered 14 nurses, 5 cooks, and 4 female laundresses.[68] In the next 17
months the number of colored attendants was never lower than 20.
Among its colored attendants in November 1864 were 11 nurses, 3
cooks, and 7 laundresses. One slaveowner, R. J. Christian, notified the
hospital that "Marion has permission to collect her pay for services"
at the hospital. Generally the owners themselves received the $25
monthly wages paid for each servant they made available to the
hospital.

Negro attendants were essential to the successful operation of
every general hospital. Though much of their work was classified as
unskilled labor, they were trained to be efficient workers. Occasionally orders from the medical director and the Surgeon General out-
lined special duties they were to perform. Some were assigned to

work on ambulance trains or canal boats that were used to transport the wounded. Others had to assist in unloading operations or to transport patients to military hospitals. Negro personnel were expected to wash and mend clothing, prepare food, maintain wards, attend fires, feed the sick, and carry out other assigned duties.

In April 1862 they were required to assist in procuring medicinal plants. The Surgeon General issued a circular "urging upon medical officers the necessity for collecting the indigenous botanical remedies of the South and employing them liberally in the treatment of the sick."[69] Another circular instructed medical officers to have both hospital attendants and convalescents gather indigenous medicinal plants which could be found growing in the vicinity of the hospital.[70] During the fall of 1862 an acute shortage of drugs made it necessary for Negro attendants to collect and to prepare indigenous medicinal plants for tonics, astringents, narcotics, and sedatives. Surgeon General Moore pointed out that "those charged with collecting should be impressed with the vital importance of exercising a careful discretion in the recognition of the different articles to be collected."[71]

As the war went on, General Hospitals Nos. 1, 8, 9, and 21 apparently employed many more Negro attendants than the other 24 general hospitals around Richmond. In the fall of 1862 they employed respectively 33, 29, 36, and 33 Negro nurses; and 11, 13, 16, and 10 Negro cooks.[72] Frequently the hospital stewards used the Richmond press to notify slaveowners of their needs for additional attendants. On December 5, 1862, the Richmond *Examiner* announced for General Hospital No. 11: "Wanted—four or five good active Negro Boys, or Men" to serve as nurses.

Perhaps not one of Richmond's general hospitals had more responsibility to retain an efficient corps of Negro nurses than that of the Receiving and Wayside Hospital or General Hospital No. 9. This hospital was opened in the late spring of 1862. It was primarily a receiving hospital because of its nearness to the Virginia Central Railroad depot. Directed by Dr. J. J. Gravatt, this hospital, originally a large tobacco warehouse, had a capacity for 900 patients. Sick and wounded soldiers were received and eventually distributed among the general hospitals in the city. Since the number of inmates varied daily, many Negro attendants were kept on hand. For example, in July, August, and September 1864 it admitted 10,100 patients, but 9,663 of this number were eventually transferred to other hospitals. A kitchen, bakery, laundry, barbershop, and large bathhouse with warm and cold water were installed for the patients' needs; and each of these facilities was attended by Negro employees. During the winter months colored hospital attendants maintained 25 wood and 22 coal fires, which consumed over 20 cords of wood and 550 bushels of coal. Throughout the war the receiving hospital's colored attendants averaged between 30 and 40 nurses, never fewer than 7 cooks, and from 10 to 20 female laundresses. For example, in July 1862 the hospital's employees numbered 51 Negroes—34 nurses, 7 cooks, and 10 laundresses—and 40 whites—2 stewards, 8 ward masters, 3 matrons, and 27 detailed nurses.[73] By October the number of colored attendants had increased to 59, while the number of white attendants was reduced to 22.[74] Medical regulations permitted the admission of wounded Negroes into the receiving hospital if medical attention could not be secured elsewhere. Of the 72 admitted in 1863, four slaves—Richard, Spain, Henry, and William—were treated for gunshot wounds.[75]

Usually surgeons from general hospitals were dispatched to attend to the medical needs of Negroes working for the government. In March 1864, Medical Director Carrington issued orders that a surgeon from the general hospital be assigned to attend the 300 whites and blacks working the niter beds at Bacon Feather, as well as the 50 whites and Negroes employed in the Confederate States Ambulance Shops located on the outskirts of Richmond. In the spring of 1864 the Medical Director informed the Surgeon General that both surgeons attended 2,268 Negro and white employees—Ordnance, 1,256; Quartermaster, 932; and niter works, 80.[76] Assistant Surgeon W. F. Richardson, in addition to his regular duties at General Hospital No. 9, was directed "to visit and prescribe for approximately 130 Negroes employed by James Grant, a government contractor for the manufacture of tobacco." Carrington also informed Dr. Gravatt: "You are instructed hereafter not to receive sick Negroes hired by the Quartermaster Department unless they are on duty with Major Archer, at Bacon Quarter Branch, and to receive those until Major Archer can have a hospital prepared for them."[77] Surgeon General Moore added that sick Negroes now in the hospital who are employed by the Quartermaster Department are "to be turned over to the Quartermaster with whom they are on duty."[78] Four days later Dr. Gravatt as well as the commandants of other hospitals were instructed by the Surgeon General that "hired men of the army have no claim to be treated and maintained in the hospitals established for soldiers. The Department by whom they are employed should establish hospitals."[79]

Later records seem to indicate that the Surgeon General rescinded his order prohibiting military hospitals from admitting sick and wounded Negroes. On December 20, 1864, Surgeon L. Guild, Army of Northern Virginia, wrote to the Surgeon General:

> The employment of Negroes as teamsters, ambulance drivers, and laborers in the place of enlisted men, has made it necessary to provide special Hospital accommodations for them. I have directed that two or three hospital tents at each Division infirmary be reserved for the use of the Negro employees who may need Medical or surgical treatment.
>
> The General Commanding directs me to communicate with you on the subject of their proper care at Richmond as it will doubtless become necessary to send some of the severely sick to that city, and regards that arrangements if you have not already ordered them, be made for their accommodation.[80]

During the winter of 1864–1865 sick and wounded Negroes attached to the Army of Northern Virginia were sent to the Richmond hospitals. Medical Director Carrington instructed Surgeon Gravatt as follows:

> You are directed without delay to have Hospital Shirts and drawers provided for each bed in the Ward appointed by you for the Negroes in the Hospital under your charge. This ward is too dark and badly ventilated and could be exchanged for the ward on 18th Street with advantage. You will have their own clothing carefully washed, mended, and preserved, and returned to them when well.
>
> You are directed to provide suitable utensils for washing the person of these sick and wounded Negroes and direct that the Medical officer in charge of them see that their nurses attend to washing them when necessary. It would, I think, be well if you would assign several colored nurses to the duty of washing the feet of each sick and wounded soldier for this purpose they should go from bed to bed with buckets or tubs of warm water.[81]

Sharply contrasting with the Receiving Hospital, which had a single ward for Negro patients, was Richmond's Engineer Bureau Hospital, which regularly treated slaves and free Negroes who were injured or became ill while working on fortifications in the vicinity of Richmond. If disease was the deadliest foe that Confederate soldiers had to face, then neglect was the deadly foe to be faced by the Negro inmates in the Richmond Engineer Hospital. This three-story institution, opened in the fall of 1861, had formerly been a brick factory, approximately 44 by 57 feet. The basement was used for a kitchen and other purposes; the first floor had an office, an apothecary shop, and small rooms partitioned off for storage of utensils; the second and third floors were used for wards, each accommodating 60 to 120 beds.

On December 10, 1862, the Richmond *Examiner* reported, "The Negro Hospital . . . is wretchedly managed. Stench and filth abound in untolerable quantities . . . and the poor Negroes are dying off like penned sheep, afflicted with rot. It is a disgrace to humanity to behold their utter neglect." The following day Lieutenant John B. Stanard, an engineer officer, and C. H. Ryland, the hospital's steward, wrote to the editor that "there is no hospital in the city or elsewhere (white or black) which is kept cleaner and better managed." Ryland added that "The Hospital is thoroughly cleaned with water and broom every day." He assured the editor that there are a sufficient number of Negro nurses in each ward "to administer the medicine proper," to keep the patients clean, and if necessary "their underclothing is removed and washed" by the laundresses.

Eventually, the Surgeon General issued an oral order to have the hospital inspected. On January 9, 1863, W. A. Carrington, serving as Inspector of Hospitals, reported his findings to Thomas H. Williams, Medical Director of the Army of Northern Virginia. Carrington first noted that the inmates "are generally slaves impressed into service for a term of two months, in accordance with an enactment of Congress. Dr. W. S. Vest in charge of this Hospital, is a private physician contracted with and paid by the Engineer Bureau. He reports to Lieutenant Stanard weekly and monthly (not daily) the deaths, discharges, returns to duty, and admissions." Next Carrington remarked:

The persons and clothing of patients are very uncleanly, there being no Hospital clothing, they are generally in their working garments. At my first visit to this Hospital, I saw 3 Negroes lying moribund in this condition, without beds save the sacking of cots and bedding, save their blankets, brought from home. There has been great suffering and great mortality from these influences. . . .[82]

In 1862 from June to December, 220 of the 861 Negroes admitted were discharged and declared unfit for any future work on fortifications. In December, 42 deaths were reported among the 290 patients admitted, representing a loss of almost $63,000 to the owners of the deceased slaves. Carrington recommended:

> Immediate steps be taken to turn this Hospital over to the control of the Chief Surgeon of this division, who will assign a Commissioned Officer to take charge of it, put it in the best condition for the comfort and health of the patients, (drawing by requisition bed sacks, bedding, straw, and Hospital clothing, and constructing suitable bathing arrangements) that morning, monthly, and Quarterly Reports of the sick and wounded, and all other reports required of military Hospitals be made to and through the Chief Surgeon's Office, and that the Colored employees of the different departments be hired with this condition, and be treated at this and [other Hospitals] if the No. will require it for the economy and efficiency of the service and the benefit of the employees.[83]

In December 1862, as Carrington inspected the hospital, he noted that 3 whites—1 steward and 2 ward masters—and 16 Negroes—13 nurses and 3 cooks—were employed by the Engineer Bureau as attendants.[84] Shortly afterward 3 female slaves—Elvy, Lucy, and Mary—were hired as laundresses, and Jordan, Lee, and Charles were hired from their owners as attendants.[85]

Aside from serving in Richmond's military hospitals, Negro nurses, cooks, and laundresses served in the care of Confederate soldiers in six well-known but small private hospitals: Robertson, African Church, Samaritan, Soldiers Home, Small Pox, and Saint Francis De Sailes. Perhaps the most famous of the Confederacy's smaller private hospitals was the Robertson Hospital. Miss Sally Louisa Tompkins, the "Heroine of the Confederacy," was its founder. It is significant that this hospital was not included among the 35 small hospitals in Richmond that were closed between September 1862 and March 1864. Although its bed capacity was limited to 25, over 1,300 patients were admitted during the war. Many stories have been written about "Captain Sally Tompkins," or the little lady with the "milk-white hands," and the other noble women of the South who gathered daily at the hospital to care for the sick and wounded. Her attendants, however, except for the steward, were all Negroes. There were only two nurses —female slaves owned by Sally Tompkins—for each of whom she was paid $20 per month. Both slave nurses were named Betsy, referred to as "Gay" and "Sad" Betsy. Then there were two slave cooks, Phoebe and Sally, and a slave laundress, Patsy Williams. Early in the war Peter and Churchill Smith, the two orderlies, ran away. Eventually, John Taylor, a free Negro, was hired at $33.33 monthly for nursing duties, along with his other job as a messenger for the Medical Examination Board.[86]

The story of the attendants in the African Church, the Samaritan, and the Soldiers Home hospitals parallels that of the Robertson Hospital. For example, during its limited existence the African Church Hospital had among its 10 employees in June 1862, 3 whites—a steward, a druggist, and a ward master—and 7 Negroes—4 nurses, 2 cooks, and a wagon driver.[87] Only 2 Negroes—Ned, a cook, and Lucinda, a laundress—and two whites—a ward master and a steward —assisted Mrs. Philip Mayo, the manager of the Samaritan Hospital.[88] Finally, the Soldiers Home Hospital, which could care for 40 patients, employed 3 Negroes—James, a slave nurse, and John and Peter, cooks.[89]

Virginia's epidemics, such as smallpox in the fall of 1862 and the winter of 1863–1864, afford some idea of the vital services rendered by Negro nurses and other hospital employees. During the single week ending December 19, 1862, H. H. Cunningham asserted, the "Smallpox Hospitals in Richmond reported two hundred fifty admissions and one hundred ten deaths." In January 1863 the City Hospital reported that 109 white and 191 Negro smallpox victims had crowded the hospital to its utmost capacity. By April 1863 the crisis appears to have passed, and 32 Negroes—20 nurses, 8 cooks, and 4 laundresses —were retained to care for the victims still confined to the hospital. Within eight months a second epidemic found the medical authorities, once again, gravely dependent upon colored hospital attendants. The hiring of 20 additional Negroes increased the number of colored employees to 34 nurses (5 females), 6 cooks, and 12 laundresses. All available space was eventually filled with smallpox victims. To prevent the patients' clothing from sticking to the sores, the nurses were expected to cover them with ointments. This, as well as other treatments administered to the sick, demanded much of the nurses' time, and required extreme patience. As the epidemic reached its peak, 90 Negroes—55 nurses, 17 cooks, and 18 laundresses—were kept busy providing for the physical needs of smallpox victims in the Richmond area.[90]

Similarly, Saint Francis De Sailes Hospital provides another example of the acceptance of Negro nurses, cooks, and laundresses as full partners in the South's heroic efforts to care for the sick and wounded. Opened in June 1862, Saint Francis De Sailes was a small religiously operated hospital (capacity, 30 patients), financially subsidized by the Confederate government. Like the Louisiana Hospital, this hospital was also staffed with the "Catholic Sisterhoods." Sisters Juliana, Theresa, and Francis served as matron, assistant matron, and ward matron respectively. Of the four male nurses assisting the sisters, three were Negroes—John Brooks and Robert Cooper were free blacks, and Henry was a slave. Two female slaves, Hannah and Maria, served as laundresses. In December 1864 all four of the male nurses were Negroes. Daniel, John, and Henry were slaves hired for $25 monthly, and Robert Cooper was free, as was the hospital's cook, Moses.[91]

Closely related to nursing and the preparation of food for the sick and wounded was the matter of washing the gowns, linen, and clothing of inmates. Therefore, in December 1861 the Confederate Congress authorized military hospitals to employ laundresses "at such rates and in such numbers as may be approved by the War Department."[92] The next eighteen months, however, were characterized by many efforts to have the salary of laundresses increased to a level comparable with those of hospital nurses and cooks. Less than a month after Congress authorized their employment, General Lee's medical director notified the Surgeon General, "If it is decided that no more than $8 per month can be paid to Hospital laundresses then the act of Congress . . . will prove of little benefit to our General hospitals, at least this side of Richmond."[93] Again, in November 1862, Medical Director Williams wrote to George W. Randolph, the Secretary of War, "that monthly pay allowed to laundresses . . . is insufficient," and he requested a pay increase to $18 per month. Within a few days he was notified that a monthly pay increase to $12 had been authorized.[94] Finally, in May 1863, the Confederate Congress enacted new legislation that "the pay to be hereafter allowed to all laundresses in hospitals or other places . . . shall be $25 per month, with rations and quarters."[95]

To relieve military hospitals in the Richmond area from the responsibility of washing clothing and linens, a Confederate States Steam Laundry was opened in August 1862. Existing medical regulations permitted the employment of "one laundress to every twenty patients entitled to washing." Consequently, the 26 general hospitals which sent items to the steam laundry were authorized to employ 156 laundresses. Eighteen of these hospitals, however, found it expedient to employ 69 laundresses while using the facilities of the steam laundry. During the first four months of its existence the Confederate States Steam Laundry washed 96,522 items at a total cost of $18,509.11 (a little over 19 cents for each piece washed).[96] The laundry employed 51 laundresses, 3 clerks, 2 porters, a fireman, and a delivery man. Unquestionably the high cost of keeping it in operation concerned the Surgeon General. Neither Chimborazo nor Winder nor Howard's Grove hospital used the laundry's facilities, while Jackson, Stuart, and Louisiana hospitals reported that their use of the steam laundry was restricted to cases of emergency. Several reports indicated that the laundry was poorly managed. After one year of operation, an inspection by William A. Carrington resulted in its discontinuance by order of the Surgeon General, issued on August 3, 1863. Quite naturally the closing of the laundry was reflected by a sudden increase, in the fall of 1863, in the number of Negro laundresses employed by military hospitals within Richmond. Within a general hospital laundry two assistant matrons—one supervising the laundry and the other in charge of linen and clothing—directed the activities of many Negro female laundresses employed. Instructions were given by both matrons to have the clothes carefully marked before they were washed and ironed. If necessary they were to be mended. Negro males were hired to maintain fires, supply water, deliver linens, and to perform numerous other tasks. From time to time the employees were engaged in the manufacture of soap.

III

Except for Richmond, the hospital center of the Confederacy, practically all of the military hospitals in Virginia were located in the

Piedmont and mountainous sections of the state. In these areas serious efforts were made by the Medical Department to provide several hundred Negroes, free and slave, to serve as nurses, ambulance drivers, cooks, and laundresses. From 1862 to the end of the war these general hospitals had little respite from the steady trickle of diseased and wounded Confederate soldiers. During a fifteen-month interval from January 1862 to March 1863, approximately 113,914 cases were treated. Medical Director Carrington reported in October 1864 that "accommodations for 2000 sick and wounded is needed in this state, 1200 beds in Richmond and 10,000 out of Richmond at the various hospital posts. When filled about 2000 nurses are wanted and as many cooks, ward masters, and guards." Carrington indicated that the overwhelming majority of these would have to be hired Negroes.[97]

The transfer of wounded men from impromptu field hospitals to the nearest general hospital often involved transportation problems. Whenever a sufficient number of ambulances were not available, commanding generals frequently authorized the impressment of Negro drivers, as well as wagons and horses or mules to transport the wounded to railroad depots, steamer landings, and canal waterways.[98] A portion of the hundreds of Negro teamsters employed by the Quartermaster Department were also called upon to serve as ambulance drivers. Frequently it was necessary to carry war casualties the entire distance to an interior hospital by some means of wagon transportation. By the spring of 1862 the medical corps provided nurses to accompany the ambulance trains on Virginia's railroads. Usually one nurse was assigned to each car and was responsible for its cleanliness and for keeping it "properly supplied with fresh water and clean bandages." Surgeon F. W. Roddy, who was in charge of one of the ambulance trains, employed five free Negroes as nurses—Joe Allen, James Brown, Robert Adams, Joe Ford, and Joe Mason.[99] Charles, a slave owned by N. Buck of Fairfax county, was employed as an ambulance driver for the Second Corps of the Army of Northern Virginia.[100] In fact, complaints by field surgeons that the lack of ambulances and drivers compelled them to keep wounded men in open fields unprotected from the inclement weather resulted in the employment of additional Negroes by the Army of Northern Virginia to serve as stretcher-bearers and ambulance drivers.

Although there were over twenty major general hospitals throughout the Department of Virginia, notably those in Farmville, Danville, Petersburg, and Staunton, none was as carefully planned as the large

Lynchburg hospital complex commanded by Surgeon W. O. Owen. It contained three general hospitals in addition to the Ladies Relief, Pratt, and Wayside hospitals. Once opened, each hospital had to be staffed, and here again the Negro, free and slave, was employed. In meeting the problems of securing hospital attendants for other hospitals, Surgeon Owens apparently cooperated with the medical director. Early in December 1861, Medical Director Williams sent a telegram from Manassas Junction to Owens stating, "I wanted Negro men, not Negro women," but asking him to send the six Negro women already hired. Williams reminded Owens that Negro males could perform duties in our hospitals which females could not, and "the latter are needed only as cooks and laundresses."[101] On December 30 Owens informed Williams, "I have not been able to hire Negro men for your hospital at the rate mentioned, no effort shall be spared" to secure them.[102] Occasionally a Negro hospital attendant was illegally impressed, and it became the duty of the medical director to take steps to insure that Negroes with passes would not be molested. For example, in November 1862 a slave hospital attendant was impressed and put to work unloading freight cars at the Lynchburg depot "notwithstanding his exhibition of a pass." Captain John M. Galt, the Post Commander, was immediately informed by the medical director that he was not to interfere with Negro attendants on official duty for hospitals.[103]

It is noteworthy that the labor needs of both the large government shops in Lynchburg and the quartermaster officers who were in

Table 5.5 *Negro attendants in Lynchburg hospitals, 1862*[104]

Name	Nurse	Cook	Laundress
General Hospital No. 1	102	19	28
General Hospital No. 2	56	19	29
General Hospital No. 3	61	18	33
Ladies Relief	10	1	2
Pratt	11	4	10
Wayside	13	2	2
	253	63	104

charge of collecting forage increased greatly the demand for Negro workers in the Lynchburg area. Nevertheless, over 400 workers were employed in Lynchburg's military hospitals (Table 5.5). By way of comparison, the white attendants in Lynchburg's military hospitals numbered 18 civilian stewards and 144 detailed men who served as nurses, ward masters, and guards. The three general hospitals had a total capacity of almost 3,000 beds. The Ladies Relief, Pratt, and Wayside hospitals could each accommodate about 100 inmates.

In the summer and the autumn of 1861, six military hospitals, with a capacity of more than 3,000 patients, were located in northern Virginia—Front Royal, Warrenton, Gordonsville, Culpeper Court House, Manassas, and Orange Court House. Each one, however, except for the hospital in Gordonsville, was abandoned within six to nine months after it opened. In spite of the presence of a large slave population, it appears that each of these hospitals experienced great difficulties in securing Negro attendants. Surgeon Benjamin Blackford, in charge of the Front Royal hospital, wrote to Medical Director Williams on December 17, 1861, that he was unable to hire civilians and Negroes as nurses. The following day the medical director notified the surgeon that if he could not hire or impress Negroes in the vicinity of Front Royal he should "try in the adjoining counties. Send an agent to see what he can do. Try every method before resorting to applications for details from the army."[105] On the same day the medical director dispatched a letter to surgeon J. M. C. Smith, in charge of the Warrenton Hospital, in which he indicated, "If Negroes cannot be hired or pressed in the vicinity of Warrenton, you must see what can be done in the adjoining counties. Free Negroes not already in the service of the government will be pressed wherever found, if they refuse to be hired. No exertions must be spared." Within a week General Joseph E. Johnston disapproved a request by Williams to retain detailed soldiers serving as nurses.[106] Shortly before the general hospital at Culpeper Court House was closed, Dr. D. S. Green complained that among the hospital's urgent needs was to increase the number of Negro nurses, cooks, and washwomen.[107]

Established in November 1861, Moore Hospital at Manassas was the largest military hospital in northern Virginia. Composed of wooden pavilions, it contained in all about 1,400 beds. Here also the hospital was confronted with the vexing problem of securing Negro attendants. On November 16, 1861, Medical Director Williams notified Major Thomas G. Rhett, Acting Adjutant General of the Army of the Potomac, that "nurses are required without delay." He also reported that General Jackson prevented Surgeon Anderson from leaving Winchester with fifteen Negro nurses he had recently hired. The General was enforcing a military order, issued by the Commanding General of the Army of the Potomac, which prohibited Negroes "from being hired outside the Winchester area." On November 19, 1861, the matter was finally brought to the attention of General Johnston, who ruled that "negroes required as Hospital nurses must be hired within this district."[108] during the four months of Moore Hospital's existence, it is clear that the hospital made continual efforts to secure colored attendants from other parts of the state. Several were hired from distant areas such as Farmville, Virginia. Early in 1862 Medical Director Williams notified Thomas L. Martin, an agent from Farmville:

> Enclosed find pass and tickets for transportation over the Lynchburg and Manassas R.R. for six Negroes you mention, and also an order on the Superintendent of the South Side R.R. passing them from Farmville to Lynchburg. Endeavor to get as many more as you can, and inform me as fast as you procure them, and I will send transportation. All the Negroes from Farmville to the Moore Hospital near Manassas, and will therefore be together.[109]

In March 1862 Moore Hospital was abandoned, but it was re-established at Gordonsville on a site not far from the Receiving and Wayside Hospital already in operation. The Gordonsville Receiving Hospital alone admitted 23,642 patients from June 1, 1863, to May 5, 1864. In June 1864 it admitted 6,278 inmates. Most of the Negro attendants were brought from Manassas to the new Gordonsville institution, some fifty odd miles to the south. Immediate steps were taken to secure additional Negro personnel. In November 1862 Surgeon B. M. Libby, in charge of the Gordonsville Receiving and Wayside Hospital, received orders from the medical director to "send your Negro attendants to this place as rapidly as their services can be dispensed with."[110]

On the whole, there was no marked difference in the availability of Negroes to serve as attendants in the general hospitals located at Danville and Farmville. The presence of a large Negro population to draw upon for hospital employees, along with existing railroad lines to transport the sick and wounded, were two of the outstanding advantages attached to locating military hospitals in these cities. The Danville hospital, which had a capacity of 2,400 patients, was by far the larger. In January 1862 the surgeon in charge was "authorized to hire Negroes by the year at prices not to exceed Twenty dollars per month without clothing." Yet, in spite of the presence of Negro labor, there were times when the hospital reported its inability to secure the large number of Negro attendants required to operate the vast institution. For example, in June 1862 the Surgeon General was informed:

> Having failed after diligent efforts to procure colored men and women in sufficient number to meet the demands of the hospital, I respectfully suggest the expediency of authorizing the Quartermaster of this Post to impress the hands of Planters engaged in cultivating tobacco. It would I presume be inexpedient to cripple the agricultural force of the farmers who are raising breadstuffs and other subsistence supplies, but there is a very considerable number of persons in this region . . . who have turned a deaf ear to every appeal to the patriotism and have appropriated their best hands to the production of tobacco during the present season. It would be fit and proper to make these men bear a share of the necessary burdens of the war. For want of nurses . . . is exceedingly urgent. I respectfully request that the proper measure be taken to procure a supply in the only way in which the demand can be promptly met.[111]

Medical Director Williams took note of the suggestion made by the surgeon in charge of the Danville hospital, and asserted that he favored the plan "to impress a portion of the Negroes of the Tobacco planters."

Good administration and effective utilization of Negro attendants were frequently combined in the operation of the Danville hospital. As a rule the needs of this hospital required the employment of over 100 Negro attendants. For example, in March 1863 the 122 Negro employees consisted of 67 nurses, 21 cooks, and 34 laundresses. During the next two months the colored attendants numbered from 121 to 116. At this time Surgeon G. F. Carmichael, in charge of one of the hospital's divisions, was instructed to return "Carrington, the baker, to his regiment," and to transfer two other Negro bakers to Division No. 4, to assist in baking bread for the hospital. Several weeks later he was requested to "furnish what hands can be spared to work in the ice pond."[112] However, in the fall of 1863 the surgeons in charge of each hospital division were directed to discharge all colored attendants whose services were unnecessary. During the following months a substantial decrease in the number of hospital patients prompted another reduction of Negro nurses to fewer than 40.[113] In some cases the released Negro attendants were immediately transferred to other hospitals, but usually they were sent to the Quartermaster Department to assist in the collection of forage or to the Engineer Bureau to labor on the Danville and Richmond fortifications. For example, on October 3, 1864, a telegram sent to surgeon H. R. Davidson contained instructions to provide all the able-bodied surplus Negro men "with one day's rations and send them down by the next train to Richmond . . . to report to the Engineer Headquarters." Three weeks later Dr. Davidson was directed "to return to Petersburg all the colored employees from the Petersburg hospital not required."[114]

In some cases, as in that of the Danville hospital, colored attendants would leave their jobs and seek employment in hospitals near their homes. Late in July 1862, four Negroes—Cyrus, James, Samuel, and Laura—who resided in the vicinity of Farmville left the Danville hospital. Surgeon H. D. Taliaferro, in charge of the general hospital at Farmville, was "instructed to employ none of them . . . nor any other servant who may have deserted the Hospital in this District."[115] Aside from restrictions dealing with slaves and free Negroes who walked off their jobs in other military hospitals, Surgeon Taliaferro was free to hire the large number of Negro attendants required for the Farmville general hospital. Opened in May 1862, this hospital had a capacity of 1,200 beds. At first, free Negroes from surrounding counties were detailed for hospital service. Theoretically, they had resort to seek employment of their choice, but in actual practice this was not always true. Many were unwillingly impressed for noncombat military duty. In mid-July 1862, Dr. Taliaferro submitted a requisition for 30 male free blacks, and the sheriff of neighboring Cumberland County was instructed to see that they "reported to Colonel Parrish who will send them to Farmville for service."[116] Subsequent legislation soon increased the number of slaves available for hospital service. Under the authority of the provisions of the act of September 27, 1862, the Farmville hospital, during the following six months, was able to hire several slave attendants. During the first five months of 1863, 61 Negro nurses were employed. Among the 24 free blacks serving as nurses were 7 females—Amanda, Mary, Eliza, Agnes, Nannie, Clara, and Mary. Likewise, there were 11 females among the 37 slave nurses. Hence 29.5 percent of the Negro nurses in the Farmville hospital were females.[117] By the end of 1863 the hospital had more than doubled its number of Negro attendants. For example, during the months of November and December there were 139 slaves and free Negroes—100 nurses, 31 laundresses, 7 cooks, and 1 baker. Thirty of these attendants were free blacks—20 males and 10 female laundresses. In the same months 7 of the hospital's surgeons hired out their slaves (13 in all) as hospital attendants.[118]

On December 15, 1863, sixteen days prior to the opening of the hiring season, Dr. Taliaferro was notified that $20 per month should be a maximum for Negroes as hospital attendants when clothing, rations, and quarters are provided. Hospital laundresses could be paid as high as $25 per month including rations and quarters, but not clothing. By January 1, 1864, ten free Negroes—6 nurses, 2 cooks, and 2 laundresses—and 77 slaves—54 nurses, 7 cooks, and 16 laundresses—were hired.[119] Once again 7 of the hospital's surgeons hired their slaves as attendants. Such slaves composed 19.5 per cent of the slave employees. The 7 cooks included 6 slaves and a free Negro. By April 1864, Surgeon Taliaferro was reminded that he had more attendants than were allowed for the number of inmates confined to the hospital. The medical director suggested that if they could not "be employed in the gardens" that they "should be temporarily hired to some of the farmers or manufactures in the vicinity."[120] The medical director's instructions did not indicate that unneeded attendants should be sent to the local engineers in charge of erecting fortifications. Yet, during the periods that Negroes worked on defensive works at High Bridge or other areas within a fifty-mile radius of Farmville, a ward was provided in the hospital for Negroes who became sick or were injured.

Not only were colored nurses employed in the Danville and Farmville hospitals, but they also worked in the Staunton and Charlottesville military hospitals. In July 1862 the Staunton institution was established under the direction of Surgeon William Hay. Within three months, hundreds of ambulance wagons were engaged in transporting over 500 sick and wounded soldiers from Winchester to the newly opened hospital. Surgeon Hay expressed grave concern to the medical director of Lee's army about the shortage of Negro hospital attendants. Meanwhile, from the winter of 1862 to the fall of 1864, over a hundred slaves, free Negroes, and detailed soldiers served in various capacities. At least 16 Negro nurses were employed in January 1863, and by September the hospital's attendants numbered 36 Negroes and 35 detailed soldiers.[121] The latter served largely as ward masters, stewards, and guards. In April 1864 Surgeon Hay reported only 211 patients, although 514 beds were available. The medical director notified Surgeon Hay that the 150 attendants employed for the hospital exceeded the number authorized for the number of patients confined to the hospital. Eventually the surplus colored attendants were released (subject to recall), and the detailed soldiers were directed to report to the medical director.

Significance of colored nurses in the Charlottesville general hospital is evidenced by one of its former surgeons, Dr. Edward Warren, who after serving early in the war was appointed the Surgeon General of North Carolina. Dr. Warren wrote, "I can see before me the great rotunda filled with hastily-constructed beds . . . surgeons . . . and the faithful Negro attendants."[122] This large institution, opened in July 1861, was administered by surgeon James L. Cabell, who was assisted by 30 surgeons and assistant surgeons. The hospital was constantly faced with the problem of securing sufficient attendants. As early as October 1861 Surgeon Cabell was still seeking "to secure civilians and colored hirelings" to staff the hospital. Medical Director Williams then declared that "it is only in case suitable nurses cannot be hired, that enlisted men may be detailed." He added, "It is to the interest of the service to have as few men detailed from their regiments as possible."[123] During the November hiring season Cabell was notified that Negro nurses hired or impressed would receive the maximum monthly pay of $18.50 each.[124] By February 1862 the hospital managed to employ 61 nurses, cooks, and laundresses to attend the 320 inmates.[125] At no time during 1863 was the hospital sufficiently staffed with attendants. In November the medical director wired Surgeon Cabell:

> You are authorized to hire servants such as can use soldiers' clothing by the month or year, on the best terms you can, giving clothes, rations, and a maximum of $300 per annum—$20 per month is the price generally given elsewhere for the best attendants, and is only exceeded in cases of extreme efficacy.[126]

The following month Cabell requested the medical director to "procure an order to impress slaves as hospital nurses." The surgeon explained, "I find an unexpected difficulty in hiring them."[127] Since the hiring season for 1864 was less than three weeks away, Cabell was anxious to have the authority to retain his present attendants and to take whatever additional steps were necessary to secure others. Despite the wartime shortage of hospital personnel, the physicians, nurses, and other employees struggled to provide adequately for the physical welfare of diseased and wounded soldiers.

Several hospitals, notably those in rural Virginia, for the most part proved to be most valuable during the periods when campaigns were waged in their vicinities or when other military hospitals were overcrowded. Colored nurses, cooks, and laundresses figured prominently in the smaller military hospitals (Table 5.6). The medical institutions in this category within the Department of Virginia proved to be a valuable asset to the sick and the wounded of the Army of Northern Virginia.

Most of the thousands of Negroes—nurses, ambulance drivers, stretcher-bearers, cooks, bakers, and other hospital attendants—are now nameless. Yet they bathed patients, fed the sick and wounded, administered medicines, aired and made beds, cleaned wards, maintained fires, and performed numerous other tasks. Other colored hospital attendants prepared food, washed clothing, whitewashed and repaired buildings, worked in the purveyor's office and the commissary, labored in the gardens, dairies, and icehouses maintained by the

Table 5.6 *Small military hospitals, Department of Virginia, 1862–1865*[128]

Hospital	Location	Year	Negroes	Whites
White Oak	Dinwiddie County	1862	7	4
Episcopal Church	Williamsburg	1862	2	8
General	Montgomery Springs	1864	26	13
Wayside	Dublin	1864	2	5
General	Parisburg	1865	2	3
Breckenridge	Marion	1865	25	10
Washington	Abingdon	1864	12	10
Parker's Store	Spotsylvania County	1864	57	0
			133	53

hospitals, drove wagons, and so forth. Seldom were they mentioned in the journals of their day, and only a few were named or described in the memoirs of Confederate surgeons. On the other hand they never engaged in wholesale desertions. The decision to place them as attendants in military hospitals not only freed many thousands of soldiers for military duty but considerably lightened the burden of caring for the sick and wounded in Confederate armies. Now wholly forgotten, these Negroes' names have no meaning today. Confederate medical histories seldom discuss the Negro. For the same reason, too, the story of Confederate logistics is incomplete.

CHAPTER SIX

Confederate Labor Troops

Union soldiers . . . sallied up to Rebel breastworks that were often impregnable. They began to complain, finding the Negro with his pick and spade, a greater hindrance to their progress than the Rebel's cannon balls.

The narrator is Joseph T. Wilson who, after serving in both the Confederate and Union armies, expressed the war sentiment of Federal fighting forces.[1] As the Confederate armies were being mustered for combat, the South marshaled a vast army of blacks for the erection of defensive works. In vivid portrayal of this epic event, Bell I. Wiley wrote:

The roar of cannon, the rattle of muskets, and the clatter of the sword in the hand of the white was accompanied by the thud of the sledge hammer, the ring of the axe, and the clank of the shovel wielded by the strong ebony arm . . . as he worked to make impregnable the endangered positions of the South. . . . Together they worked, white and black, through the halcyon days of '61 and '62 and the dark periods of '64 and '65, an army of soldiers and an army of laborers.[2]

For the warring Confederate States of America, the years 1861–1865 were a period characterized by constant construction of defensive works designed to repel attacks by Union armies. This was especially true in Virginia, where Negroes, free and slave, were continually called upon to toil on land and river defenses. Virginia, as the northern boundary of the Confederacy, was in a very exposed location and subject to invasion by Union forces. Her northern and western borders measured about 1,000 miles; her eastern boundary consisted of 342 miles of navigable coastal waters. The vulnerability of Virginia's borders was largely a product of uncertainty as to where to expect a Federal attack. The task of erecting fortifications became the responsibility of the Corps of Engineers by act of the Confederate Congress on March 6, 1861.[3] In the ensuing eight months, Virginia's Engineer Department took initial steps for defense of the state.

Extensive defensive preparations were ordered by Governor John Letcher immediately after secession.[4] On April 26 he dispatched Colonel Andrew Talcott, state engineer, to lay out batteries on Virginia's vulnerable sea coast. For the next six months Virginia's corps of state engineers was largely responsible for locating and designing the state's fortifications. The primary object of the artificially constructed defensive works was to protect rivers, to protect Confederate troops from enemy fire, and to enable the Confederate soldiers to deliver their own fire with devastating effect. Hence, the successful repulse of Union attacks and the construction of satisfactory entrenchments were directly related. However, the engineers could set the stakes only at chosen locations, where it was left to others to do the digging and construct batteries, entrenchments, and redoubts. Consequently the six months that followed Virginia's secession are the least known but the most interesting of the war for the mobilization of black manpower in the preparation of defensive works. In the first wave of war patriotism state engineers found at their disposal practically all of the adult males among Virginia's 58,042 free Negroes and 491,031 slaves.[5] The possibility of a fleet movement of Federal gunboats up the Rappahannock, York, or James rivers—all of which were navigable to points within striking distance of Richmond—prompted the fortification of rivers as the initial step in the defense of the state. Negro labor, under the supervision of state engineers, was immediately committed to the construction of river batteries and defensive lines.

In digging entrenchments the majority of Negro workmen were distributed to excavate the ditch and to form the parapet and the glacis embankments. One Negro swinging a pick could loosen sufficient earth to keep two others busy shoveling and heaving. The men were spaced from 4 to 6 feet apart in order to prevent interference. Each shovelful of earth could be pitched about 12 feet in a horizontal direction, or 6 feet in a vertical direction. An expert ditcher could throw up from 8 to 10 cubic yards during a ten-hour period; but for Negroes unaccustomed to the use of ditching tools, the removal of 6 cubic yards of earth was considered an average day's work in ordinary soils. When a relay of shovelers was placed in an offset in the ditch, however, from 4 to 5 cubic yards was sufficient.

The excavation began with the pick breaking the ground far enough from the counterscarp crest (outer edge of the ditch) that by digging vertically for 3 feet the digger ultimately reached the upper edge of the ditch (see Plate 3). The digging continued for an additional 3 feet in depth; the earth thrown out was used to form that parapet and the glacis (specially constructed large embankments) on both sides of the ditch. The dirt was then spread evenly and tamped. For convenience of entering the ditch while working, steps were formed, and another 3 feet of earth was removed. When the ditch had been excavated to the bottom, the offsets were cut away, and both sides of the ditch were properly sloped. The earth thrown from the offsets, if not required to complete the parapet (usually an 8-foot inclined embankment supported by wooden beams to protect soldiers when firing), was used to form the glacis (a sloping mound beyond the outer edge of the ditch). In the construction of the parapet great care was taken to provide drainage at some suitable point. Erosion was avoided by carrying off the water and preventing it from running down the side of the ditch. Hard labor and dexterity were required for proper construction of the defensive works, with their many slopes, platforms, and powder magazines.[6] Hence, the value of such work depended to a great extent upon the ability of the labor crews and the care they took in making the entrenchments impregnable.

Table 6.1 *Free Negro laborers on river batteries, 1861*[7]

Location	May	June	July	Aug.	Sept.	Oct.	Remarks
Fort Boykins	—	—	65	104	94	94	1 carpenter
Fort Huger	—	—	—	—	153	117	10 carpenters
Fort Lowry	68	138	138	49	46	66	5 carpenters
Gloucester Point	79	56	96	—	—	—	3 carpenters
Hardy's Bluff	—	—	76	88	—	—	2 carpenters
Jamestown	231	276	192	192	26	—	5 carpenters
Mulberry Island	—	—	—	103	115	113	3 bricklayers
Yorktown	—	51	51	67	71	76	2 carpenters

Throughout the war Virginia committed her Negro auxiliary force to the erection of batteries and entrenchments. On April 26, 1861, Colonel Andrew Talcott, the state engineer, was dispatched by Governor John Letcher to Gloucester Point and to Yorktown, at the mouth of the York River, to lay out batteries. General Lee also pushed both defensive works with the utmost vigor. At Gloucester Point's fortifications, slave and free Negro laborers—turfers, carpenters, bricklayers, sawyers, wagon drivers, and ditchers—were engaged in the construction of batteries. Lee was anxious to obstruct enemy gunboats from moving up the York River and thus prevent an attack on Richmond, except by long land marches.

Lee advised Colonel W. B. Taliaferro, Commanding Officer at Gloucester Point, to utilize Negro labor to fortify the land approaches to his rear.[8] Across the river from Gloucester Point, several hundred additional Negroes were engaged in constructing the batteries of Yorktown, designed to complete the command of the York River. By June the slaveowners of York, Warwick, and Elizabeth City counties had responded favorably to an urgent request for half of their slaves to erect defensive works.[9] Slaveowners were paid 50 cents a day for the labor of each slave. Those who sent carpenters and bricklayers received $1.00 a day. In October General Magruder asked the citizens of King and Queen, Gloucester, and Mathews counties to send "one-third of their efficient male slaves" to work on the York River, Yorktown, and Williamsburg entrenchments.[10] Although the owners responded promptly to Magruder's request, they complained about the harsh treatment of their slaves and the lack of a proper diet and adequate amounts of food.

From the York River and Gloucester Point batteries and entrenchments Talcott proceeded to Norfolk to superintend and to hasten the construction of essential defensive works. Upon his arrival he effectively organized and supervised the deployment of several gangs of slave laborers. At the Naval Hospital batteries there were 131 slaves; at Pit Point, 72; at Sewall's Point, 115; at Craney Island, 82; at St. Helena, 42; at Fort Boykins, 118; at Lambert's Point, 30; at Tanner's Creek, 27; and at Fort Norfolk, 197.[11] Sixty others were also employed in the obstruction of the Elizabeth River and the Norfolk Harbors.

Obstruction of rivers was sometimes accomplished by felling or laying huge piles of trees across the stream. Another method involved the sinking of small craft or the anchoring of rafts across a narrow place in the river. The 874 slave laborers at Norfolk were buttressed by another labor force of at least 350 free Negroes from the surrounding counties who volunteered their services. In reply to a telegram sent by T. P. Gwynn, chief engineer of the Norfolk defenses, for 600 free Negroes from Petersburg, Petersburg authorities informed the governor that at least 300 would be sent.[12]

Colonel Talcott left the Norfolk defenses for several days to locate and stake out the best site for a battery, which he deemed necessary to prevent the enemy from ascending the Nansemond River and cutting the Norfolk and Petersburg Railroad. Three batteries were staked out at the mouth of the Nansemond River. By September 1861 the construction of Fort Huger, designed to control entry into the Nansemond River, was well under way with slave and free Negro labor.[13]

Once the Norfolk defenses were started, State Engineer Talcott proceeded up the James River to select suitable sites for batteries. Talcott decided upon the immediate fortification of Jamestown Island. Several hundred slaves and free Negroes, with ditching tools, carts, and horses, were marshaled to perform the necessary work. A few months later other batteries were constructed at Mulberry Island, south of the Jamestown Island defensive works. The Mulberry works were to become the chief defense on the lower James River.[14]

Life for Negroes working on Confederate defenses was extremely harsh and physically exhausting. This was especially true during the winter months, when there was constant exposure in obstructing rivers and building batteries or earthworks such as those of Jamestown and Mulberry Islands. The tedious work of digging, shoveling, and heaving earth, as well as the erection of massive embankments, demanded tremendous physical stamina. Likewise, the placing of heavy logs for revetments and the mounting of heavy guns contributed to a high rate of injury and mortality among Negro laborers at defensive works. While construction was in progress, the James River works, like those at the Naval Hospital, utilized almost 200 bales of cotton to provide a temporary cover for troops in case of emergency. Each bale, weighing 500 pounds, had to be positioned to form a protective wall. In this swampy area the building of batteries proved to be extremely difficult. Negro laborers were frequently forced to work in mud or water up to their waists. Tons of dirt, sand, or stones used to reinforce the heavy wooden beams had to be procured and put in place. Often, unduly heavy labor, improper diet, brutal punishment, neglect, and poor medical care combined to seriously impair (sometimes permanently) a slave's ability to perform his regular duties, once he was returned to his owner. The same was true for many free Negroes who labored on Virginia's defensive works.

Despite frequent complaints about the poor physical condition of slaves returned from defensive works, slave labor was continually utilized during the summer and fall of 1861. General Lee directed that a small battery of four guns be erected on the Rappahannock River, below the city of Rappahannock, to allay the fears of the people that the enemy might ascend the river. Thus, at Lowry's Point a fort was constructed by Negro manpower. During the months of June and July, Essex and Richmond counties supplied 138 free Negroes, whose labor was compensated at 50 cents a day. Achilles and John Henry, both slave carpenters, were hired for $1.00 a day. Twenty-five Negro turfers and turf cutters were paid between 60 and 75 cents daily. Approximately 150 slaves were supplied by planters from surrounding counties to labor on the defensive works at Lowry's Point.[15]

With batteries strategically located to prevent enemy gunboats from ascending the Virginia rivers, the governor ordered Colonel Talcott to make preparations for the precautionary defenses of Richmond. The state engineer dispersed topographic survey parties to prepare up-to-date maps of the city's environs, from which a decision could be made as to the best location for redoubts and entrenchments on the outskirts of the capital city. The state engineers also moved to lay out the Williamsburg and Yorktown lines of defense. Eventually by proclamation of the governor on June 8, 1861, Virginia's forces and defenses were turned over to Confederate authorities in Richmond. The final and formal transfer, however, was not completed until another five months had elapsed. A report of General Robert E. Lee summarizes Virginia defenses as they existed at Confederate accession: (1) on the lower James, two batteries armed with 32-pounders and lighter guns; (2) on the York, three batteries with a total of 30 guns; (3) on the Potomac, no guns except the 12 guns on Aquia Creek Landing; (4) on the lower Rappahannock, a four-gun battery of 32-pounders and 8-inch columbiads; (5) at Norfolk, six batteries on the Elizabeth River with 85 guns, and fieldworks on the bay side of the city; (6) at Richmond, fieldworks planned for 60 guns; and (7) on the Peninsula, the Williamsburg and Yorktown lines.[16]

Some construction actually commenced on the Williamsburg defensive lines as early as May 1861, when state engineers and several hundred slave and free Negro laborers were dispatched to stake out and erect fortifications. General Lee was aware that he had little time to prepare Virginia for the first shock of an invasion that was inevitable, because of the state's proximity to Federal lines. He postulated his war plans on the maintenance of a strict defense, where Virginia forces could be dispersed to meet effectively the advance of a superior enemy that not only controlled the Chesapeake Bay but was able to move into the state simultaneously from the north, the east, and the west. The heart of Virginia was also open to invasion by her long tidal rivers. Moreover Lee's defensive policy called for the immediate and continual construction of entrenchments. The success of the general's basic strategy depended, to a large extent, upon the Negro manpower he could command to perform the physical work necessary for so huge an undertaking. Between May and August 1861, for example, 458 free Negroes from York, James City, Surry, and Prince George counties were marshaled to labor on the Williamsburg lines.[17] In September an additional 166 free Negroes arrived to continue work on the entrenchments. The slaveowners of New Kent, York, Surry, and Prince George counties sent their quota of 489 slaves.[18] At one time over 1,500 Negroes were engaged in the preparation of embankments and the ground around the entrenchments. Trees had to be felled and all the land around the works, within range of rifles or cannons, had to be cleared so that no shelter might be available to the enemy in the event of an attack.

The Richmond lines, like the Williamsburg entrenchments, were under construction when Governor Letcher transferred Virginia's defensive works and their supervision to Major Danville Ledbetter, the second ranking Confederate engineer officer.[19] In order to defend the city in case of enemy attack, elaborate plans were made for its defense. Three slaves—William, James, and Armistead—and four free Negroes accompanied topographical survey parties sent out to prepare maps of the city's environs.[20] Once the survey parties had completed their tasks, the state engineers set out stakes at the sites where the earthworks were to be constructed. Calls were issued for slave and free Negro laborers from the Piedmont counties. Work began on entrenchments on the outskirts of the city, and a vast network of earthworks broke the green landscapes. By October 1861 a major portion of the works slowly began to take shape. Negro carpenters were engaged in constructing rectangular timber platforms from which the guns were to be fired—13 slave and 15 free Negro carpenters are listed for July–October 1861.[21] In building a platform, the earth on which it rested was tamped and leveled by slave turf cutters. Three trenches were cut for the sleepers, two of which were placed under the cannon wheels, and the third under the trail. The sleepers were laid flush with the ground and firmly secured by pickets driven at their sides and ends, and the earth was firmly packed in the trenches around the guns. If necessary, wooden platforms were laid on both sides of the guns to keep the artillerymen's feet out of the soft, sticky mud. The revetments, behind which soldiers stood as they fired, were usually constructed with a facing of timber, although stone and sod would sometimes be used to sustain the earth embankment.[22] Over 700 free Negroes from nine counties were marshaled to labor on the Richmond lines.[23] This labor force was supplemented by almost 2,000 slaves—wagoners, bricklayers, sawyers, ditchers, and carpenters.[24] General Lee was extremely perceptive as to the value of Negro laborers for military purposes. Writing to President Davis, he asserted, "There is nothing so military as labour, and nothing so important to an army as to save the lives of its soldiers."[25]

Lee's views were shared by both the Richmond press and President Davis. An editorial in the Richmond *Examiner* entitled "Who'll Help to Defend the City?" called upon the citizens to send their slaves to labor on defensive works. The citizens were also asked to clean the gutters opposite their premises, since the city's Negro employees and carts (used to haul tools and provisions) were employed at the entrenchments.[26] On June 3, 1861, President Davis visited Marion Hill, on the outskirts of the capital, where redoubts were being constructed by Negro labor under the direction of Captain Even Scott, chief engineer. The Richmond press reported that as the President was shown around the bastions, the delight and gratification of the Negroes was openly manifested.[27] Each evening several hundred Negroes returned to the city "bearings flags, picks, shovels, and singing as they proceeded up Main Street."[28] In July the City Council of Richmond passed an ordinance which obligated free Negroes to labor on fortifications. Several free Negroes were brought to the City Hall, where the mayor reminded them that "it was no less their duty than that of the white people to do something for the good of the country—since they could not fight, they should work."[29] After

Mayor Mayo concluded his speech he ordered the free Negroes to return to their homes and to report to him at sunrise next day at the City Hall. The mayor later reported that 120 free Negroes had offered their services, and that he expected to have at least 300 in a very few days.[30]

Prior to November 1861, the major responsibility for the construction of river batteries and entrenchments for Virginia's defense was assumed by state engineers under the direction of the Governor, General Lee, and Colonel Andrew Talcott. On the heights around Richmond they began the erection of a system of forts and earthworks. As early as the summer of 1861, Richmond's defense was a matter of prestige and formed the basis of Lee's strategy during the months to follow. Since the city might face combined land and water attacks, its fortification was imperative, and to this task the state's engineers and Negro laborers gave themselves as assiduously as they had to the construction of defensive works at Yorktown and Williamsburg and on the James, York, Rappahannock, and other Virginia rivers.

It was not until the fall of 1861 that the Engineer Bureau of the Confederacy assumed sole responsibility for the construction of Virginia defensive works. Under the supervision of Colonel J. F. Gilmer, in command of the Engineer Bureau, and Colonel W. H. Stevens, chief engineer of the Army of Northern Virginia, earthworks rose steadily. Richmond, the capital of the Confederacy, and Petersburg, a vital industrial and rail center, were encircled by immense webs of entrenchments; in fact, the entire state was checkered with redoubts and fortifications. Additional river batteries were erected, and guns were mounted at key points along Virginia waters.

Unfortunately the zeal for the Southern cause which existed during the opening months of the conflict began to wane substantially, and both state and Confederate authorities were to experience great difficulty in obtaining a sufficiency of Negro workers. Voluntary contracts with the owners or with the Negroes themselves proved to be unsatisfactory. Consequently, Virginia was forced to find other means to tap Negro manpower before the end of the first year of conflict. Throughout the war five methods were used to obtain Negro labor to construct entrenchments: slaves were offered by their owners without request for compensation; free Negroes volunteered their services; Negroes, free and slave, were hired by the Engineer

Bureau; labor was impressed by commanding officers because of the exigencies of war; and conscription laws were passed by both the General Assembly of Virginia and the Confederate Congress. This legislation was enacted to "relieve whites for military duty, and from the obligations of production and manufacture."[31] The laws were also designed to give the governor the authority to impress slaves and free blacks in numbers sufficient for the adequate defense of Virginia, if they could not be secured by voluntary hire. These laws provided that impressment be in uniform proportion to the number of able-bodied male slaves owned, fixed the rate of compensation, prescribed the age limits, and designated the period of labor within which slaves were subject to impressment. Administration of laws was such that clashes ultimately developed between slaveowners, state officials, and Confederate officials. In March 1863 the Confederate Congress legalized the drafting of slaves. Yet ever mindful of states' rights, the lawmakers stipuated that military authorities in drafting slaves or free Negroes must conform to the rules and regulations of state law.[32]

Payrolls and other records from the Confederate Engineer Bureau contribute to a fuller understanding of the many ways in which Negro manpower was inextricably interrelated to the Virginia war effort, especially in the preparation of military defenses. Exigencies of four years of warfare prompted Virginia governors to call upon slaveowners to furnish almost fifty thousand slaves to construct defensive works. Though many planters objected, insisting that such labor was detrimental to their slaves' health, both Governor Letcher and Governor Smith were successful in securing a somewhat favorable response to the seven requisitions they submitted to county authorities for slaves to labor on fortifications. In the opening months of 1862, officials from Lunenburg and New Kent counties questioned a directive to send "all the able-bodied free Negroes and one half of the male slaves between the ages of 16 and 50" to work on the Yorktown fortifications. Governor Letcher then notified county authorities that "the requisition was made by General Magruder, and that the executive of Virginia cannot interfere." He also stated, "The public necessity demands and the people must yield their Negroes or submit to the Yankees."[33] Meanwhile Powhatan and Goochland authorities sent respectively 300 and 400 slaves to Yorktown.[34] Shortly after McClellan landed at Fortress Monroe to prepare his Peninsula Campaign of 1862, the Confederate commander Magruder issued a call for a thousand Negroes to erect entrenchments at Mulberry Island (Lee's Farm), to protect his rear.[35] Over 1,300 slaves were dispatched from fourteen counties.[36] In August, Colonel W. H. Stevens, chief of construction for the Richmond lines, informed the Secretary of War of his need for 5,340 slaves to perform the labor. President Davis wrote Governor Letcher requesting that he take the steps necessary to fulfill Steven's requisition.[37] Stevens had only recently advertised in the Richmond press for a thousand Negroes.[38]

Although Confederate authorities were reluctant to withdraw Negro labor harvesting crops, they nevertheless impressed them to labor at the Richmond defense lines. Throughout September long lines of Negroes passed through the city to work on the fortifications. The need for Negro labor was so great, however, that various wartime regulations were enacted to guarantee an adequate supply of slaves in critical industrial, military, and agricultural areas. This permitted the shifting of Negroes to war industries, railroads, hospitals, ordnance and naval works, and the Quartermaster and Commissary Departments. Even the Confederate armies in the theater of operations were able to tap successfully the Negro reservoir. Such provisions were made in October 1862 by the General Assembly of Virginia. A ceiling was put on the number of slaves the governor could impress for public defense of the state at any one time. The ceiling was 10,000, or no more than 5 per cent of the slave population. The impressment act of October 3, 1862, found Confederate authorities moving rapidly to procure slave labor.

On October 8, 1862, Gilmer wrote the Secretary of War requesting that President Davis submit a requisition of the governor of Virginia for 4,500 slaves from 14 counties.[39] The chief of engineers pointed out that "the counties specified are those which have furnished none or only a portion of the legal draft." Colonel Gilmer asked that the slaves be delivered promptly to the Richmond engineer office, and that the railroads be notified "at least three days beforehand that the necessary transportation may be furnished without delay."[41] The governor informed President Davis that the counties had been requested to respond to the requisition promptly. On October 21 the governor turned down a request from General Smith to have Petersburg and Richmond furnish respectively 300 and 500 slaves while awaiting the arrival of others recently impressed. The governor reasoned that both cities had already furnished their quotas and should not be further imposed upon.[42] Throughout October, county officials notified the governor's office that every effort was being made to supply their full quotas. Each county sheriff was expected to collect the slaves and deliver them to Julius Lamb, the engineer agent in Richmond. Each county was late, however, in supplying the number of slaves called for in the requisition. Some delayed sending their slaves for several weeks, explaining that the delay was caused by the failure of the Justices to set quotas, the need of slaves for harvesting, the smallpox epidemic, and the ineptness of the sheriff. The counties who sought exemption from the governor were turned down and were asked to comply immediately.[43]

In November 1862 the Confederate Engineer Bureau moved again to commit another block of Virginia's Negro labor market to the Richmond defensive works. Jefferson Davis sent Governor Letcher a requisition for 4,550 slaves to be taken from 26 other counties, which would make almost 10,000 slaves available to construct earthworks on the outskirts of the capital. The Engineer Bureau asked the governor to take immediate steps to have delinquent counties supply their full quotas of slaves.[45] The governor issued an order authorizing the sher-

Table 6.2 *Requisition for 4,500 slaves by counties, October 1862*[40]

County	Quota	Furnished	Deficit	Sent later	Deficit
Albemarle	540	0	540	442	98
Amherst	260	145	115	97	18
Appomattox	180	109	71	56	15
Bedford	450	274	176	176	0
Buckingham	300	204	96	2	94
Campbell	400	204	196	23	173
Charlotte	230	197	33	19	14
Cumberland	210	197	13	2	11
Fluvanna	140	101	39	14	25
Halifax	350	263	87	30	57
Louisa	350	241	109	69	40
Nelson	190	109	81	16	65
Pittsylvania	580	410	170	170	0
Prince Edward	320	303	17	13	4
Total	4,500	2,757	1,743	1,129	614

iff to take the slaves of parties who refused to send their slaves and to deliver them to Richmond.[46]

On January 13, 1863, Gilmer wrote to the Secretary of War that "a further supply of labor for fortifications . . . in Virginia is required," and recommended that another call for 4,000 slaves be made upon Governor Letcher. Twenty-two counties and the cities of Petersburg, Richmond, and Danville were included in the January requisition. On January 22 Governor Letcher addressed a letter to the affected counties and cities requesting that they "make provisions for the number of slaves they were assessed."[47] The Governor emphasized that large numbers of slaves were needed to prepare defenses for the spring campaign. Hence, eleven counties surrounding Richmond were each asked to supply from 150 to 500 slaves, and the remaining

Table 6.3 *Requisition for 4,550 slaves, by counties, November 1862*[44]

County	Quota	Furnished	Deficit
Augusta	250	231	19
Botetourt	100	97	0
Brunswick	225	100	125
Caroline	400	400	0
Culpeper	200	200	0
Essex	150	150	0
Franklin	300	289	11
Greene	75	75	0
Hanover	225	225	0
Henry	225	205	20
King and Queen	150	150	0
King William	100	100	0
Lunenburg	150	143	7
Madison	200	200	0
Mecklenburg	300	249	51
Montgomery	100	80	20
Nottoway	200	200	0
Orange	200	141	51
Page	25	25	0
Patrick	75	67	8
Pulaski	50	46	4
Rappahannock	150	150	0
Roanoke	100	84	16
Rockbridge	150	139	11
Rockingham	100	26	74
Spotsylvania	350	350	0
Total	4,550	4,150	400

counties, which were located in southwestern Virginia, were each assessed from 20 to 150 slaves. Subsequent reductions in quotas for some counties were prompted by the loss of slaves to Federal raiding parties, slaves escaping to Union lines, and inadvertent mistakes in quotas.[48] For example, Nottoway County was included in the January draft for 200 slaves, although those supplied in the November draft were still laboring on defensive works. Colonel Gilmer recommended that Nottoway be exempt from the January draft.[49] In less than two months Colonel Gilmer wrote to the Secretary of War that "an additional supply of labor . . . is absolutely necessary to complete the works, within the time desired by General Lee."[50] On March 11, 1863,

Table 6.4 *Requisition for 2,832 slaves by counties, March 11, 1863*[51]

County	Old deficit		New call	Number
Albemarle	Oct. '62	98	66	164
Amherst	Oct. '62	18	36	54
Appomattox	Oct. '62	15	20	35
Augusta	Nov. '62	19	30	49
Bedford	Oct. '62	175	58	233
Botetourt	Nov. '62	3	38	41
Brunswick	Nov. '62	125	97	222
Buckingham	Oct. '62	94	48	141
Campbell	Oct. '62	173	58	231
Charlotte	Oct. '62	14	89	103
Cumberland	Oct. '62	11	9	20
Fluvanna	Oct. '62	25	38	63
Franklin	Nov. '62	11	17	28
Greene	Nov. '62	0	31	31
Halifax	Oct. '62	57	185	242
Henry	Nov. '62	20	37	57
Louisa	Oct. '62	40	90	130*
Lunenburg	Nov. '62	7	83	90
Mecklenburg	Nov. '62	51	38	89
Montgomery	Nov. '62	20	10	30
Nelson	Oct. '62	65	61	126
Orange	Nov. '62	51	0	50*
Patrick	Nov. '62	8	16	24
Pittsylvania	Oct. '62	170	137	307
Prince Edward	Oct. '62	4	47	51
Pulaski	Nov. '62	4	29	33
Roanoke	Nov. '62	11	53	64
Rockingham	Nov. '62	74	0	75*
Total		1,379 +	1,453 =	2,832

President Davis sent a letter to Governor Letcher stating, "I call upon you . . . for 2832 Negroes to labor . . . for 60 days on the fortifications of this state."[52] The Governor requested that Colonel Gilmer specify "what the deficiency is in each case, and what is the new requisition made on certain counties for slaves." Gilmer informed the governor that the aggregate of deficiencies in former quotas amounted to 1,379 slaves, and the new quota called for only 1,453 slaves.[53] Confederate engineer officers, however, also submitted to county and city officials a draft for 1,029 free Negroes to labor on the state's defensive works.[54]

On March 25, 1863, state action was superseded by impressment from another source, the Confederate government. Military impressment of slaves by state law was not only unpopular, its legality was openly questioned. Consequently, the Confederate Congress enacted a general impressment law legalizing the drafting of Negroes for military purposes. Such impressment was to be made "according to the laws of the state wherein they were impressed."[56] This general law was supplemented by an amendatory act of February 17, 1864, the purpose of which was to further increase the effectiveness of the original act by making the portion dealing with Negroes clearer and more specific.[57] With the passage of the March 1863 act, the coercing agent was no longer the state governor, although future requisitions for slaves were still to be made upon his office.

Table 6.5 *Requisition for free Negro labor in Virginia by counties and corporations, March 19, 1863*[55]

County and Corporation	Number	County and Corporation	Number
Bath	9	King and Queen	40
Brunswick	58	King William	20
Charles City	100	Louisa	22
Charlotte	23	Madison	7
Chesterfield	59	Nelson	9
Dinwiddie	54	New Kent	20
Essex	50	Nottoway	13
Fluvanna	31	Petersburg (city)	100
Goochland	62	Powhatan	63
Greensville	12	Prince Edward	52
Hanover	10	Prince George	50
Henrico	25	Southampton	142
		Total	1,029

The first draft in Virginia for slaves to labor on fortifications, under the newly enacted law of the Confederate Congress, occurred in August 1863, when a requisition for 4,230 slaves was submitted to

Governor Letcher. The following month R. O. Howard, clerk of the hustings court in the city of Richmond, informed the governor that "the court declined to act upon his requisition for 160 slaves." Letcher immediately sent a letter to the state legislators suggesting that the law should be amended so as to require the city officials, under severe penalties, to act without delay. The governor wrote, "I can see no reason why the Hustings Court cannot do what other courts in the state have done." He pointed out, "The law authorizes me to impress slaves where the court declines or refuses to act." Letcher threatened that he would "commence the impressment by taking slaves of the members of court and officers, by way of examples."[58] Meanwhile F. Johnston, clerk of Roanoke County, informed the governor that their deputy sheriff took 57 slaves to Richmond, and "the Confederate officer to whom the slaves were delivered, refused to pay his expenses until all 60 slaves called for were delivered. The governor replied that "the other slaves must be impressed."[59]

Like Governor Letcher, the War Department saw the need to initiate more stringent measures to procure sufficient slaves to labor on fortifications. Hence, on October 24, 1863, the Department issued General Orders No. 138 designed to supplement General Orders No. 37 of March 1863. Negro labor on fortifications and other public works was to be secured by contract if possible; but "the Commanding General or the officer of engineers in charge of the work shall have power to decide upon the necessity for making impressments of slaves." Only in cases of great urgency were slaves to be impressed from service on plantations devoted exclusively to the production of grains. The period of service was limited to sixty days, except in case of default, when the owner was penalized by an additional thirty days of service for the first five days in default, and ten days for each subsequent day's delay. The rate of compensation was fixed at $20 a month except to defaulters, who were to receive only $15. Rations and medical attention were furnished to the slaves, and indemnity was guaranteed to the owners for all losses "by the enemy or arising from negligence on the part of the army."[61]

When the engineer officer made a demand upon an owner for male slaves, he was careful to choose the ones whom he wanted to labor on defensive works. Frequently they were accompanied to the rendezvous by the owner or his overseer. There they were met by the sheriff or some other official, who took charge of them. They were examined to see if they were "able-bodied," and an appraisal of their value was made and recorded so that just compensation might be made to their owners if they died, ran off, or were captured. They were then conducted by engineer officers to the scene of their labor, where they were immediately committed to the charge of the military authori-

Table 6.6 *Requisition for 4,230 slaves by counties, August 1863*[60]

County	Quota	Furnished	Deficit
Albemarle	200	166	34
Amelia	50	45	5
Amherst	100	45[a]	55
Appomattox	90	90[a]	0
Augusta	80	0	80
Bedford	200	200[a]	0
Botetourt	60	60	0
Brunswick	130	126	4
Buckingham	180	162	18
Campbell	260	260[a]	0
Charlotte	170	169	1
Chesterfield	150	15	135
Cumberland	80	80	0
Fluvanna	80	57	123
Franklin	70	63	7
Goochland	50	33	117
Halifax	300	300	10
Hanover	30	23	17
Henrico	140	0	140
Henry	100	88	12
Louisa	150	134	16
Lunenburg	120	111	9
Mecklenburg	200	168	332
Montgomery	50	0	50
Nelson	150	136	14
Nottoway	100	100	20
Pittsylvania	300	0	300
Powhatan	50	43	7
Prince Edward	150	147	3
Richmond (city)	160	0	160
Roanoke	60	60	0
Rockbridge	90	64	26
Russell	50	0	50
Spottsylvania	30	0	30
Sussex	50	35	15
Total	4,230	3,035	1,250

[a] 650 slaves furnished for Lynchburg defenses; deficit of 55 slaves.

ties.[62] Bell I. Wiley reports that the slaves were supervised through many officials. The lowest in rank was the Negro foreman or driver (one for every 25 slaves); the foreman was responsible to a white overseer (one for every 50 slaves); the overseer was subject to the orders of a manager (one for every 100 slaves); over the manager was a superintendent (one for every 800 slaves), who took his orders from a director (one for every 3,400 slaves). The director was responsible to the chief engineer.[63]

In January 1864 Letcher's successor, Governor William Smith, was called upon by President Davis to administer promptly a requisition for 5,019 slaves. On January 22 George Mumford, Secretary of the Commonwealth of Virginia, dispatched a directive to each clerk of the state's county courts which read:

> By direction of the Governor, I enclose herein a copy of the act . . . to further provide for the public defense. You will see, by the terms of the act, what is required of you. . . . The Governor is informed by the Engineer in charge of fortifications of Richmond, that in the event of the failure of the County courts to respond promptly . . . he will be obliged, in the discharge of his duty, to apply the terms of General Orders No. 138, Adjutant and Inspector General's Office, of date October 24, 1863, to carry into effect the 9th section of the act of March 26, 1863, to regulate impressments in respect to labor on fortifications and other public works.[64]
>
> The Governor hopes that the officer of the Confederate States of America may not find it necessary to apply any law but that enacted by the State Legislature. . . .

Colonel Stevens, chief of the Engineer Bureau, asked the governor to include in his remarks to the county courts his offer to "hire for 12 months, or for any less period, not less than 120 days, from any parties sending slaves under said call, 10,000 Negroes, to be paid $300 per year, with clothing and rations furnished by the government."[65] If the owners furnished clothing and rations, they were to be paid $550 yearly. Fifty-three counties and the cities of Richmond and Petersburg were asked to furnish the more than 5,000 slaves called for on the engineer requisition. The justice of Campbell County argued to no avail that 188 slaves were already employed in three government stables and hospitals. They sought release from the call made upon them for 140 slaves.[66] Officials from Augusta County contended that over 100 of their slaves were employed at the government blast furnaces in western Virginia. Cumberland, Halifax, Pulaski, and several other counties responded promptly to a draft for a portion of their slaves.[67]

In a fiery editorial the Richmond *Examiner* stated, "No outcry or intrigue should prevent the levy of Negro hands from all parts of the country to do the work with speed. . . . If Richmond is taken what will those farms and Negroes be worth?"[68] The Richmond *Whig* reported that "a Yankee revelation, hailing 'Just from Richmond,' furnished the New York *World* with an elaborate description of the defense of Richmond, which he described as the most stupendous, perfect, and formidable that Military Art and Negro labor could make them."[69] Beginning with January 1864, each month contributed to swell the ranks of Negro laborers for "digging and throwing dirt" at the Richmond fortifications. Yet, in October still another call was made by General Lee for approximately 1,590 slaves from 14 counties surrounding the Confederate capita.[70] Negro men found walking the streets of Richmond were immediately impressed to labor on earthworks. The Richmond *Examiner* reported,

> Yesterday was a real day of excitement among the able bodied male Negro population bond and free, in consequence of an order impressing them for defense purposes. . . . The Negroes were taken unaware on the street, at the market, from the shops, and at every point where they were found doing errands for themselves or their masters.
>
> . . . At an early hour the Negroes began to snuff something in the wind, and, rolling the whites of their eyes, began to betake themselves to indoors and more secluded retreats of Negro dens downtown. At noon an able bodied Negro, save those under escort, of impressment guards, was rare upon the streets . . . . In some cases the impressment agents acted with considerable indiscretion, snatching the Negro from the marketing of his master and leaving the markcting to take care of itself; taking the Negro from his perch on the cart and leaving the cart driverless behind. Castle Thunder was made the temporary depot of Negroes, and they were sent from this point to points where they were needed.
>
> Notwithstanding the sudden and summary manner of their taking off, the Negroes were in Jubilant spirit, and sang and halloed on

their way through the streets . . . but . . . made to do the country a service . . . which patriotic citizens should not begrudge for the sake of the common cause.[71]

On December 14, 1864, Major General Gilmer wrote Secretary of War Seddon that "upon the urgent solicitations of General Lee I . . . recommend that a further call be made upon . . . Virginia for 5000 slaves to labor on fortifications for 60 days." The following day President Davis submitted Gilmer's request to Governor Smith.[72] Shortly after the governor issued his call, officials from approximately eleven affected counties wrote to him seeking exemption from the draft of their slaves. Still other county officials complained bitterly that such a requisition would drain the counties of their labor supply.[73] As Federal forces prepared to lay siege to Richmond and Petersburg in February 1864, Lee urged the governor to take the necessary steps to procure the labor called for in the December draft. Lee wrote, "I regret to inform you that of the 5000 laborers requested in December last, we have received but 502. . . . Unless I can get a strong force of laborers at once, I see no prospect of having our extensive lines in the conditions they should be."[74] In March 1865 the chief of the Engineer Bureau submitted another requisition to the governor for 3,000 slaves to be furnished from the derelict counties under the December 1864 draft for laborers.[75] Forty-four counties were called upon for the December draft, and by March 9, 1865, sixteen had failed to comply with the requisition. Hanover, Madison, and Rockbridge counties were eventually exempted from the December call, but Hanover County was expected to furnish fifty slaves at a future date. As early as January the governor had requested that each county submit to his office "a full and correct statement of all such requisitions for slaves made and complied with" from the outset of the war. Patrick, Greene, Nelson, Amelia, and Halifax counties reported that from the spring of 1862 to December 1864, they had sent a total of 3,089 slaves to labor on fortifications.[78] Mecklenburg County reported that including the December 1864 draft, it had sent 1,546 slaves to construct earthworks.[79]

Records of the Engineer Bureau, coupled with those of Virginia's governors, seem to indicate that at least 35,000 Negroes, free and slave, responded to the various calls to construct Confederate entrenchments and batteries within the state. By the close of 1864, however, the reluctance of slaveowners to comply promptly and fully with the calls of military authorities for the Negroes angered both state and Confederate authorities. In January 1865 Governor Smith wrote the officials of Greene County that "the tendency of these delays and disputes of the Courts over the call for their slaves is to defeat General Lee's earnest efforts to be in complete readiness in the spring, and their certain effect if continued will be to require the slaves to be taken away so late in the year as to influence later injury on the interest of agriculture, than if set to work on the fortifications at once."[80]

In his February 1865 report to Governor Smith, Chief of Engineers Gilmer indicated that the total number of slaves furnished in the December 1864 draft was "entirely insufficient for the necessities of the service." Governor Smith, however, had already informed the

Table 6.7 *Requisition for 5,000 slaves by counties, December 1864*[76]

County	Number of slaves furnished	County	Number of slaves furnished
Amelia	97	Powhatan	61
Amherst	62	Prince Edward	44
Augusta	5	Roanoke	42
Bedford	2	Wythe	21
Buckingham	85	Albemarle	0
Carroll	8	Appomattox	0
Charlotte	92	Botetourt	0
Chesterfield	10	Brunswick	0
Cumberland	86	Campbell	0
Floyd	9	Caroline	0
Fluvanna	15	Dinwiddie	0
Franklin	29	Goochland	0
Grayson	10	Greene	0
Halifax	130	Greensville	0
Henrico	22	Henry	0
Louisa	53	Orange	0
Lunenburg	56	Patrick	0
Mecklenburg	98	Pittsylvania	0
Montgomery	17	Pulaski	0
Nelson	21	Washington	0
Nottoway	87	*Total*	1,162

General Assembly that additional legislation was necessary and asserted that he was overwhelmed by the excuses presented by the various counties.[81] "From all I can learn," the governor wrote, "the safety of this city depends upon the prompt supply of the necessary labor. It cannot be had with the requisite promptness without further and immediate legislation."[82] On March 4, 1865, the Virginia lawmakers enacted a law prescribing the mode of apportioning slaves to work on fortifications. The act stipulated:

> It shall be the duty of the governor, and he is hereby authorized and required, whenever thereto requested by the president of the Confederate States, to call into the service . . . for labor on fortifications . . . from time to time, for a period not exceeding sixty days, a number of male slaves between the ages of eighteen and fifty-five, not exceeding 10,000 at any one time, and not exceeding in any county or corporation, one-fifth of the . . . slaves.[83]

Resistance of Virginia slaveowners to compliance with requisitions for the labor of their slaves was based chiefly on the pecuniary loss involved for the actual value of the slaves. Planters also felt that military labor was injurious to health, and they complained that their slaves were treated harshly. The Richmond press contributed to the reluctance of planters to send their chattels to labor on earthworks.

Table 6.8 *Slaves sent to labor on fortifications, Cumberland and Brunswick counties, 1862–1863*[77]

Cumberland County			Brunswick County		
Date	Number	Period	Date	Number	Period
Spring 1862	105	60 days	May 1862	293	60 days
October 11, 1862	210	60 days	November 1862	140	60 days
September 16, 1863	80	60 days	August 1862	147	60 days
February 10, 1864	110	60 days	May 1864	152	60 days
October 24, 1864	69	30 days	October 1864	105	60 days
July 20, 1864	126	60 days	November 1864	73	60 days
November 17, 1864	48	12 months	December 1864	104	60 days
Hired to quarter-master, 1864	54	12 months		1,014	
December 1864	28	60 days			
	830				

Early in January 1862 the *Examiner* stated, "The whole condition of the management of our city fortifications needs investigation." The newspaper reported that a free Negro "had his back actually cut into a mangle of bleeding flesh, the driver having given him, as we were told by a policeman, 561 lashes with the whip, until the poor victim sank exhausted."[84] In a second editorial the *Examiner* stated that the Negro Engineer Hospital was wretchedly managed, and "stench and filth abound in intolerable quantities, and as a legitimate result much sickness prevails." Describing the slave inmates of the Hospital, the *Examiner* read:

> And the poor Negroes are dying off like penned sheep, afflicted with the rot. Owners should look after their slaves, and see that they are not wholly neglected by those appointed to see to their wants while temporarily in the employ of the Government. The Negroes have been for the most part, engaged in the Brooke defenses. It is a disgrace to humanity to behold their utter neglect.[85]

The hospital's steward accused the *Examiner* of misrepresentation "well calculated to excite the anxiety of the owners." Acknowledging that many of the patients needed a change of clothing, the steward insisted that "whenever the condition of the patients will admit of it their underclothing is removed and washed. If their persons need cleansing it is always promptly done."[86] In January 1863 a resolution from the House of Delegates was sent to Governor Letcher pointing out that the slaves "are not provided with sufficient and proper food, although the law expressly requires that they should be furnished with soldiers rations."[87] A copy of the resolution was sent to Gilmer, who notified the governor that "from inquiries recently made into the justice of the complaint alluded to in the resolution, and with the consent of the Secretary of War, it has been determined to increase the supply of breadstuffs by an additional allowance of meal." The chief of the Engineer Bureau was careful to point out that "as the law requires, soldiers rations have been and are regularly drawn and issued to Negroes."[88] Once again the *Examiner* reported

> We doubt if the government is aware of the treatment of Negroes, sent by the patriotic planters of the counties to work on fortifications around Richmond. . . . On Saturday several owners anxious to note the condition of their slaves, visited the place and saw for themselves the rations issued, and brought away several as specimens. These they weighed with the following results: For dinner, meat rations, three quarters of an ounce; bread rations,

three ounces and three quarters; for supper and breakfast the same. The bread is simple ingredients of flour and water, heavy and indigestible.

They saw one Negro snatch rations from the plate of another. They appealed to the overseers, who said they had the same rations and were not permitted to see those issued to the Negroes. Some owners . . . purchased bacon and sent it out for their use; . . . all they ask is that full soldiers rations may be issued to the Negroes. . . . It is, moreover, insinuated that the full rations are drawn by the Commissary, but find their way into other mouths than those of the poor starving Negroes.

It is idle to attempt to get labor out of a half fed Negro, while the inhumanity of the evil complained of should insure its immediate correction. The matter, we see, is to be made a matter of inquiry by the Legislature of the State.[89]

The Richmond *Whig* reported that the Negroes working on fortifications "around this city, are, in some instances, so badly fed that they desert and run off either to their masters or into the woods."[90]

Both Governors Letcher and Smith received numerous letters from owners requesting compensation for their slaves who had been working on fortifications and were lost because of disease, accident, exposure, and neglect. For example, John B. Baldwin, a legislator from Staunton, wrote that "no payment has been made for any of about 30 slaves from Augusta and Rockbridge Counties who died in January and February, 1863."[91] In another letter affidavits submitted by the overseer and the examining physician supported the petition of Mary Clark of Alexandria County for compensation for loss of her slave, who was sick while employed in ditching in water up to his waist.[92] Most of the letters sent to the governor were careful to point out that "slaves heretofore sent suffered much from exposure . . . and brought back most unfavorable accounts of their treatment and neglect, and impressed their fellow slaves with the hardships and trials while working on fortifications."[93] J. B. Davis from Greene County wrote Governor Smith that his slaves insisted that their treatment while working on fortifications was such that "no torment could be worse." He indicated that six slaves had died, and many returned totally unfit and unable to perform even light tasks.[94] Citizens of Lunenburg County sent a resolution to Governor Smith protesting that in almost every instance where they sent slaves to labor on entrenchments they were "returned to their owners in a feeble and exhausted condition."[95] Tazewell County officials informed the governor that "it can with truth be asserted that adult slaves remain here with their masters through choice, not necessity." They pointed out that their slaves "entertain a kind of legendary dread of going to Lynchburg or Petersburg" to labor on defensive works.[96]

Undoubtedly the frenzy to complete the Richmond lines, an engineering marvel, involved strenuous work for the many thousands of Negroes, free and slave, who labored on Confederate defenses. As far as the eyes could scan, long lines of blacks could be seen swinging pickaxes and heaving dirt. Few opportunities, if any, existed for relaxation; discipline was rigid, and frequently the Negroes were brutally treated by their military supervisors. Meanwhile thousands of other Negroes were employed in constructing defensive works in other parts of the state. Those located at Petersburg and Drewry's Bluff also involved countless man hours of labor by the Virginia Negro. The Dimmock Line, for example, with its fifty-five artillery batteries, extended in a ten-mile arc east, west, and south of Petersburg, below the Appomattox River. The Dimmock Line was constructed to protect Petersburg, whose strategic importance became apparent after the first year of the war.

The work was begun in 1862 under Captain Charles H. Dimmock, and that spring the Petersburg Common Council complied with his request for several slaves and free Negroes to expedite construction. From May to June 1862, Brunswick, Nottoway, and Mecklenburg counties furnished 253 slaves to assist in obstructing the Appomattox River and to erect batteries at Fort Clifton.[97] In August and September, Amelia, Greensville, Sussex, Halifax, and Northampton counties supplied 264 slaves to labor on the Petersburg defenses.[98] On December 12, 1862, Engineer Dimmock addressed a letter to the mayor of Petersburg, stating:

> The early completion of the defensive works around your city must be a matter of paramount interest to yourself. It has been found impossible to secure an immediate and adequate force to meet the demands for labor upon your defenses.
>
> The following suggestions . . . will afford means to push our works to an early completion.

It is proposed that you secure a force of 200 Negroes by such means as may in your judgment seem best. . . . This force to report each morning upon their work—which is two miles from the city—at 8:00 o'clock, to be permitted to return home at 4:00 P.M. With this force, for two or three weeks, more can be accomplished than in as many months of the rapidly approaching bad weather.[99]

The same day Major General French also dispatched a letter to the mayor which pointed out that "this call on the citizens to contribute some labor for the early completion of the defenses of your city, is made at my suggestion and meets my approval."[100] The Common Council complied with Dimmock's request and sent over 200 slaves and free Negroes. Residents of Petersburg also sent several of their slaves to labor on the Dimmock Lines for twenty days. By the beginning of 1863 extensive earthworks were taking shape on every hill, creek, or position that would enhance the defense of the city. In March, Negroes from Petersburg were still employed by the city to work on entrenchments, and the Common Council passed a resolution that they be retained an additional month.[101] As the months passed hundreds of Negroes were impressed from surrounding counties to complete the Petersburg lines. Early in September 1864 General Lee called for an additional 2,000 Negroes to supplement the colored labor force.

Among the many projects assigned to the Corps of Engineers was that of fortifying Drewry's Bluff. Seven miles below Richmond, where the James River is less than a mile wide, a vital shore battery was erected on a 200-foot cliff on the south bank known as Drewry's Bluff. Since no point on the James River above Jamestown Island had been fortified by state engineers from May to October 1861, Lee ordered the obstruction of the river at this site to impair passage by any hostile vessel. In the spring of 1862, Negro laborers began pouring into the area. They toiled ceaselessly in bottomless mud, in chilly water, and in constant rain. They hauled planks and stone ballast, constructed cribs, began ditching operations, and assisted in mounting heavy guns. New freshets damaged portions of the barriers, but the river was finally obstructed with logs, stones, and iron rubbish. Piles were driven in the bottom of the river, and several schooners and sloops were sunk in the main channel—leaving only a narrow, intricate passage directly under Confederate guns. Work commenced on several bombproof emplacements in which 8-inch cannons and other artillery were mounted.[102]

When McClellan pushed up the Peninsula in May 1862, the Confederate high command sensed the danger of rapid Federal crossings of the James River below Drewry's Bluff to be followed by an unopposed march on Richmond. The only bridges available to Con-

Table 6.9 *Slave laborer contributions at Drewry's Bluff, 1862–1863*[103]

Date	Number	County	Period
March	21	King George	4 to 14 days
April	23	Henrico	26 days
April	11	Hanover	20 days
April	21	King George	43 days
April	2	James City	3½ months
April	35	Henrico	26 days
April	14	Charles City	90 days
May	23	King George	45 days
May	19	Surry	7 days
May	23	Prince George	50 days
May	21	Frederick	45 days
May	9	Hanover	10 days (obstructing river)
May	20	Nottoway	10 days (obstructing river)
July	10	Pittsylvania	73 days (obstructing river)
July	46	King George	47 to 90 days
July	5	Charlotte	57 to 70 days
July	123	Halifax	58 to 60 days
July	340	Lunenburg, etc.	40 to 60 days
July	21	Henrico	25 to 90 days
Sept.	21	Chesterfield	60 days
Sept.	20	Fluvanna	20 days
Oct.	77	Buckingham	60 days
Oct.	59	Prince Edward	60 days
Oct.	21	Campbell	60 days
Oct.	20	Fluvanna	60 days
Oct.	80	Pittsylvania	60 days
Jan.	41	Augusta	60 days
Jan.	80	Pittsylvania	60 days
Jan.	4	Alleghany	60 days (obstructing river)
Total	1,198		

federate forces were at Richmond, and a decision was made to construct one just above Drewry's Bluff. Captain W. W. Blackford suggested a "pontoon" bridge of canalboats and river craft, and received orders to commence construction. Both Negro and white carpenters were immediately hired. The provost marshal impressed over 500 laborers of both races.[104] Large rocks from local stonecutters and quarries served as anchors for the fleet of canalboats and schooners. The laborers worked toward the center of the river from both sides of the bank, and within five days the bridge had been constructed.

The desirability of improving the fortifications at Drewry's Bluff resulted in continual drafts for Negro laborers from the summer of 1862 to the spring of 1865. In August 1862 Gilmer notified Lieutenant C. T. Mason, provisional engineer, "All the Negro force employed at the works will be retained—none must be released or discharged without orders from this office."[105] Chief of Engineers Gilmer wrote his wife that "Lee thought it essential for me to remain at Richmond and to press up the defenses around the city—also at Petersburg."[106] Gilmer made a thorough inspection at Drewry's Bluff (on the south side of the James River) and then crossed over to inspect Chaffin's Bluff, nearly opposite Drewry's Bluff. He explained to his wife that within range of the heavy guns located on both sides of the bluff the laborers had sunk heavy obstructions in the form of log houses (cribs) filled with rock, forming a strong barrier to the passage of all vessels.

During 1864 Colonel Stevens, chief engineer of the Army of Northern Virginia, procured several hundred Negroes to strengthen the defensive works surrounding Drewry's Bluff. In June he sent 100 Richmond Negroes to extend the clearing in front of the earthworks.[107] Four months later Stevens was responsible for drastic steps taken by Governor Smith to secure an adequate number of Negroes to enlarge the works at the bluff, without delay. On October 1, 1864, Governor Smith wrote William A. Dietrick:

> A great public exigency is upon us . . . labor is necessary at Drewry's Bluff. The ordinary forms of law cannot, for want of time, be now resorted to, and I find myself constrained, under calls from Confederate authorities, to assume a responsibility, which otherwise I would unhesitatingly refuse. I therefore as Governor . . . constitute and appoint you as agent for the purpose to summons a sufficient force among your patriotic neighbors in . . . Henrico, Hanover, and Goochland and proceed to arrest and safely

keep all able bodied free Negroes in those counties and bring them without delay to me in this city.

You will also proceed to obtain from the good citizens . . . such slave labor as they can possibly spare and bring them to me. . . . Wages will be paid and they will be discharged in two weeks.[108]

Four days later the governor notified his aide, Lieutenant Colonel P. B. Smith, that he desired a list of all the Negroes retained—free and slave—to be sent to Drewry's Bluff. The colonel was ordered to "see that the boat is ready to send down a cargo this evening. I wish you to go down with the Negroes, or get Captain Lee to go."[109] On October 6, 1864, Captain C. R. Mason sent a telegram to the governor requesting that he order "the next Negroes to be sent to General Stevens at Chaffins Bluff."[110] A few weeks later Mason was asked to furnish fifty Negroes to assist in mounting seven-inch guns at the recently constructed shore batteries.[111]

In its Negro population Virginia possessed an indispensable source of military labor. Early laws enacted by the state legislature and the Confederate Congress, however, failed to provide sufficient labor for defensive works. Finally the Congress on February 17, 1864, authorized the organization of labor troops to be composed of free Negroes and slaves of ages eighteen to fifty years. The former were to be given the pay and allowance of a private of infantry—that is, $11 monthly, rations, medical attention and clothing—and were to serve for the duration of the war. The term for slaves was twelve months.[113] The owners of slaves were to be compensated at the prevailing impress-

Table 6.10 *Slave employees at Drewry's Bluff, 1864*[112]

Name	Occupation	Annual Wages	Name	Occupation	Annual Wages
Nelson	Wagon driver	$300	Henry	Wagon driver	$300
Henry	Cook	$300	Thomas	Wagon driver	$300
Dick	Wagon driver	$300	William	Wagon driver	$300
Arthur	Boatman	$300	George	Hostler	$300
Edward	Wagon driver	$300	Jacob	Boatman	$300
Jacob	Cook	$300	William	Boatman	$300
William	Blacksmith	$300	Cyrus	Cook	$300

ment schedules. On March 19 the Bureau of Conscription issued Circular No. 9, directing the enrollment of all Negroes subject to the act. The law permitted the impressment of as many as 20,000 slaves.[114]

During the next few months, however, the bulk of Negro laborers were procured under the old short-time impressment method, as may be concluded from examining the requisitions submitted to Governor Smith by Confederate engineers.

On December 5, 1864, the Adjutant and Inspector General issued General Orders No. 86, directing that 20,000 slave troops be brought into service with the utmost dispatch. A week later the Bureau of Conscription, in Circular No. 36, announced that Virginia's quota was 2,250 slaves.[115] The Superintendent of Conscription (Brigadier General John S. Preston), in an informal letter to the Secretary of War, recommended the passage of an act by Congress to authorize the War Department "to negotiate with the States for the impressment of slaves on such terms as may be agreed." Preston's letter was referred to Chief of Engineers Gilmer for comment. General Gilmer returned it with his concurrence on February 1, 1865, and four weeks later President Davis approved a new labor troop bill.[116] This act reduced the age limit from fifty-five to forty years, but increased the quota of slaves from 20,000 to 40,000. Governor Smith took prompt steps to supply his state's quota.

Southern sentiment had changed somewhat prior to the passage in February 1865 of the new labor troop bill, calling for 40,000 slaves. In the fall of 1864 the Confederacy moved to adopt a more realistic attitude toward her vast Negro population. Although there was no real change in racial attitudes, Southerners manifested a higher degree of racial tolerance. Incentives were extended to Negroes to identify with the Southern war effort. Perhaps strangest of all was the bold pronouncement of President Davis regarding "the propriety of a radical modification in the theory of the law." Davis asserted:

> Viewed merely as property, and therefore as the subject of impressment, the service or labor of the slaves has been frequently claimed for short periods in the construction of defensive works.
>
> The slave, however, bears another relation to the State—that of a person. The law of February, 1864, contemplates only the relation of the slave to the master (as property) and limits the impressment to a certain time of service. . . . Hazard is also encountered in all the positions to which Negroes can be assigned for service with the army, and the duties required of them demand loyalty and zeal.
>
> In this aspect the relation of person predominates so far as to

render it doubtful whether the private right of property can consistently and beneficially be continued. . . .

Whenever the entire property in the service of a slave is thus acquired by the Government, the question is presented by what tenure he should be held. Should he be retained in servitude, or should his emancipation be held out to him as a reward for faithful service, or should it be granted at once on the promise of such service, and if emancipated, what action should be taken to secure for the freedman the permission of the State from which he was drawn to reside within its limits after the close of his public service[?] The permission would serve as a double motive for zealous discharge of duty . . . their freedom and the gratification of the local attachment which is so marked a characteristic of the Negro, and forms so powerful an incentive to his action.

President Davis concluded his message to Congress by indicating that "the policy of engaging to liberate the Negro on his discharge after service faithfully rendered, seems to me preferable to that of granting immediate manumission or that of retaining him in servitude."[117] Top military commanders also evidenced the need to offer strong incentives to retain the loyalty of Negro laborers, as well as to improve their morale. On November 25, 1864, General Gilmer informed Secretary of War Seddon that he fully concurred with General Lee's views that "kind treatment should be secured to the Negroes." Lee wrote Gilmer:

Every precaution should be taken to insure proper and kind treatment of the Negroes and to render them contented in the service. The code of punishments should be distinctly defined, and the graver punishments should not be left in the hands of the managers and overseers. . . .

There should be a system of rewards, too, for good conduct and industry, these rewards to be paid to the meritorious over and above the hire paid to their masters. . . .[118]

On December 5, 1864, S. Cooper, Adjutant and Inspector General, released General Orders No. 86, which stated:

Every effort will be made to induce contentment in the slaves. Their discipline will be considerate and mild for minor offenses. Cases of a grave character will be forwarded for the determination and instructions of the chief of engineers of the army or department, who will in the meantime prepare and submit for the approval of his commanding general a code for the government of managers and others in charge of the slaves.

The commanding general of each army or department will promptly remove and order to the ranks any manager or other employee having the supervision of slaves who is guilty of cruelty toward them, or malfeasance or of malpractice, and will impose such other penalties as the offense would justify under the Ninety-ninth Rule and Article of War.[119]

Even some high officials of the Confederate government expressed a willingness to make other concessions to the Negro. Secretary of State Judah P. Benjamin, for example, wrote in 1864 of the necessity to modify and to improve existing conditions for Negroes by providing for them a certain degree of personal liberty. Benjamin made mention of the need to remove from Southern institutions "much that is unjust and impolitic" lest it "draw down on us the odium and reprobation of civilized man."[120] In December 1864 Governor Smith said, "I do not hesitate to say that I would arm such portion of our able bodied slave population, as may be necessary, and put them in the field . . . even if it resulted in the freedom of those thus organized."[121] General Lee, in a letter to Senator Hunter on January 11, 1865, commented: "If it ends in subverting slavery, it will be accomplished by ourselves, and we can devise the means of alleviating the evil consequences to both races. I think, therefore, we must decide whether slavery shall be extinguished by our enemies and the slave be used against us, or use them ourselves at the risk of the effects which may be produced upon our social institutions."[122] Lee expressed the belief that it "would be neither just nor wise" to ask the Negroes to serve as slaves. He therefore proposed a gradual and a general emancipation. The Richmond *Examiner* reported, "The Senate and House have not yet agreed upon the provisions of another important military bill—the provision for the employment" of Negroes to perform labor connected with the defense of the country. The *Examiner* asserted that the Confederacy "in its present temper, will not sustain any hesitation or resistance to this . . . measure, founded on cupidity, or reluctance to sacrifice property—any amount of property—in the common cause."[123]

Although the designation "labor troops" did not become official until February 1865, Negroes worked with engineer troops early in the war. Richmond's engineer workshops for the manufacture of tools, implements, and preparation of materials for pontoon bridges utilized Negro laborers. Such workshops served the needs of the Army of Northern Virginia. In June 1862 General Lee ordered the rebuilding of a bridge across the Chickahominy River. A detachment of soldiers assigned to complete the bridge made little progress. Fortunately Captain C. R. Mason arrived with his "Negro navvies" who had a knack for the rapid construction of rough, stout bridges. The soldiers were relieved, and the Negroes constructed the bridge.[124] In September 1863, Chief of Engineers Gilmer inspected a bridge under construction by Negro laborers over the James River.[125] The following month the Richmond press reported that another large workyard at Eighteenth and Clay streets had been established by the Engineer Corps for the manufacture of "ready-made bridges for spanning streams." The *Examiner* stated that "a large number of Negroes are now daily employed in getting out and shaping timber,"[126] and 11 free Negroes are listed with the Third Regiment of Engineer Troops in 1864.[127] In February 1865 Chief of Engineers Gilmer reported to the Secretary of War that the repair of railroad bridges was done by "fatigue parties, by engineer troops, and Negroes, hired and impressed."[128]

Not until February 1865, the sunset of the Confederacy, was the structure of Negro labor troops devised. Each company or "gang" consisted of 100 Negroes, under a manager and two overseers, with four of the best Negroes selected as foremen. Eight companies constituted a section under a superintendent; and three sections composed a force under a director. A section or battalion consisted of 800 Negroes and 38 white men; and the force or regiment comprised 2,400 Negroes and 88 white men.[129] But it was too late! The approach of Appomattox never permitted the infant Negro labor troops to fulfill the glowing expectations of Confederate engineers and military commanders.

Virginia's fortifications and the labor force responsible for their construction have received less attention than other phases of the Civil War. Yet, from every part of Virginia, thousands of Negroes were called upon to encircle cities and vulnerable areas with cordons of earthworks, and their labor undoubtedly prolonged the war by preventing Federal invasions from seriously affecting the resources of the state. Their story not only provides new insights into the history of the warring South, but contributes to an understanding of the many ways in which the Virginia Negro was inextricably related with the Southern war effort. When weighed against the tragic theme of the stunted existence which resulted from his enslavement, the war discloses that he had a compelling effect on the course of the war and that his service was a key piece in the mechanism of Southern defenses.

Conclusion

Unlike Johnny Reb or Billy Yank the Confederate Negro is a historical enigma. Historians today are far from acknowledging his essential importance to the Confederate war effort, nor do they claim that his brawn and skill enhanced the fighting potential of Southern armies. Yet, looking through existing war records, one finds something else. The Negro was an inseparable part of the economic machinery which supported and sustained the Southern forces in the vital fields of logistics, ordnance production, medical care, and military fortifications. Behind the fighting lines he bore a multitude of burdens. He augmented the manufacture of naval and military ordnance; he built ships, wagons, bridges, and freight cars; he hauled essential war supplies; he loaded and unloaded shot, shell, heavy guns, plate and bar iron, and other freight at wharves and railroad depots; he maintained and constructed lines of transportation; and he hammered out strong wrought iron.

While the overwhelming majority of Virginia Negroes were common laborers, there were also many highly skilled craftsmen. The laborers provided essential manpower for the procurement of food, forage, and raw materials such as coal, iron ore, limestone, timber, niter, hides, salt, and various organic products. Dexterous Negro artisans provided their skills in subsequent stages of refinement and processing of commodities into manufactured items in arsenals, armories, government shops, blast furnaces, ironworks, and machine shops.

Yet, who was the Confederate Negro? He was the man that he was —denigrated, corroded by degradation, and psychologically disabled by oppression. Nevertheless, he had a definite influence on the War for Southern Independence. Moreover, Confederate officials and top military commanders insisted that every black man as well as every white had to contribute to the success of the cause for which the war was inaugurated. Consequently, with the enrollment of whites for combat duty, there began the employment of dark-hued hands for supporting military and domestic purposes.

This was especially true in Virginia, whose industries were more diversified and more highly developed than those of any other Southern state. Richmond—the capital, the industrial center, and the nerve center of the Confederacy—was destined to become a major military target. Virginia's strong commitment to the war effort, therefore, found the state making extensive use of the physical and mental capacities of its large Negro population. Nowhere is this manifested more dramatically than in the employment of male and female Negro nurses who composed the largest single nursing force in Virginia's military hospitals.

Virginia Negroes also labored assiduously in the construction of defensive works throughout the state to repel land and water attacks by Federal forces. Many thousands were called upon to build river obstructions and to erect river batteries, and thousands of others encircled cities and strategic areas with vast cordons of earthworks. These tasks were physically exhausting, injurious to health, and monotonous; there was an unusually high mortality rate among the workers. The facts, however, have been obscured because attention is focused on slaveholders, their bitter opposition to slave impressment, and their subsequent failure to comply fully with the urgent and continual military requisitions for slaves. Slaves as well as free Negroes were successfully marshaled, and together they frequently managed to complete vital earthworks within time limits which normally would have required many more laborers than were available. Hence the conventional emphasis on the slaveholders' resistance to the impressment of their chattels should not obscure the tangible results produced by the many thousands of Negroes drafted for earthworks and fortifications.

During the fast-moving developments of the war years, thousands of Negro teamsters, stevedores, and boatmen expedited the stockpiling and steady flow of countless tons of supplies to the fighting forces. Construction and repair shops at quartermaster and ordnance depots required the retention of a large labor force of Negro craftsmen. To procure these much needed Negro laborers, hiring agents and impressment officers constantly combed the Virginia countryside.

It was in Virginia, the major Civil War battleground, that the war served most as a catalyst for the rapid development of Southern industry and technology. Voluntary enlistment and conscription stampeded white skilled workers into Confederate armies. Therefore, the Virginia Negro, whether free or slave, was forced in an unprecedented way into the arena of Southern technology. Virginia's vast army of skilled, semiskilled, and common Negro laborers manfully struggled to produce the sinews of war. They worked successfully in producing iron. In the Shenandoah Valley thousands of blacks, superintended by a few whites, successfully operated pig iron furnaces. In Richmond, many others puddled and squeezed iron and rolled iron plate for Confederate ironclads. In blacksmith shops equipped with steam hammers, muscular blacks forged an assortment of fittings. Slave technicians cast cannons and wheels and worked as grinders and core makers. Slave miners in the Richmond bituminous coalfields supplied the fuel necessary for the new processes for making iron.

Virginia's grand design for solving the problems of war production was ended abruptly at Appomattox, but within the state's war program germinated an exciting and adventurous experiment with strong and skilled arms of sable. Negro commitment in the beleaguered Southland varied—for some it was with mingled feelings, for others it was sincere, and for many it was necessity—but throughout, the war response of the Negro and his creditable performance are historically unique.

Caught in the web of an invidious stereotype—that he was irresponsible, childlike, and racially inferior—his lacerated historical image continues to remain repugnant. Yet, in assessing the Civil War scene, one finds no similarity between this stereotype and the facts disclosed by Civil War documents bearing on his vital responsibilities, craftsmanship, and economic demeanor.

Today, in a lonely unmarked grave, forgotten and unknown, lies the Confederate Negro—a casualty of history.

Notes

CHAPTER ONE

1. See Tinsley Lee Spraggins, "Mobilization of Negro Labor for The Department of Virginia and North Carolina, 1861–1865," *North Carolina Historical Review*, XXIV, No. 2 (April 1947), 173.
2. From 1840 to 1861 the rapidly changing pattern of the state's economic growth and life resulted from the rapid development of urban areas and industries. In 1860 the South contained only 10 of the 102 American cities with a population of more than 10,000 people, and 30 per cent of the Southern cities in this category were located in Virginia (Richmond had a population of about 40,000). Virginia also ranked first among the Southern states, with its 5,385 manufacturing establishments.
3. See Clement Eaton, "Slave-Hiring in the Upper South: A Step Toward Freedom," *Mississippi Valley Historical Review*, XLVI, 663 ff.
4. *Ibid.*, p. 663.
5. See James H. Brewer, "Legislation Designed to Control Slavery in Wilmington and Fayetteville," *North Carolina Historical Review*, XXX, No. 2, pp. 155–166.
6. See Luther P. Jackson, *Free Negro Labor and Property Holding in Virginia, 1830–1860* (New York: D. Appleton-Century Company, 1942), p. 55.
7. Spraggins, "Mobilization of Negro Labor," p. 171. In order to avoid the Impressment Act of 1862, some free Negroes took advantage of a Virginia statute enacted in 1853 which allowed any free Negro of mixed blood to have himself legally declared "not a Negro by the testimony of a white person." Subsequently, the Virginia courts certified many free Negroes, claiming less than one fourth Negro blood, to be "persons of mixed blood and not Negroes." In December 1862 Albert S. Gentry, a free Negro of Richmond, was arrested "for want of a register, and brought before the court on a writ of habeas corpus." After hearing the argument of Gentry's lawyer (Virginia Code, 17th Section, Chapter 107), the judge ruled that "Gentry had less than ¼ Negro blood" and discharged him. On January 26, 1863, Gentry was again arrested and his case was tried in the Richmond hustings court. Gentry's counsel again argued that his client was not a Negro and secured his release. After the trial the mayor of Richmond questioned whether "the legislature had the constitutional right to make white men out of mixed bloods." See the Richmond *Examiner*, Dec. 5, 1862; Jan. 26, 1863. Also see Jackson, *Free Negro Labor and Property Holding.*
8. Spraggins, "Mobilization of Negro Labor," p. 173.
9. *Journal of the Congress of the Confederate States of America, 1861–1865*

(7 vols., Washington, 1904–1905), III, 191. See Chapter 6 for a full discussion of slaves impressed to labor on fortifications and defensive works. Even before this law, the Confederate Congress in 1862 authorized the employment of Negroes as cooks and musicians in the army. Subsequently the majority of cooks in Southern armies were Negroes; each company was entitled to four cooks. Owners were paid $15 monthly for slave furnished, and their chattels were entitled to clothing and rations.

10. *The War of the Rebellion: A Compilation of the Official Records of the Union and Confederate Armies* (Washington, 1880–1901), Ser. IV, Vol. III, p. 547; hereinafter cited as *Official Records.*

11. *Ibid.*, II, 947.

12. *Ibid.*, p. 998.

13. *Ibid.*, p. 208.

14. *Ibid.*, pp. 716–17.

15. *Ibid.*, p. 665.

16. *War Department Collection of Confederate Records*, Record Group 109, Chap. 1, Vol. 241, Register of Free Negroes Enrolled, 1864–1865. See also Chap. 1, Vol. 240. This collection is hereinafter cited as *Confederate Records.*

17. *Ibid.*

18. Richmond *Whig*, Oct. 10, 1862.

19. Richmond *Examiner*, May 5, 1863.

20. Existing records indicate that the greatest loss of slaves occurred in the western counties of Virginia. Most historians agree that slaves usually fled whenever a reasonable chance presented itself. Some evidence exists to sustain this point of view, especially during the last sixteen months of the war. There is, however, little evidence to sustain the position that Virginia Negroes, free and slave, showed an appreciable disposition to desert or to impair the war effort. Virginia's desertion problem or slave losses did not contribute to the general breakdown of Confederate industry. This study is not designed to treat thoroughly the question of slave losses, although such a study should be made to ascertain the effect desertion had upon the Confederate war effort.

21. See "Communication from the Auditor of Public Accounts, Virginia State Library, Richmond, Virginia." *Documents of the Senate, 1863–1864*, No. 19.

CHAPTER TWO

1. The responsibility for provisioning the Confederate armies was a function of the Commissary and Quartermaster departments. The duties of the commissary were limited to the procurement and issuance of food and feed; transportation of these commodities was the responsibility of the quartermaster. The Quartermaster Department also provided uniforms, shoes, blankets, tents, cooking utensils, fuel, forage for livestock, and nonmedicinal hospital supplies. It was also charged with providing quarters, storage for army supplies, and army transportation by whatever means. Other responsibilities included securing artillery and cavalry horses and the payment of army troops and nonmilitary personnel. The first quartermaster general was Abraham C. Myers; he occupied this

position until August 1863, when President Davis replaced him with General Alexander R. Lawton. The first commissary general was Lucius B. Northrop, who resigned in February 1865 and was succeeded by General Isaac N. St. John.

2. On April 24, 1863, the Confederate Congress legislated that farmers and planters, after reserving for their own use stipulated amounts of their products, should pay and deliver to the Confederate government one tenth of the products remaining. This act further provided that tax assessors should transmit estimates of the products—or tax in kind—due from each person and that quartermasters should collect such taxes in kind and distribute them, except for cotton and tobacco, to the proper points for supplying the army. These products were to be delivered to agents of the Secretary of the Treasury. A second act of June 14, 1864, authorized the President to appoint a quartermaster for each Congressional district in the state to execute the duties relating to the tax in kind.

3. The organization of the Confederate Quartermaster and Commissary departments paralleled that of corresponding departments in the United States in that they were geographical units commanded by quartermaster officers. In Virginia these units were occasionally subdivided into districts to serve strategic areas such as the Shenandoah Valley.

4. In Virginia five geographical departments constituted the primary zones in which Southern troops were stationed. The first, the Department of the Peninsula, was established in May 1861. It embraced the troops and military operations in Hampton, Gloucester Point, West Point, Yorktown, and Jamestown Island, as well as the counties of Gloucester, Mathews, and Middlesex. In April 1862 this command occupied a position as the right wing of the Army of Northern Virginia. Next, the Department of Northern Virginia, established in October 1861, comprised the districts of Aquia, Potomac, and the Valley. The Army of the Potomac (later called the Army of Northern Virginia) and the Army of the Kanawha made up this second command. During April and June 1862 this zone was extended to include three other departments—Norfolk, the Peninsula, and eastern Virginia. In the spring of 1863 the post at Staunton was added to the Department of Northern Virginia.

The third military zone, the Department of Henrico, was also organized in October 1861. In March 1862 this department was extended to include Petersburg and the surrounding area for ten miles. In May 1864 the Henrico Department was absorbed by the new fourth military zone, namely, the Department of Richmond, which included all of Virginia north of the James River. Organized in April 1863, the Department of Richmond was eventually enlarged to include the defenses of Drewry's Bluff and Manchester. The fifth military command was the Department of North Carolina and Southern Virginia. Established in September 1862, its operations extended to the south bank of the James River. In April 1863 this department was divided into the Departments of Richmond, Southern Virginia, and North Carolina.

Throughout the war, repeated changes were made in the geographical and military boundaries of these five departments. Departments were merged or enlarged, and in a few instances two or more military commands were grouped together to form a single department or command. The armies of the Kanawha and the Peninsula, for example, were merged under the command of Lee's Army of Northern Virginia.

5. Persons employed by J. B. Harvie, Major, A. QM., *Confederate Records*, Manuscript Rolls, Nos. 4822, 5544, 5523, 5828. Twenty-eight whites (18 ship captains, 5 carpenters, 2 clerks, 1 agent, 1 watchman, and 1 yard boy) were employed by Major Harvie. See Register of free Negroes enrolled, *ibid.*, Chap. i, Vol. 241.

6. T. C. De Leon. *Four Years in the Rebel Capitals* (Mobile: Gossip Printing Co., 1890).

7. See also Adjutant and Inspector General Office, inspection reports, Entry No. 15, 73-H-26, *Confederate Records*, Chap. vi, Vol. 416.

8. *Ibid.*, Manuscript Rolls, No. 5912.

9. *Ibid.*, Chap. vi, Vol. 416.

10. *Ibid.*, Manuscript Rolls, No. 5912.

11. *Ibid.*

12. *Ibid.*, Nos. 4152, 5202, 5921.

13. Adjutant and Inspector General Office, inspection reports, *ibid.*, Entry No. 15, 118-H-26, *ibid.*

14. *Ibid.*, Manuscript Rolls, No. 5912.

15. Adjutant and Inspector General Office, inspection reports, Entry No. 15, 119-H-26, *ibid.*

16. *Ibid.*

17. *Official Records*, iv, II, 719.

18. See Charles W. Ramsdell, "General Robert E. Lee's Horse Supply, 1862–1865," *American Historical Review*, XXX, No. 4: 772.

19. Adjutant and Inspector General Office, inspection reports, Entry No. 15, 224-C-61, *Confederate Records*.

20. *Ibid.*, Manuscript Rolls, No. 6452.

21. *Ibid.*, Manuscript Rolls, No. 6068.

22. Governor John Letcher, *Executive Papers*, Archives of Virginia, State Library, Richmond, Virginia. Telegram to Governor Letcher, November 7, 1862.

23. *Confederate Records*, Manuscript Rolls, No. 4208.

24. Adjutant and Inspector General Office, inspection reports, 1-C-46, *ibid.*

25. Richmond *Examiner*, Jan. 21, 1865.

26. Adjutant and Inspector General Office, letters received Aug. 13, 1863, *Confederate Records*.

27. *Ibid.*, Aug. 6, 1863. See Manuscript Rolls, No. 5602.

28. *Ibid.*, Manuscript Rolls, Nos. 6447, 6460.

29. *Ibid.*, No. 5796.

30. *Ibid.*, No. 4339.

31. *Ibid.*, No. 4319.

32. *Ibid.*, No. 5372.

33. *Ibid.*, No. 5706.

34. Adjutant and Inspector General Office, inspection reports, Entry No. 15, 9-C-38, *ibid.*

35. *Ibid.*, Manuscript Rolls, Nos. 5038, 5669, 6109.

36. *Ibid.*, No. 5926.

37. *Ibid.*, No. 4352.

38. Adjutant and Inspector General Office, inspection reports, Entry No. 15, 28-C-62, *ibid.*
39. *Ibid.*, Manuscript Rolls, Nos. 4202, 5364, 6133, 6346.
40. Adjutant and Inspector General Office, inspection reports, Entry No. 15, 72-C-36, 27-C-36, *ibid.*
41. *Ibid.*, 3–6–57.
42. *Ibid.* For slaves impressed in the field, see Manuscript Rolls, Nos. 3712, 3812, 3834, 6136, 6339, 6341, 6364. For slave teamsters attached to the Army of Northern Virginia, see Nos. 3638, 4277, 5110, 5296, 5378, 5413, 5475, 5795, 5938, 6081, 6135, 6423, 6454.
43. *Ibid.*, Nos. 6294, 4161.
44. *Ibid.*, Nos. 4735, 4414, 5120.
45. *Ibid.*, Nos. 4283, 5413, 5470, 5471, 5623, 5654, 5103.
46. *Ibid.*, No. 5807.
47. *Ibid.*, No. 3640. See also Nos. 3630, 5605, 6332–6335.
48. *Ibid.*, Nos. 3629, 4806, 5386.
49. *Ibid.*, Nos. 5901, 5374, 5277.

CHAPTER THREE

1. Luther P. Jackson, *Free Negro Labor and Property Holding in Virginia, 1830–1860* (New York: D. Appleton-Century Company, 1942), pp. 97, 219. See chap. vii, "Property in Slaves."
2. See Payroll, Confederate States Naval Ordnance, Richmond, Virginia, *Naval Records Collection of the Office of Naval Records and Library*, Record Group 45; hereinafter cited as *Naval Records*. Slaveholders who hired out their slaves to the Bureau of Ordnance and Hydrography received the wages paid to their slaves.
3. See William N. Still, Jr., "Facilities for the Construction of War Vessels in the Confederacy," *Journal of Southern History*, XXXI (Aug. 1965), 285–287. The Richmond naval laboratory had a very small labor force of 17 whites and 3 slaves in October 1861. This laboratory became a testing ground for many new developments in naval war technology such as ironclad warships, floating and anchored torpedoes, and Brooke rifled naval guns. See E. Merton Coulter, *The Confederate States of America, 1861–1865*, in A History of the South Series, Vol. VII (Baton Rouge: Louisiana State University Press, 1950), pp. 208–209.
4. Payroll of mechanics, Rocketts Navy Yard, Richmond, Virginia, *Naval Records*. The Naval Secretary took personal charge of the shipbuilding program and appointed John L. Porter the Chief Naval Contractor.
5. Payroll of mechanics, Naval Station, Richmond, *ibid.* Negro laborers transported heavy guns and munitions from the navy yard to various points where river batteries were located. These guns weighed from five to ten thousand pounds each. Slave carpenters constructed gun carriages and platforms to mount guns. The environs of Richmond provided an adequate supply of sawmills for cutting timber for ship construction.
6. Adjutant and Inspector General Office, Register of free Negroes enrolled and assigned, 1864–1865, *Confederate Records*, Chap. i, Vol. 241. Scattered information pertaining to Virginia's navy yards may be found in Subject File, Record Group 45 (National Archives). At Richmond the

yard known as Rocketts completed three ironclads, and others were under construction when the war ended.

7. Naval Powder Works and Rope Walk, Petersburg, Virginia, *Naval Records*.

8. Mechanics, West Point Boat Yard, *ibid*. There were many small boatyards operating, but the exact number is impossible to determine because of frequent abandonment and loss of records. Mallory followed three plans in his shipbuilding program: (1) naval officers were the supervisors, (2) agents were hired to supervise construction, and (3) contracts were signed with owners of private yards to construct vessels.

9. Slave Roll, Fluvanna County Naval Station, *ibid*.

10. Slave Roll, Mosely Farm, Powhatan County, *ibid*.

11. Payroll, C. S. Naval Coal Mines, Botetourt County, *ibid*.

12. Accession Nos. 247686, 29768, Virginia State Library, Richmond, Virginia.

13. Vessel Papers, H-15, P-6, Muster roll of men on Battery Buchanan, *Naval Records*; Richmond *Examiner*, Nov. 11, 1862; Sept. 2, 1863; July 1, 1864; Aug. 1, 1864. Robert Cole, a slave belonging to Jefferson Davis, was assigned to the steamer *Patrick Henry*.

14. Payroll, C. S. Naval Station, Norfolk, Virginia, Steamer *Hampton*, James River Squadron, *Naval Records*.

15. The records of the headquarters of the Ordnance Department and of the Niter and Mining Bureau in Richmond were presumably destroyed at Charlotte, North Carolina, or Fort Mill, South Carolina.

16. *Official Records*, IV, II, 957.

17. *Ibid.*, III, 1054.

18. *Ibid.*, 1071.

19. See Frank E. Vandiver, *Ploughshares into Swords: Josiah Gorgas and Confederate Ordnance* (Austin: University of Texas Press, 1952), p. 148.

20. Slave rolls, Richmond Arsenal, Oct. 1862, *Confederate Records*, Manuscript Rolls, No. 6403.

21. See the Richmond *Examiner*, Dec. 23, 1862; Aug. 1, 1863; July 30, 1864; Nov. 24, 1864. See also the Richmond *Whig*, 1862–1864.

22. *The Confederate Veteran*, XIX, No. 1, p. 22.

23. Payroll, Richmond Arsenal, *Confederate Records*, Manuscript Rolls, No. 5804.

24. *Ibid.*, Nos. 26, 27, 6398, 6401. In April 1864 Daniel received $85 monthly, and the other Negro packers $80 each per month.

25. Letters received, Richmond Arsenal, *ibid.*, Chap. IV, Vol. 93, p. 55.

26. *Ibid.*, p. 157.

27. List of free Negroes taken from the Confederate States Central Laboratory, Richmond, Virginia, *ibid.*, Manuscript Rolls, No. 5971.

28. *Official Records*, IV, III, 987.

29. *Confederate Records*, Manuscript Rolls, Nos. 4829, 4830, and Slave Rolls, Nos. 24, 245.

30. Richmond Armory, *ibid.*, Manuscript Rolls, No. 6306.

31. *Ibid.*

32. *Ibid.*, No. 800. The Petersburg Lead Works was eventually turned over to the Niter and Mining Bureau.

33. *Ibid.*, Nos. 3582, 6397.

34. *Ibid.*, Slave Rolls No. 343.

35. Letcher, *Executive Papers*, November 14, 1862.
36. Register of free Negroes enrolled, *Confederate Records*, Chap. VI, Vol. 241.
37. Adjutant and Inspector General Office, inspection reports, Entry No. 15, Lynchburg Arsenal, *ibid.*
38. Letters received, Richmond Arsenal, *ibid.*, Chap. IV, Vol. 94, pp. 105, 113.
39. *Ibid.*, p. 180.
40. *Ibid.*, Vol. 93, p. 136.
41. *Ibid.*, p. 152.
42. *Ibid.*, p. 115.
43. *Ibid.*
44. One cave in Tazewell, one in Giles, and six small caves in Wythe, Smyth, Pulaski, and Montgomery.
45. *Official Records*, IV, II, pp. 27–29.
46. In May 1862 Major St. John was paying 75 cents a pound for niter, while at the same time the Federal government was paying only 13 cents a pound. At this time Confederate currency had not depreciated noticeably in value. It is plain that Confederate niter deposits were very expensive to work.
47. *Confederate Records*, Selected Slave Rolls. Also Niter Works at Petersburg, District No. 4, *ibid.*, Manuscript Rolls, Nos. 6396, 6402.
48. *Official Records*, IV, III, 699.
49. *Ibid.*, p. 733.
50. *Ibid.*, p. 698. For complaints to the governor see Governor Letcher, *Executive Papers*, Feb., 1863.
51. *Official Records*, IV, III, 696.
52. For an excellent summary of coal mining in ante-bellum Virginia see Howard N. Eavenson, *American Coal Industry* (Baltimore: Waverly Press, Inc., 1942).
53. *Ibid.*, p. 130.
54. *Ibid.*, p. 121.
55. Richmond *Examiner*, Dec. 16, 1863.
56. *Ibid.*, Sept. 12, 1862.
57. Kathleen Bruce, *Virginia Iron Manufacture in the Slave Era* (New York: The Century Co., 1931), p. 232. See especially chap. vi, "Slave Labor."
58. *The Eighth Census of the United States: Manufactures* (Washington, 1864), CLXXIX–CLXXXIII. Other iron-producing Southern states were Maryland, Kentucky, and Tennessee; but they came under Federal control early in the war. In 1860 Tennessee, the largest producer of pig iron in the South, had seventeen furnaces which smelted 22,302 tons annually. In 1863 the Confederate government acquired an iron foundry at Selma, Alabama, and developed a huge ordnance including an arsenal and a naval foundry. In addition to casting heavy cannons, the Alabama works made machinery and plate iron.
59. Bruce, *Virginia Iron Manufacture*, p. 232.
60. Richmond *Dispatch*, Jan. 11, 1859; Richmond *Inquirer*, Sept. 5, 1860.
61. Bruce, *Virginia Iron Manufacture*, p. 239.
62. Richmond *Whig*; Richmond *Examiner*, Oct. 29, 1861.

63. Richmond *Examiner*, Dec. 19, 1862.
64. Select Slave Rolls, Westham Furnace; Westham Furnace at Richmond, Niter and Mining Service, 1864, *Confederate Records*, Manuscript Roll, No. 3578.
65. Letcher, *Executive Papers*, Aug. 31, 1861.
66. *Ibid.*, Feb. 22, 1862.
67. *Ibid.*, Aug. 29, 1864.
68. *Ibid.*, Jan. 7, 1863.
69. *Ibid.*, Feb. 14, 1863.
70. *Official Records*, iv, III, 989.
71. *Ibid.*, p. 832.
72. Adjutant and Inspector General Office, inspection reports, 5-C-28, List of Employees, District No. 1, Wythe County, Nov. 8, 1864, *Confederate Records.*
73. Letcher, *Executive Papers*, Sept. 10, 1864.
74. List of employees engaged in manufacturing of iron in District No. 1, furnished by request of Lieutenant Colonel Chandler, Inspector, Adjutant and Inspector General Office, inspection reports, Entry No. 15, 5-C-28, *Confederate Records.*
75. Charles B. Dew, "Southern Industry in the Civil War Era: Joseph Reid Anderson and the Tredegar Iron Works, 1859–67," (Ph.D. dissertation, Johns Hopkins University, 1964), pp. 24–27. Among the studies on Southern ironworks this is perhaps the most definitive.
76. *Ibid.*, p. 29. Anderson personally owned twenty-eight skilled rolling mill hands, and Dr. Robert Archer owned four. Slaves who worked overtime or produced more than their work required could earn extra money for themselves. Foreign and Northern whites, however, dominated the skilled positions throughout the Tredegar works.
77. James Aston and Edward B. Story, *Wrought Iron: Its Manufacture, Characteristics and Applications* (Pittsburgh: A. M. Byers Company, 1939), pp. 12–13.
78. *Tredegar Journal*, Joseph R. Anderson Papers, Virginia State Library, Richmond, Virginia, Aug. 24 to Dec. 1, 1861, p. 1113.
79. Dew, "Southern Industry in the Civil War Era," p. 133.
80. *Tredegar Journal*, March 1862 to Jan. 1864, pp. 62, 103, 279, 389, 490, 560, 1164.
81. *Ibid.*, pp. 15, 235, 265, 332, 452, 453.
82. Dew, "Southern Industry in the Civil War Era," p. 384.
83. *Tredegar Letter Book*, Joseph R. Anderson Papers, Virginia State Library, Richmond, Virginia, May 1 to Aug. 24, 1861, p. 650.
84. Dew, "Southern Industry in the Civil War Era," p. 133.
85. *Tredegar Letter Book*, Nov. 28, 1862, to Feb. 18, 1863, p. 446.
86. Dew, "Southern Industry in the Civil War Era," p. 384.
87. *Tredegar Letter Book*, Feb. 18 to July 29, 1863, p. 264.
88. *Tredegar Journal*, Dec. 7, 1864, to February 14, 1865, p. 769.
89. *Ibid.*, Feb. 20 to May 19, 1864, p. 583.
90. *Tredegar Letter Book*, Feb. 18 to July 29, 1863, p. 260.
91. Dew, "Southern Industry in the Civil War Era," p. 384.
92. *Ibid.*
93. *Ibid.*

94. *Tredegar Journal,* Feb. 18 to July 29, 1862, p. 55.
95. *Ibid.,* Aug. 24 to Dec. 1, 1861, pp. 1108, 1229.
96. *Ibid.,* p. 1233.
97. *Ibid.,* Nov. 28, 1861, to Feb. 18, 1862, p. 15.
98. *Ibid.,* May 17 to Dec. 19, 1863, p. 391.
99. *Ibid.,* Nov. 28, 1861, to Feb. 18, 1862, pp. 1–7.
100. *Tredegar Day Book,* p. 323.
101. *Ibid.*
102. *Ibid.,* Feb. 18 to July 29, 1863, p. 83.
103. Register of free Negroes enrolled, 1864–1865, *Confederate Records,* Chap. I, Vol. 241.
104. *Tredegar Letter Book,* Aug. 20 to Dec. 7, 1864, p. 338.
105. *Foundry Sales Book* and *Rolling Mill Sales Book,* Tredegar Iron Works, 1861–1865, Joseph R. Anderson Papers, Virginia State Library, Richmond, Virginia.
106. *Tredegar Journals,* 1861–1865; *Tredegar Day Book,* 1863–1865.
107. For the importance of the Clover Hill and Midlothian coal mines to the Confederacy see the letter from J. R. Anderson to Hon. James A. Seddon, Secretary of War, *Tredegar Letter Book,* Dec. 11, 1862. Between March 1 and March 24, 1864, the Midlothian Coal Company delivered 8,287 bushels of coal to the Tredegar foundry. See *Tredegar Day Book,* 1861–1865, p. 401.
108. *Tredegar Letter Book,* Nov. 28, 1862, to Feb. 18, 1863, p. 473.
109. *Ibid.,* p. 474.
110. *Ibid.,* p. 215.
111. *Ibid.,* p. 210.
112. *Ibid.,* p. 269; *Tredegar Journal,* 1863, pp. 156, 171, 197, 223, 231. Anderson offered a slaveowner of Buckingham Court House $1,200 per year for the hire of his blacksmith.
113. *Tredegar Journal,* Feb. 28, 1862, to July 29, 1863, p. 414.
114. *Ibid.*
115. *Ibid.,* p. 471.
116. *Ibid.*
117. *Tredegar Letter Book,* Jan. 9 to April 3, 1863. Giles, a slave shoemaker belonging to Mrs. Ann Smelsen of Bedford County, was hired for $150 annually.
118. Dew, "Southern Industry in the Civil War Era," pp. 221–224.
119. Bruce, *Virginia Iron Manufacture,* pp. 359, 365.
120. *Ibid.,* p. 364.
121. William Fairbairn, *Iron: Its History, Properties, and Processes of Manufacture* (Edinburgh: Adam and Charles Black Company, 1865), p. 37.
122. *Tredegar Letter Book,* Nov. 28, 1862, to Feb. 18, 1863, pp. 184, 187, 254.
123. The stone stacks were usually about 37 feet high and 9 feet across the egg-shaped bosh at the bottom. The inner chamber was round and reached the greatest diameter about one third of its height from the bottom. The widest area was called the bosh. From there upward the furnace was filled with its charge of charcoal, ore, and limestone. From the bosh downward the furnace was slowly filled with iron and slag. The roofed ground floor, or casting floor, of the furnace was covered with sand. At regular intervals the furnace was tapped and the molten metal

was dropped to the casting floor to flow through gutters into the pigs. At some furnaces the molten metal was emptied into ladles, in which it was transferred to the pigs. It was also necessary to "blow out" the furnace so that repairs could be made to the interior, which was lined with refractory stones.

124. *Tredegar Letter Book*, Feb. 18 to July 29, 1863, p. 245.
125. *Ibid.*, Nov. 28, 1862, to Feb. 18, 1863, pp. 69, 184, 294.
126. *Ibid.*, Feb. 18 to July 29, 1863, p. 105.
127. *Ibid.*, pp. 172, 475.
128. *Ibid.*, Aug. 20 to Dec. 7, 1864, p. 271.
129. *Ibid.*, Dec. 7, 1864, to Feb. 14, 1865, p. 48. The above statement shows the number of men and animals employed in producing and transporting pig metal, and the quantity of corn required to maintain the workmen for ten months and animal forage for six months. Some of the workmen brought their families with them (a total of 408 women and children). Four pecks of corn were allowed monthly for each laborer, two pecks for each female and child, and eight pounds of long forage per day for each animal.
130. *Tredegar Letter Book*, May 17 to Dec. 19, 1863, p. 536. Iron from the Shenandoah blast furnaces was shipped to Richmond by rail until the Manassas Railroad was destroyed. The metal was then hauled by Negro teamsters sixty miles to Staunton for rail delivery.
131. *Ibid.*
132. *Ibid.*, Feb. 18 to May 17, 1863.
133. *Ibid.*, Nov. 28, 1862, to Feb. 18, 1863, p. 43.
134. *Ibid.*

CHAPTER FOUR

1. The remaining 170 whites were employed as gatekeepers, agents, toll collectors, clerks, lockkeepers, overseers, inspectors, dockmasters, and engineers. Thomas H. Ellis was president, and Edward Lorraine was chief engineer of the company. Reports of the James River and Kanawha Company. *Twenty-Sixth Annual Report*, p. 45. Virginia State Library, Richmond, Virginia; hereinafter cited as *Reports, J. R. & K. C.*
2. Compliance with the Code of Virginia dealt the company a blow from which it never recovered. The code provided that in time of war the tolls collected on troops should not exceed one fourth the rate of other persons. With this provision enforced, and the loss of normal profits to the company, revenue was insufficient to keep the canal in repair. On the eve of the war the company, with an annual income of approximately $310,000, was one of the most powerful corporations in the state. Its tonnage exceeded the combined tonnage of four railroads entering Richmond, making it the largest freight carrier in Virginia. The railroads were to deprive the company of tonnage and revenue, however, until bankruptcy was inevitable.
3. Board of Public Works, *Reports*, Virginia State Library, Richmond, Virginia, Document No. 17, pp. 86, 90; hereinafter cited as B. P. W. *Reports*.
4. *Reports, J. R. & K. C.* Document No. 43, pp. 45–46.

5. Wayland F. Dunaway, "History of the James River and Kanawha Company," *Studies in History, Economics and Public Law*, CIV, No. 2 (Columbia University), p. 164. The Richmond dock was 4,100 feet long from the ship lock to Seventeenth Street and had a continuous wharf, protected by a granite wall. Its depth was from 11 to 15 feet, and its average width was 100 feet.

6. *Ibid.*, p. 166. The berm bank, or berm ditch, was described as follows. "Along the entire canal, on the lower or river side, there is a ditch, called the soakage ditch, which is intended to prevent damage to the adjacent land by percolation from the canal; while on the upper or hill side, there is commonly a ditch, called the berm ditch, intended to catch the washing from the neighboring slopes or streams, to prevent its passing into the canal, and convey it off through culverts, at suitable points along the canal." The cost of construction for the first division, from Richmond to Lynchburg, was $5,837,628, or $39,082 per mile; that of the second, from Lynchburg to Buchanan, $2,422,556, or $48,451 per mile. In the second division there were 28 miles of canal and 22 miles of slack-water navigation. The heaviest traffic was between Richmond and Lynchburg, and the time ordinarily taken by the freight boats for an uninterrupted trip between the two points was 3½ days up, and 3 days down. Boats regularly engaged in transportation on the canal as freight carriers were decked boats, open boats, and batteaux. Packet boats were used for passenger traffic.

7. B. P. W. *Reports*, Doc. No. 17, p. 86.

8. *Ibid.*, p. 90.

9. *Ibid.*

10. *Ibid.*

11. *Ibid.*, p. 92. Use was made of a flat-bottomed barge which contained a mechanical device (usually hand-operated) that was lowered into the canalway and scooped the mud and residue from the bottom of the canal.

12. *Ibid.*, p. 93.

13. *Ibid.* The carpenters also replaced eleven lock gates; built a new house-boat; constructed one large and one small flatboat, six bridges, and a new toll office at Lynchburg; framed a timber house; and did all the timber work on the repairs of dams.

14. Richmond *Examiner*, March 26, 1862.

15. Register of free Negroes enrolled, 1861–1865, *Confederate Records*, Chap. 1, Vol. 241, p. 1.

16. See Robert C. Black, III, *Railroads of the Confederacy* (Chapel Hill: University of North Carolina Press, 1952); John F. Stover, *The Railroads of the South, 1865–1900* (Chapel Hill: University of North Carolina Press, 1955); Angus J. Johnston, *Virginia Railroads in the Civil War* (Chapel Hill: University of North Carolina Press, 1961). Black asserts that the happy partnership of steam and government perhaps achieved its highest development in Virginia: "The Old Dominion commonly subscribed three-fifths of the equity capital invested in her railroad companies; she had extended them loans to the sum of $3,904,918 by 1861. She had endorsed, or guaranteed, $300,000 of their bonds; she had constructed one railroad on her own account; and she was playing a major role in

building another. Virginia directors dominated the board rooms of a majority of the carriers within her limits; her proxies wielded decisive influence at stockholders' meetings. All intra-state rates and fares were obliged to seek the approval of Richmond, while the State Board of Public Works carefully watched the financial condition of each carrier, even to the extent of specifying the format of its annual report. Railroading was no free enterprise in Virginia in 1861. It was not even private. By September, 1865, Virginia had expended more than $18,000,000 in the purchase of railroad stock." See Black, *Railroads of the Confederacy*, p. 42.

17. Letcher, *Executive Papers*, Jan. 30, 1863.
18. *Ibid.* Of the estimated total railroad mileage in the United States in 1861 (specifically, 31,256) the States of the Confederacy contained 9,283, or less than 30 per cent. This figure was soon reduced by Federal inroads to something over 6,000 miles, or roughly one fifth of the country's total mileage. Virginia led the Southern states with over 1,800 miles of track spanning the state.
19. Black, *Railroads of the Confederacy*, pp. 12, 13. The rails possessed neither the strength nor the stamina of the steel rails of today. They had the advantage, however, of being suitable for re-rolling and return to the track. Heavy war traffic made frequent replacement of the wrought-iron rails a necessity. Rails were spiked directly to the ties, without benefit of tie plates. The joints were not connected, as they are today, by angle bars; rather they were connected by a device called a "chair." Generally the roads were built through a sparsely settled region. Heavy grading was avoided wherever possible, and many of the railroads laid rail upon the thinnest practicable embankment of raw earth. A line was constructed tangent when it encountered hills. In swampy and coastal areas the track was carried forward occasionally upon dirt fills, but more often upon pile trestlework that was poorly drained. Bridges were usually wooden trestles and had stone abutments. Nearly all the railroad bridges of the state were thus highly susceptible to damage by floods and fires. Fortunately, raw material for sleepers or crossties grew abundantly and bordered nearly every right-of-way. The climate, however, was not conducive to a long life for the ties. The capacity for a freight car was usually eight to ten tons.
20. The two principal officers of the Virginia Central were Edmund Fontane, president, and Henry D. Whitcomb, chief engineer and superintendent. The employees consisted of ticket agents, conductors, freight runners, road and section masters, shop mechanics, watchmen, engineers, firemen, brakemen, train hands, and laborers. However, conscription took its toll early in the war, for railroad employees were not exempt from military service until the spring of 1864, when the Confederate Congress passed an act exempting a certain number of skilled railroad laborers. The Virginia Central hauled approximately one half of the supplies for the Army of Northern Virginia.
21. See Isaac Hammond Collection, *Accession* No. 24335, Virginia State Library, Richmond, Virginia. It was not until 1865 that the company adopted a system of track maintenance in which rail mileage was broken down into divisions or sections, with a foreman responsible for each

section. Labor equipment shortages caused constant repair and replacement of bridges, ties, roadbeds, and rails. Frequent repairs were also needed when Federal raiders frequently destroyed sections of line.

22. See Virginia Central Railroad, *Twenty-Seventh Annual Report,* Virginia State Library, Richmond, Virginia, p. 79. Slaves were secured on a rental basis, and their rate of hire varied according to their abilities.

23. Richmond *Daily Dispatch,* Aug. 8, 1862. The bridge over the South Anna River and the trestles near Hanover Court House were destroyed.

24. *Official Records,* XXV, Part 2, p. 683.

25. *Ibid.,* p. 703.

26. General Assembly of Virginia, *Documents,* Doc. No. 1, 1863, p. 16.

27. *Ibid.* See also the Virginia Central Railroad, *Twenty-Eighth Annual Report* (1863), pp. 9, 10, 24, 25.

28. *Ibid.*

29. See Virginia Central Railroad, *Twenty-Ninth Annual Report* (Nov. 1864), pp. 47–48. See also Register of free Negroes enrolled, 1864–1865. *Confederate Records,* Chap. 1, Vol. 241.

30. See Virginia and Tennessee Railroad Company, *Seventeenth Annual Report* (Lynchburg, 1864), pp. 12, 106. In October 1865 the expenses for Negro hire amounted to $194,957.99.

31. *Ibid.* Four slaves—Bob, Emanuel, Fred, and Joe—and two free Negroes —James Finney and Abraham Pleasants—lost their lives in accidents.

32. See Virginia and Tennessee Railroad Company, *Eighteenth Annual Report* (Oct. 1865).

33. See Southside Railroad Company, *Twelfth Annual Report* (Nov. 1861). Also B.P.W. *Documents,* Doc. No. 17, p. 28.

34. Every Virginia locomotive utilized wood as fuel, and the number of miles produced by the combustion of a single cord varied widely, but a reasonable average was between 50 and 60 miles. Animal oil and tallow were used in large quantities as lubricants. Sperm oil fed the enormous headlights. See Black, *Railroads of the Confederacy,* p. 21.

35. Letcher, *Executive Papers,* Nov. 3, 1862.

36. *Ibid.,* Feb. 18, 1863.

37. *Ibid.,* Feb. 1, 1864.

38. See Southside Railroad Company, *Fourteenth Annual Report* (Nov. 1863). The Negro employees were fed bacon cured in Cincinnati. The company also erected a large smokehouse and killed and cured its own pork. Almost 14,000 tons of freight were hauled during the year.

39. Before the war ended, all but eleven miles of strap rail southwest of Burkeville had been replaced.

40. See Richmond and Danville Railroad Company, *Fourteenth Annual Report* (Dec. 11, 1861).

41. *Ibid.*

42. See B. P. W. *Reports,* Doc. No. 15, Richmond and Danville Annual Report (Sept. 1862), pp. 15, 142.

43. Letcher, *Executive Papers,* Oct. 20, 1862.

44. Richmond and Danville Railroad Company, *Sixteenth Annual Report* (Dec. 10, 1863), p. 358.

45. *Ibid.,* p. 339. Lewis E. Harvie, president of the line, was injured as he

traveled down the road on a handcar worked by Negroes, when the car collided with some passenger cars left standing on the track at Manchester. The cars were not seen because of darkness. See the Richmond *Examiner*, Oct. 4, 1864.

46. Richmond and Danville Railroad Company, *Seventeenth Annual Report* (Dec. 1864) and *Eighteenth Annual Report* (Dec. 1865).

47. Richmond *Examiner*, Dec. 19, 1864; Richmond *Daily Enquirer*, Jan. 3, 1865.

48. The wisdom of constructing this line became evident during the last year of the war; it was over this line that the bulk of the supplies for Lee's army were transported. The other vital supply line, the Petersburg and Weldon, was permanently disrupted by Federal troops. President Davis advocated public assistance for the scheme as early as the fall of 1861, only to see his recommendation bypassed by the stubborn Congress, which—perhaps influenced by the many opponents of the measure —feared the diverting of the commerce of western North Carolina into Virginia. Sentiment for the project eventually became overwhelming. On February 8, 1862, the State Convention of North Carolina approved a charter for the Piedmont Railroad Company, provided that the same was certified by the Legislature of Virginia. The new Piedmont Company attained legal status on March 27, 1862, when the General Assembly of Virginia gave its formal sanction. By May 1862, a satisfactory construction agreement was worked out between the Confederate government and the officials of the Richmond and Danville Railroad Company. In June the Piedmont Company was fully organized, and the Richmond and Danville line agreed to undertake the erection and operation of the new line. The Confederate Congress enacted a law which appropriated $1,000,000 for connecting the Richmond and Danville and the North Carolina Central railroads. Surveys of exploration under the direction of the Engineer Bureau were ordered to determine the most satisfactory connection.

49. Richmond and Danville Railroad Company, *Fifteenth Annual Report* (Dec. 10, 1862).

50. *Ibid.* Captain E. T. D. Myers, a young engineer officer and son of the Quartermaster General, dispatched a bevy of agents into the countryside to secure teams, carts, tools, and Negro laborers. He also invited bids on portions of the line. Myers was chief engineer and chief of construction of the Danville-Greensboro extension.

51. *Ibid.*

52. Black, *Railroads of the Confederacy*, 151.

53. Letcher, *Executive Papers*, March 11, 1863.

54. *Ibid.*, Feb. 18, 1864.

55. B. P. W. *Reports*, Annual Reports (1861), p. 180; Petersburg Railroad Company, *Annual Report* (1861), p. 17.

56. Petersburg Railroad Company, *Thirteenth Annual Report*, p. 29.

57. Petersburg Railroad Company, *Thirty-First Annual Report*.

58. B. P. W. *Reports*, Annual Reports, Doc. No. 17, p. 145; Richmond and Petersburg Railroad Company, *Twenty-Seventh Annual Report* (1862).

59. *Ibid.*

60. *Ibid.* In 1862 the company transported 32,259 tons of coal to Richmond, and over 80,000 tons of freight.
61. Richmond *Examiner*, Dec. 6, 1862.
62. Letcher, *Executive Papers*, Feb. 18, 1863.
63. Richmond *Whig*, Aug. 15, 1863; Dec. 22, 1863.
64. Richmond *Examiner*, Nov. 10, 1864.
65. Richmond and Petersburg Railroad Company, *Twenty-Ninth Annual Report* (April 1864), p. 506.
66. *Ibid.*, p. 478. The Richmond and Petersburg Railroad Company owned 17 engines, 12 passenger cars, 3 baggage cars, 46 box and flat cars, and 146 sand, coal, and gravel cars. Repairs on machinery, depots, and the road came to over $175,000 in 1864. A total of 78,092 tons of freight was transported.
67. Richmond *Examiner*, July 26, 1861. Archie, slave of Mrs. L. Redd, was killed while engaged in coupling cars on freight train at Guinea Station. See B. P. W. *Reports*, Doc. No. 15, p. 187.
68. Richmond and York River Railroad Company, *Eighth Annual Report* (1862), p. 24.
69. *Ibid.* An inventory of rolling stock disclosed that the line had 5 engines and 80 cars (flat, dump, passenger, baggage, and freight).
70. Richmond and York River Railroad Company, *Tenth Annual Report* (Oct. 1864), p. 5.
71. B. P. W. *Reports*, Annual Reports, Doc. Nos. 15, 17, 1861–1863, pp. 227, 173, 187. See Richmond, Fredericksburg and Potomac Railroad Company, *Annual Reports* (1861–1863).
72. See Richmond, Fredericksburg and Potomac Railroad Company, *Thirty-Third Annual Report.*
73. Charles W. Turner, "Richmond, Fredericksburg and Potomac, 1861–1865," *Civil War History*, VII, 256.

CHAPTER FIVE

1. A more popular subject is that of Confederate medical history. See Wyndham B. Blanton, *Medicine in Virginia in the Nineteenth Century* (Richmond: Garrett and Massie, 1933); and H. H. Cunningham, *Doctors in Gray. The Confederate Medical Service* (Baton Rouge: Louisiana State University Press, 1958). Both Blanton and Cunningham disclosed that Virginia's contribution to the medical care of Confederate wounded exceeded that of any other Southern state. Nearly one half of the 190,000 wounded Confederate soldiers were injured in Virginia, and some 60 per cent of these passed through Virginia's hospitals.
2. On February 26, 1861, the Medical Department was organized by an act of the Confederate Congress, and eventually $50,000 was appropriated for hospital construction. The Medical Department, headed by Surgeon General Samuel Preston Moore, became a division in the War Department. The Surgeon General was charged with the administration of his department, the government of hospitals, and the regulation of medical officers. Other major responsibilities included the supervision of hospital inspectors, all medical officers, and field and general hospitals. See Blanton, *Medicine in Virginia*, p. 274. Other administrative officers

included an assistant surgeon general, a medical director, an assistant medical director, an inspector of hospitals, a medical inspector, and the chief surgeon of the department of Richmond. Each general hospital was staffed with a director or chief surgeon, surgeons, assistant surgeons, and acting assistant surgeons.

3. After the Battle of Manassas in July 1861, thousands of wounded poured into the city of Richmond, where hospitals to accommodate such large numbers were unavailable. The hundreds of makeshift hospitals—tobacco factories, churches, schools, warehouses, private houses—used to treat the wounded were unsatisfactory. In the fall of 1861, hospital encampments in the Richmond suburbs were under construction, and as soon as possible many of the temporary hospital buildings were closed. See Robert W. Waitt, Jr., *Confederate Military Hospitals in Richmond* (Richmond, 1964). Waitt's study lists 54 military hospitals: 6 general hospital encampments (Chimborazo, Howard's Grove, Jackson, Stuart, Louisiana, and Winder), 20 smaller hospitals, and 28 general hospitals. Some of the 54 military hospitals were used for emergencies, many were used off and on, and the others were in continual operation. An additional 20 large general hospitals were located throughout the Piedmont, the Valley, and the western part of Virginia. The largest of these hospitals, staffed with from 7 to 20 surgeons, were found in cities such as Petersburg, Lynchburg, Danville, Farmville, and Charlottesville. A general hospital was one that contained three or more divisions. The table of organization for the Medical Department in the Field was headed by a medical director for each army or corps. Directly under him were the chief surgeons, one for each division; senior surgeons, one for each brigade; and regimental surgeons, a surgeon and assistant surgeon to each regiment.

4. By 1862 the Surgeon General had eliminated much of the confusion and impromptu efforts to make provisions for the immediate care of the sick and wounded. Many private hospitals scattered throughout the state were incorporated into the Medical Department. Receiving and wayside hospitals were located near important railroad junctions. By 1863, wayside hospitals for wounded and sick soldiers on furlough or honorably discharged from the service were maintained in Richmond, Petersburg, Danville, Farmville, Lynchburg, Charlottesville, Liberty, and Staunton. In 1864 two receiving hospitals were located in Gordonsville and City Point.

Legislation enacted by the Confederate Congress provided for the allotment to each hospital of two matrons, two assistant matrons, and two matrons for each ward (with rations and suitable places of lodging), giving preference in all cases to females. The two head matrons were required to see that the food or diet was properly prepared and to perform all other duties that might be necessary. The assistant matrons were charged with the supervision of the hospital laundry and the care of patients' clothing. The two ward matrons authorized for each ward of 100 patients were responsible for the preparation and cleanliness of beds, for ascertaining that food was carefully prepared and furnished to the sick, for seeing that medicines were administered, and for assuring that patients were receiving medical attention (Act of September, 1861). It was generally recognized that women made better nurses than men, yet full-time service in military hospitals was not considered respectable work for white women.

5. Despite the large number of wounded, sickness was far more of a problem for the hospitals. During the first year of the war almost 50,000 troops in Virginia averaged three illnesses per man. Blanton, *Medicine in Virginia,* concluded that "on the average, each Confederate soldier was wounded or sick about six times during the Civil War." According to Blanton, in 1862 most of the 9,000 sick of General Joseph Johnston's inactive army were sent to Richmond hospitals. In one group of general hospitals between September and December, there were 48,544 admissions, of which 34,890 were for illness. Among the disabling diseases were malaria, typhoid fever, smallpox, and pulmonary tuberculosis.

A consolidated report of hospital admissions in the Department of Virginia from September 1862 to December 1863 listed 293,165 patients. For a period of 23 months between September 1862 and August 1864 a grand total of 412,958 sick and wounded were admitted into Virginia's general hospitals. See Cunningham, *Doctors in Gray,* p. 277.

6. *Official Records,* IV, I, 580. The nurses and cooks hired or impressed were to be paid on hospital muster rolls by the Quartermaster Department at rates not to exceed $18.50 per month. In March 1863 this figure was increased to $25.00.

7. *Journal of the Congress of the Confederate States of America, 1861–1865,* I, 793. Inasmuch as 25 per cent of the battles and an overwhelming majority of Confederate army casualties occurred within a 75-mile radius of Richmond, this city naturally became the center for the reception, treatment, and convalescence of military casualties. The total forces of the Confederate Army were estimated at 600,000 men, and there were fewer than 3,000 medical officers—834 surgeons and 1,668 assistant surgeons, of which number 755 came from Virginia.

8. Each building was 150 feet in length, 30 feet in width, and one story high. Five divisions were organized with 30 wards to each division. These ward rooms were arranged with cots on each side of a central aisle to accommodate from 40 to 60 patients.

9. List of employees, Chimborazo Hospital, 1862–1863, *Confederate Records,* Chap. VI, Vol. 79.

10. The supply of milk and kid meat was nutritious and palatable for the patients.

11. List of employees, Chimborazo No. 2, 1862–1865, *Confederate Records,* Chap. VI, Vol. 85, p. 15.

12. See J. Julian Chisolm, *A Manual of Military Surgery for the Use of Surgeons in the Confederate Army* (Richmond: West and Johnson, 1861), pp. 66–67.

13. List of detailed men, Chimborazo Hospitals Nos. 1–5, Jan. 1, 1863, *Confederate Records,* Chap. VI, Vol. 98.

14. *Ibid.* Mike, a slave cooper belonging to John Greanor, was employed by the Naval Medical Purveyor's Department to cooper barrels to store sugar. See the Richmond *Examiner,* Feb. 10, 1864.

15. *Ibid.*
16. *Confederate Records*, Letters received and sent, Chimborazo Hospital, 1861–1864, Chap. VI, Vol. 707, p. 212.
17. Richmond *Examiner*, Dec. 8, 1862. James, a slave belonging to George W. Phillips, was employed as a packer in the Medical Purveyor's office. See *Confederate Records*, Manuscript No. 4270. Bose Valentine, a free Negro, was employed in the Medical Purveyor's office in Wytheville, Virginia. See Adjutant and Inspector General Office, inspection reports, Dec. 1864, *Confederate Records*, Entry No. 15, 39–C–36.
18. Letters received and sent, Chimborazo Hospital, 1861–1864, *Confederate Records*, Chap. VI, Vol. 707, p. 223.
19. *Ibid.*, Vol. 709, p. 130.
20. *Ibid.*
21. *Ibid.*
22. Letcher, *Executive Papers*, October 3, 1864.
23. Adjutant and Inspector General Office, inspection reports, S-45: Hospitals in and near Richmond, *Confederate Records*.
24. *Ibid.*
25. Letters received and sent, Medical Director, Richmond, Virginia, 1861–1864, *Confederate Records*, Chap. VI, Vol. 364, p. 309.
26. *Ibid.*, Vol. 709, p. 271.
27. *Ibid.*, Vol. 364, p. 285. See Memorandum book, William E. Toombs, Steward, Chimborazo No. 1, 1862–1863, *ibid.*, Vol. 316.
28. Daily morning reports, Divisions 1–6, Winder Hospital, 1863–1864, Richmond, Virginia, *ibid.*, Vol. 710. In January 1863 the Richmond *Examiner* advertised for forty Negroes to serve as hospital attendants in the first division of Winder Hospital.
29. List of employees, Division No. 2, Winder Hospital, 1863, *ibid.*, Vol. 218.
30. Daily morning reports, Winder Hospital, 1864, *ibid.*, Vol. 710.
31. List of employees, Division No. 2, Winder Hospital, 1864, *ibid.*, Vol. 218.
32. Confederate information index, Slaves, March 1865, *ibid.* Bell I. Wiley asserts that "there seems to be no evidence that the Negro soldiers authorized by the Confederate Government in 1865 ever went into battle." A careful probe into existing Confederate records reveals that the Jackson and Winder hospitals' Negro troops were in actual combat. These records provide the only documentary evidence which might serve as an exception to Wiley's contention.
33. J. B. Roden, "Experience in Richmond Hospitals," *Confederate Veteran*, XVI, 222.
34. Letters sent and received, Medical Director, Richmond, Virginia, *Confederate Records*, Chap. VI, Vol. 364, pp. 271, 274. Surgeon Palmer was ordered to relieve all able-bodied men and detailed soldiers fit for field duty.
35. The Negro nurse received instructions from the ward master, who in turn was responsible to his immediate superior, the steward, for the cleanliness of the ward and the well-being of the patients. Both the cook and laundress looked to their respective matrons for direction and orders. See Record book, Division No. 1, *Confederate Records*, Chap. VI,

Vol. 197, pp. 198–205; Howard's Grove General Hospital, *ibid.*, Vol. 355, pp. 166–174.

36. Requisitions for hospital attendants, Howard's Grove Hospital, Richmond, Virginia, 1863, *ibid.*, Vol. 470.

37. Morning report of sick and wounded, Howard's Grove, Division Nos. 1–3, 1864, *ibid.*, Vol. 713.

38. Record book, Division No. 1, Howard's Grove General Hospital, *ibid.*, Vol. 203.

39. *Ibid.*, p. 15.

40. *Ibid.*, p. 102.

41. Morning reports of attendants, Howard's Grove Hospital, 1864, *ibid.*, Vol. 429, p. 90.

42. *Ibid.*

43. *Ibid.* The surgeons usually received $300 yearly for the hire of their slaves as cooks, nurses, and laundresses.

44. Richmond *Examiner*, Jan. 12, 1863. City Hall, the Third Division of Howard's Grove, and General Hospital No. 21 were the three smallpox hospitals in Richmond.

45. *Ibid.*, Jan. 13, 1863. As this epidemic reached its peak in the capital city, 137 Negroes were engaged to provide for the physical needs of smallpox victims.

46. Letters and orders issued, Howard's Grove General Hospital, *Confederate Records*, Chap. VI, Vol. 429, p. 15.

47. *Ibid.*, p. 24.

48. *Ibid.*, p. 25.

49. Morning report of attendants, Smallpox Hospital, Howard's Grove, *ibid.*, Vol. 713, p. 4.

50. *Ibid.*

51. Letters and orders issued, Howard's Grove, *ibid.*, Vol. 203, pp. 112–115; Record book, Division No. 1, Howard's Grove, Chap. VI, Vol. 197, pp. 198–205.

52. *Ibid.*

53. Letters, orders, and circulars sent, Surgeon General's Office, Richmond Virginia, 1861–1865, *ibid.*, Vol. 740, p. 440.

54. *Ibid.*

55. Requisitions for hospital supplies, laborers, and funds, Howard's Grove, Division Nos. 1–3, 1862–1865, Richmond, Virginia, *ibid.*, Vol. 470.

56. Letters sent and received, Medical Director, Richmond, Virginia, *ibid.*, Vol. 364, p. 47.

57. Letters and orders issued, Howard's Grove Hospital, *ibid.*, Vol. 429, p. 7.

58. Cunningham, *Doctors in Gray*, pp. 52–53.

59. List of employees and attendants (Negroes), Jackson Hospital, *Confederate Records*, Chap. VI, Vol. 187, pp. 1–7.

60. Muster and payroll, Jackson Hospital, Richmond, Virginia, 1864, *ibid.*, Manuscript Rolls, Nos. 6064–6065. The Negro payroll for October, November, and December 1864 amounted to $18,161.55, while the payroll for white employees amounted to $4,807.16.

61. Adjutant and Inspector General Office, inspection reports, S-45: Hospitals in and near Richmond, *ibid.*, p. 40.

62. *Ibid.*, Chap. VI, Vol. 187.

63. *Ibid.*
64. Adjutant and Inspector General Office, inspection reports, S-45, *ibid.*, p. 20.
65. Letters sent, Medical Director, Richmond, Virginia, *ibid.*, Chap. vi, Vol. 364, p. 307.
66. *Ibid.*, pp. 328, 331, 332.
67. Adjutant and Inspector General Office, inspection reports, S-45: Hospitals in and near Richmond, *ibid.*, p. 45.
68. Account book, General Hospital No. 24, Richmond, Virginia, *ibid.*, Chap. vi, Vol. 653.
69. *Official Records*, iv, II, 13. The Medical Department published a pamphlet describing the useful plants and herbs that could be utilized.
70. *Ibid.*, p. 467.
71. *Ibid.*, p. 569.
72. Adjutant and Inspector General Office, inspection reports, S-45: Hospitals in and near Richmond, *Confederate Records*, Chap. vi, Vols. 123, 327, 331, 339, 711, 718, General Hospitals, Richmond, Virginia.
73. Virginia hospital rolls, General Hospital No. 9, Richmond, Virginia, *ibid.*
74. Receiving and wayside hospital, General Hospital No. 9, Richmond, Virginia, *ibid.*, Vol. 339, pp. 19, 21, 25, 27, 29, 31.
75. Record book, General Hospital No. 9, Richmond, Virginia, *ibid.*, Vol. 110, pp. 303–304. Paragraph 46 of the Medical Regulations provided that officers were to attend hired Negroes at stations where other medical attention could not be received.
76. Letters sent and received, Medical Director, Richmond, Virginia, *ibid.*, Vol. 364, pp. 29, 45. The Quartermaster Headquarters in Richmond employed 19 Negro ambulance drivers to assist in the rapid movement of the wounded from hospital trains to the receiving hospitals. Each owner was paid $380 yearly for the hire of his slave. See Slave Rolls, No. 5912, Richmond, Virginia, *ibid.* For a discussion of the Negro employees of the Confederate States Ambulance Shops see Chapter 2. This shop was located on the outskirts of Richmond.
77. Letters sent, Medical Director, Richmond, Virginia, *ibid.*, Vol. 364, p. 321.
78. Letters sent and received, General Hospital No. 9, Richmond, Virginia, *ibid.*, Vol. 423, p. 104.
79. Circular No. 16, *ibid.*, p. 120.
80. Orders and letters, Medical Director's Office, Army of Northern Virginia, April 1863 to May 1865, *ibid.*, Vol. 642, p. 102. Surgeon L. Guild was the medical director of the Army of Northern Virginia.
81. Letters sent, Medical Director, Richmond, Virginia, *ibid.*, Vol. 364, p. 351.
82. Report of inspection of Engineer Bureau Hospital, *ibid.*, Vol. 416, pp. 27, 28.
83. *Ibid.*, p. 31.
84. *Ibid.*, p. 28.
85. Selected slave rolls, Engineer Bureau, Engineer Hospital, Richmond, Virginia, *ibid.*

86. Hospital rolls, Virginia, Robertson Hospital, Richmond, Virginia, *ibid*. See Elizabeth Dabney Coleman, "The Captain Was a Lacy," *Virginia Cavalcade*, VI, No. 1, 31–35.
87. Selected Slave Rolls, African Church Hospital, Richmond, Virginia, *Confederate Records*, Chap. VI, Vol. 416.
88. Virginia hospital rolls, Richmond, Virginia, April 1863, *ibid*.
89. *Ibid*.
90. Smallpox Hospital, Richmond, Virginia, *ibid*., Chap. VI, Vol. 247. See also Virginia hospital rolls, Richmond, Virginia.
91. Hospital rolls, Saint Francis De Sailes Hospital, Richmond, Virginia, *ibid*.
92. *Official Records*, IV, I, 777.
93. Letters sent, Medical Director's Office, Manassas Junction, *Confederate Records*, Chap. VI, Vol. 739.
94. *Ibid*., Vol. 461.
95. *Official Records*, IV, II, 533.
96. Inspection reports of Virginia Hospitals, *Confederate Records*, Chapter VI, Vol. 416, pp. 11–13.
97. Letters sent and received, Medical Director, Richmond, Virginia, 1862–1865. *ibid*., Vols. 364, 367, 369.
98. In May 1864 nine slaves were impressed to assist in transporting the sick and wounded across the New River. Several other slaves were impressed by Major E. Crutchfield to transport the wounded to the general hospitals in southwestern Virginia. See Slaves impressed in the field, *Confederate Records*, Manuscripts, Slave Roll No. 4352. When slaves were needed to drive ambulance wagons, a quartermaster officer called upon the slaveowners in the vicinity for their slaves. If necessary they were impressed solely on the grounds of urgent needs imposed by war.
99. *Ibid*., Manuscripts, Slave Roll No. 5158. See Chap. VI, Vol. 187.
100. *Ibid*., Manuscripts, Slave Roll No. 3832. The Richmond Ambulance Corps, a volunteer organization of about fifty citizens, exempt from military duty, was active in many major battles in Virginia. Its major services included the transportation of wounded to hospitals. A free Negro from Richmond, I. Roberts, was detailed to the Ambulance Corps. Both slaves and free Negroes served as ambulance drivers. See Register of free Negroes enrolled, *Confederate Records*, Chap. I, Vols. 240–241.
101. Letters sent, Medical Director, Manassas Junction, Virginia, *ibid*., Chap. VI, Vol. 367, p. 205.
102. Letters received, Medical Director, Army of Northern Virginia, *ibid*., Vol. 369, p. 83.
103. Letters sent, Thomas H. Williams, Medical Director, *ibid*., Vol. 461, p. 49.
104. Report of attendants, Lynchburg Hospitals, 1862, *ibid*., Vol. 724.
105. Letters sent, Medical Director, Manassas Junction, *ibid*., Vol. 367, p. 198.
106. *Ibid*., pp. 194, 197, 209.
107. Letters sent, Thomas H. Williams, Medical Director, Army of the Potomac, *ibid*., Vol. 369, p. 17.
108. *Ibid*., Vol. 367, p. 128.

109. *Ibid.*, p. 254.
110. Letters sent, Thomas H. Williams, Medical Director, Army of Northern Virginia, *ibid.*, Vol. 461, p. 45.
111. Letters received, Thomas H. Williams, Medical Director, *ibid.*, Vol. 369, p. 125.
112. *Ibid.*, Vol. 436.
113. *Ibid.*, Vol. 550.
114. *Ibid.*, Vol. 436.
115. Letters sent, Medical Director, Richmond, Virginia, *ibid.*, Vol. 366, p. 76.
116. List of free blacks detailed, *Cumberland County, Miscellaneous Papers*, Virginia State Library, Richmond, Virginia.
117. Hospital rolls, free Negroes and slaves employed, Farmville General Hospital, *Confederate Records*, Chap. VI, Vol. 32.
118. *Ibid.*
119. List of Negroes employed, Farmville General Hospital, *ibid.*, Vol. 513.
120. Letters sent, Medical Director, Richmond, Virginia, *ibid.*, Vol. 364.
121. Hospital rolls, General Hospital, Staunton, Virginia, 1863, *ibid.*
122. Blanton, *Medicine in Virginia*, p. 306.
123. Letters sent, Thomas H. Williams, Medical Director, Army of Northern Virginia, *Confederate Records*, Chap. VI, Vol. 367.
124. *Ibid.*
125. *Ibid.*, Vol. 369. In October 1862 the hospital received a substantial portion of the 5,000 sick and wounded transferred from Winchester.
126. Orders, telegrams, circulars issued and received, Medical Director's Office, Richmond, Virginia, *ibid.*, Vol. 368.
127. *Ibid.*
128. See Records of hospitals in Virginia, *ibid.*, Chap. VI, Vol. I, pp. 1–85.

CHAPTER SIX

1. Joseph T. Wilson, *The Black Phalanx: A History of the Negro Soldiers of the United States, 1775–1865* (Hartford, Conn.: American Publishing Company, 1888), p. 103.
2. Bell I. Wiley, *Southern Negroes, 1861–1865* (New York: Rinehart and Company, 1938), p. 113.
3. William M. Robinson noted that in a total authorized strength of 477 officers and 9,920 enlisted men, the Confederate "Engineers amounted to but two per cent of the officers and one per cent of the soldiers." See "The Confederate Engineers," *Military Engineer*, XXII (July–Aug. 1930), 297. Engineer troops in the Confederate armies were very informally organized during the first two years of the war. The organization of four regiments contemplated in the plans of the Chief of Engineers began in the summer of 1863. The headquarters of the First Engineers was established at Richmond. Colonel T. M. R. Talcott was appointed regimental commander, and Special Order 189, Adjutant and Inspector General Office, issued August 10, 1863, permitted him to handpick his quota of recruits at the conscription camps. The First Engineer Regiment became an excellent unit.
4. On April 23, 1861, Robert E. Lee, with the Virginia rank of Major

General, assumed command of the state's military and naval forces. Already Virginia had committed "acts of war": Harpers Ferry, in a very exposed location, was seized; and Norfolk, with its great naval yard, ordnance shops, and stores intact, came under state control. See James L. Nichols, *Confederate Engineer* (Tuscaloosa, Ala.: Confederate Publishing Company, 1957), p. 20.

5. Governor Letcher received several offers from slaveholders to provide slaves to labor on fortifications. Free Negroes also volunteered their services, as can be seen from the chart.

6. See D. H. Mahan, *A Treatise on Field Fortifications* (New York: John Wiley, 1848). During the month of April 1861, about three hundred free Negroes assembled at the Petersburg Court House to hear a speech by John Dodson, former mayor. The free Negroes were about to leave town to work on Confederate fortifications at Norfolk. In reply to Dodson's speech, Charles Tinsley, a free Negro, said, "We are willing to aid Virginia's cause to the utmost extent of our ability." Tinsley then stepped forward to receive the Confederate flag, stating, "I could feel no greater pride, no more genuine gratification, than to be able to plant it upon Fortress Monroe." See Petersburg *Daily Express*, April 26, 1861.

7. Engineer Department of Virginia, Payroll of slaves and free negroes, May-Oct. 1861, Doc. No. 62-787, Virginia State Library, Richmond, Virginia; hereinafter cited as *State Engineers*. The General Assembly of Virginia enacted legislation authorizing the governor to employ an engineer to plan and construct coast, harbor, and river defenses. Colonel A. Talcott was selected for this position, and $200,000 was appropriated in January 1861. On April 30, 1861, $2,000,000 was authorized by the legislators for the defense of the state. See *The Calendar of Virginia State Papers, 1652–1869* (11 vols.; Richmond: 1875–1893) XI, 157.

8. *Official Records*, IV, II, 857. In December 1861, almost fifty slaves were

Slaveowner	Location	Number of Slaves
J. M. Rucker	Bedford	2
B. D. Cogbill	Boydton	50 (free Negroes)
L. Battaile	Caroline	1
G. B. Hammath	Clarksville	40
John Taylor	Culpeper	100
	Danville	100 (free Negroes)
W. J. Henry	Louisa	5
W. D. Branch (Mayor)	Lynchburg	70 (free Negroes)
J. H. Lee	Orange	50
	Petersburg	300 (free Negroes)
N. Dadaman	S. W. Virginia	50
C. R. Mason	Staunton	200
T. McCarrin	Sulphur Springs	40
E. L. Layton	Tye River	7
C. L. Crockett	Wytheville	60

engaged in erecting entrenchments to protect Taliaferro's rear. See *Confederate Records*, Manuscript No. 4212, Gloucester Point, Dec. 24, 1861.

9. For an excellent discussion of the mobilization of Negro labor see Tinsley Spraggins, "Mobilization of Negro Labor," p. 169.

10. Richmond *Examiner*, Oct. 3, 1861. The slaves were fed only rice for breakfast and half a pint of meal per man for dinner. The lack of meat, fresh vegetables, etc., contributed to a continual breakdown of the slaves' physical stamina during their periods of employment. The owners demanded an improvement in the daily rations issued to their slaves, who were expected to perform hard physical labor for ten hours daily.

11. *State Engineers*, Payroll. Twenty-eight slaves were employed in June 1861, on defensive works at Chamberlain's Depot. See Letcher, *Executive Papers*, June 28, 1861.

12. Letcher, *Executive Papers*, April 22, 1861. Many of the batteries along the rivers were armed and manned by the Confederate Navy. Because of a lack of naval vessels, at the beginning of the war, naval officers were assigned to shore batteries. They were especially fitted for mounting the guns, since these were mainly naval types from the Norfolk Navy Yard. See *The Official Records of the Union and Confederate Navies in the War of Rebellion* (26 vols.; Washington, 1894–1922).

13. *State Engineers, Payroll.*

14. *Ibid.* Batteries were also located on Burwell's Bay on the James River and at the mouth of the Appomattox River. Several hundred slaves and free Negroes were engaged to construct batteries and earthworks at Fort Boykins and Hardy's Bluff, located near Smithfield in Isle of Wight County. Six slave carpenters—Anthony, Jeffrey, Bill, Randall, Robert, and Dawson—and two slave bricklayers—Big Tom and Little Tom— were hired at Fort Boykin's. See *Confederate Records*, Slave Roll No. 404, Fort Boykin (Day's Neck). In November 1861, sixty-seven slaves labored at Fort Boykin.

15. *Ibid.* In August 1861, twenty-eight free Negroes from Spotsylvania County and the city of Fredericksburg were employed in loading and unloading ammunition at Fredericksburg for Fort Lowry. On August 21, 1861, the New York *Herald* reported, "A battery is being erected at Mosquitoe Point, on the Rappahannock River, on which were employed no less than 500 darkies." Actually the Mosquitoe Point alluded to was Cherry Point in Lancaster, nearly opposite Gray's Point in Middlesex. See Letcher, *Executive Papers*, Sept. 11, 1861.

16. Nichols, *Confederate Engineer*, p. 20. On November 1, 1861, Virginia transferred its defensive works and supervision of state engineers over to Confederate Engineer Bureau officers. President Davis also appointed Jeremy F. Gilmer, a lieutenant colonel in the permanent Corps of Engineers. By September 1862, Gilmer had assumed command of the Engineer Bureau, a position he held throughout the war.

17. *State Engineers*, Payroll. On April 23, 1861, $150 was appropriated by the Common Council of Petersburg for the benefit of the families of free Negroes who volunteered to go into the service of the state. Additional appropriations were made for the next three years. See Petersburg Common Council, *Minute Books*, April 1861 to April 1864. In October 1861 the mayor of Petersburg was authorized to draw $100 to purchase clothing for free Negroes sent to Yorktown to dig entrenchments for General Magruder.

18. *Ibid.* Washington and John, slave carpenters, worked at West Point. Seventy-nine slaves were also employed at the Oak Grove Entrenchments in October 1861. See *Confederate Records*, Slave Roll No. 425.

19. Shortly after, Ledbetter was ordered to assume troop command in East Tennessee, and Captain Alfred L. Rives assumed the duties of acting Chief of Engineers.

20. Selected Slave Rolls, Richmond, Virginia, *Confederate Records.* The names of four free Negroes were James Hale, Miles Potts, James Scott, and Willis Wilson.

21. *State Engineers,* Payroll. In January 1862, E. T. D. Myers, acting chief engineer of Virginia, notified Governor Letcher that he was closing the state engineer's office. See *Senate Documents,* 1861–1862, Doc. No. 14, p. 9, Richmond, Virginia. In December 1861 seven slave carpenters —Moses, William, Andrew, James, Brooks, Albert, and Manual—and four slave brickmasons—Guy, Rufus, Herman, and Charles—were hired by the Engineers. See Selected Slave Rolls, December 1861, *Confederate Records.*

22. Mahan, *Treatise on Field Fortifications,* pp. 1–6.

23. *State Engineers,* Payroll.

24. *Ibid.,* Jim, a slave belonging to P. E. Gentry, served as a messenger for the chief engineer.

25. Douglas S. Freeman, *Lee's Dispatches* (New York: G. P. Putnam's Sons, 1915), p. 8.

26. Richmond *Examiner,* June 1, 1861.

27. *Ibid.*

28. *Ibid.,* June 3, 1861; March 7, 1863.

29. *Ibid.,* June 1, 1861. General Beauregard, in December 1861, called upon Richmond for 253 free Negroes to work on the fortifications near Manassas. An additional 200 free blacks were required to labor on the fortifications on the south side of the James River. Negroes had recently constructed several batteries on the Manchester side of the James River. See Richmond *Examiner,* Dec. 21, 1861.

30. *Ibid.,* July 13 and 15, 1861. Negroes arrested for petty crimes were immediately dispatched to labor on fortifications. Those who deserted and were caught were ordered to be whipped. Free Negroes who labored on fortifications were paid $11 monthly and were provided rations. By September 1861, many of the free Negroes had been released and permitted to return to their homes.

31. *Official Records,* IV, II, 946. Slaveowners became increasingly reluctant to respond to military requests for their Negroes.

32. *Ibid.,* III, 208. See Chapter 1 for a discussion of laws enacted to impress slaves and free Negroes in Virginia. In February 1864 the Confederate Congress made all male free Negroes between the ages of eighteen and fifty liable to service "in manufactories, in erecting fortifications, and in military hospitals." See J. Matthews, ed., *Statutes at Large,* Fourth Session of the First Congress (1864).

33. Letcher, *Executive Papers,* Jan. 25, 1862; Feb. 21, 1862. Isaac M. St. John wrote that "it will not be desirable to commence work on a square redoubt with a "force of less than 40 Negroes." See the Charles T. Mason Papers (Virginia Historical Society Collection, Richmond) Aug. 2,

1862. Negro laborers were used to repair the roads approaching the battery and clear the grounds facing earthworks.
34. *Ibid.*, Feb. 1864. See Isaac Hammond Collection, Accession No. 24335. (Virginia State Library, Richmond).
35. Spraggins, "Mobilization of Negro Labor," p. 172.
36. *Confederate Records*, Slave Rolls Nos. 317–567, 1862.
37. Letcher, *Executive Papers*, Aug. 18, 22, 28, 1862. Also May 6, 1862. The governor in May 1862 informed the General Assembly of the need to obstruct the James River. He noted that the interest of the capital demanded instantaneous action, since very little had been done, leaving the city of Richmond in an exposed position. The legislature of Virginia eventually appropriated $200,000 toward the completion of the obstruction of the James River.
38. Richmond *Examiner*, April 10, 1863. The Engineer Bureau advertised that it was paying one dollar per day, rations, and medical attention. Owners were requested to deliver their slaves to Lieutenant W. G. Turpin whose office was located at Nineteenth and Cary.
39. Letcher, *Executive Papers*, Oct. 10, 11, 21, 22, 1862; Nov. 24, 1862. Negro labor was also used to construct the earthworks at Fredericksburg in the fall of 1862. General Lee reported that one thousand Negroes were fortifying the heights around the city.
40. *Ibid.* See letter dated March 19, 1863; Aug. 12, 1863. See Senate of the Commonwealth of Virginia, *Documents*, 1863–1864 (Virginia State Library at Richmond) Doc. No. 4, pp. 6–7; hereinafter cited as *Senate Documents*.
41. *Ibid.*
42. *Ibid.*, Oct. 21, 1862.
43. *Ibid.*, Oct. 22, 24, 28, 1862; Nov. 10, 20, 1862; and Dec. 1, 2, 5, 9, 11, 1862. Many counties were anxious to receive credit for the number of slaves already furnished to labor on public defenses. Some slaveowners protested that they had already supplied slaves while others who had furnished none were not being asked. The governor notified such slaveowners that their complaints would have to be taken up with local officials.
44. *Ibid.*, Nov. 21, 1862. See letter dated March 19, 1863; Aug. 12, 1863; *Senate Documents, 1863–1864*, Doc. No. 4, pp. 6–7.
45. Letcher, *Executive Papers*, Dec. 13, 16, 20, 23, 26, 1862.
46. Letcher, *Executive Papers*, Dec. 24, 1862.
47. *Ibid.*, Jan. 22, 1863. Colonel R. Withers, post commander at Danville, requested several hundred Negroes to prepare the defensive works at Danville. See letter dated Jan. 18, 1864; see also *Confederate Records*, Manuscript No. 6273.
48. *Ibid.*
49. *Ibid.*, Feb. 11, 1863. For the response of county officials to the January draft, see letters written to the governor on February 5, 6, 11, 12, 14, 24, 28, and March 2, 1863.
50. *Ibid.*, March 4, 1863.
51. *Ibid.*, March 13, 1863.
52. *Ibid.*, March 11, 1863. Bedford County officials notified the governor that in November 1862 they supplied 276 slaves, and in January 1863 they

sent 21 slaves. Sixty-nine slaves were also impressed to labor on the canal works, railroads, and ironworks. In the fall of 1861 they furnished 164 slaves as teamsters to serve at Huntersville.

53. *Ibid.*, March 13, 1863. Brunswick County officials insisted that the deficit of 222 slaves charged against them was actually only 64 slaves. The county was credited with sending 235 slaves. To correct the error they stated that 293 slaves had been sent in response to military calls, 100 slaves instead of 235 slaves. In May 1863, the sheriff of King William County was authorized by the governor to impress sufficient slaves to prevent a Union cavalry from moving through the county. The governor told the sheriff to "block up the roads . . . by felling trees, and by doing the same thing at any streams which may be forded on the line of the road." See Governor John Letcher, *Executive Papers*, May 5, 1863.

54. Spraggins, "Mobilization of Negro Labor," p. 172. The local courts were to register all free blacks between the ages of eighteen and fifty. This list was to be sent to the Adjutant General, and whenever laborers were wanted, requisitions were sent to local courts. A board of three justices selected the workers from the registration list. The sheriff was responsible for notifying the free Negroes of their call.

55. *Ibid.* The pay, rations, and allowances were borne by the Confederate States. Free Negroes were not required to serve more than 180 days without their consent.

56. Wiley, *Southern Negroes*, p. 117. The Confederacy paid the owner of each slave $30 monthly and in case of death the full value of the laborer.

57. *Ibid.* This act made all male free Negroes between the ages of eighteen and fifty liable to service in war manufactories, in erecting fortifications, and in military hospitals. It also stated that they should be taken in preference to the 20,000 slaves impressed by the same act. Not more than one fifth of the slaves of any one planter might be taken, and they should be apportioned among the planters in equal ratio in the region affected. Only under the greatest urgency should any slaves be impressed from plantations producing grain exclusively.

58. Letcher, *Executive Papers*, Sept. 9, 14, 1863. In his annual message to the General Assembly in December, the governor pointed out that Richmond had not complied with his draft of slaves and expressed concern that no action had been taken by the legislature. The lawmakers were also told that on November 26 he had received another requisition for 5,000 slaves from President Davis.

59. *Ibid.*, Sept. 28, 30, 1863.

60. *Ibid.*, Dec. 12, 1863.

61. Robinson, "The Confederate Engineers," p. 413. On February 12, 1864, General Orders No. 20 permitted impressing officers to meet the market rate for Negro laborers.

62. Wiley, *Southern Negroes*, p. 126.

63. *Ibid.*

64. Governor William Smith, *Executive Papers*, Jan. 22, 1864.

65. *Ibid.*, Jan. 18, 1864.

66. *Ibid.*, Feb. 19, 1864.

67. *Ibid.*, Feb. 6, 9, 10, 18, 1864.

68. Richmond *Examiner*, March 17, 1864.
69. Richmond *Whig*, June 21, 1864.
70. Smith, *Executive Papers*, Oct. 3, 1864.
71. Richmond *Examiner*, Oct. 6, 1864.
72. Smith, *Executive Papers*, Dec. 14, 1864. When desired by the court, one of the reserve forces of the state could be detailed for every thirty slaves to act as managers of the slaves and custodians of supplies furnished. Rations could be supplied by the owners, to be paid for by the government.
73. *Ibid.*, Jan. 7, 17, 18, 23, 26, 27, 28; Feb. 4, 6, 23; March 14, 23, 26, 1865.
74. *Ibid.*, Feb. 9, 1865.
75. *Ibid.*, March 10, 1865. Gilmer asked that the counties fulfill their quotas without delay stating that "every day that is lost may involve most serious consequences to our country."
76. *Ibid.*, March 9, 1865.
77. *Ibid.*, Feb. 6, 16, 1865.
78. *Ibid.*, Jan. 17, 24, 1865; March 20, 1865.
79. *Ibid.*, Feb. 11, 1865.
80. *Ibid.*, Jan. 28, 1865.
81. *Ibid.*, Feb. 10, 1865. Some counties insisted that they had furnished more than their quota under former requisitions, some that they had furnished slaves to officers of the government, some that they had furnished more than neighboring counties, some that they were exempt by reason of the heavy loss sustained by the public enemy, and some upon grounds of agricultural necessity.
82. *Ibid.* The governor asked county authorities for 10 per cent of their slaves.
83. *Ibid.*
84. Richmond *Examiner*, Jan. 9, 1862.
85. *Ibid.*, Dec. 10, 1862.
86. *Ibid.*, Dec. 11, 1862. C. H. Ryland, the steward of the hospital, admitted that four slaves had died during the past week, but insisted that two of them were received into the hospital in a dying condition.
87. Letcher, *Executive Papers*, Jan., 1863.
88. *Ibid.*, Jan. 12, 1863. Gilmer indicated that army rations were composed of 1½ pounds of flour and 1¼ pounds of salt meat, or 1 pound of fresh.
89. Richmond *Examiner*, Jan. 12, 1863. On January 19, the *Examiner* reported that Mr. Woolfolk of Orange County submitted a resolution which was passed, that a special committee of five be appointed to investigate the charge.
90. Richmond *Whig*, April 18, 1864. A report by Surgeon W. A. Patterson to the Board of Directors of the Penitentiary of Virginia described the awesome condition of convicts returned from fortifications. See House of Delegates of the Commonwealth of Virginia, *Documents, 1861–1862*, Doc. No. 13, p. 37.
91. Letcher, *Executive Papers*, Nov. 20, 1863; Dec. 4, 1863.
92. *Ibid.* The governor estimated that $500,000 was needed to meet the just claims for the loss of slaves. See letter, Jan. 6, 1863.
93. *Ibid.*, Feb. 5, 1864.

94. *Ibid.*, Feb. 11, 24, 1864. Goochland County officials reported that 409 able-bodied slaves were sent to General Magruder in 1862 to labor on the Peninsula for three months. They were greatly exposed, and many died, while several others returned permanently disabled or so diseased that they also died.
95. *Ibid.*, Feb. 13, 1864.
96. *Ibid.*, Feb. 26, 1864. Franklin County reported that the 117 slaves impressed in September 1864 were badly treated and poorly fed. Nineteen slaves died soon after their return, and the majority of those who survived the harsh treatment while working on fortifications were so physically disabled that they were unfit to work. The governor was asked to take steps to see that the slaves were properly treated and fed. See letter of January 11, 1865.
97. *Confederate Records*, Slave Rolls Nos. 317–565. There were 141 slaves employed in obstructing the James River. At least 235 slaves from Cumberland, Mecklenburg, and Louisa counties were sent to the stone quarries to gather rocks to make "cribs" for use in obstructing the rivers. Rocks were also used to construct redoubts.
98. *Ibid.*, Slave Rolls Nos. 1–1416.
99. Petersburg Common Council, *Minute Book*, Dec. 12, 1862, p. 480.
100. *Ibid.* The Negroes sent were under the control and supervision of Samuel Lecture. The owners were paid $2 daily by the city, with rations furnished by the government.
101. *Ibid.*, p. 492. In April the time was extended another month, providing the Negroes were required to work until 5 P.M.
102. See the Charles Taylor Mason Papers, Box No. 1 (Virginia Historical Society Collection, Richmond). On March 31, 1862, Mason wrote to Captain A. L. Rives, "We have cut and delivered . . . from 350 to 400 logs ready to be shaped for the cribs. . . . We will commence sinking them tomorrow. The piles are driven with difficulty. Today we have on the work, white and black, nearly a hundred."
103. *Confederate Records*, Slave Rolls Nos. 1–565. Cumberland, Mecklenburg, and Louisa counties furnished 235 slaves to work in the stone quarries.
104. Nichols, *Confederate Engineer*, p. 98. The assault upon Richmond would likely have been successful save for the resistance which Federal ships unexpectedly encountered at Drewry's Bluff.
105. Mason Papers, Aug. 29, 1862.
106. Jeremy F. Gilmer Papers (Southern Historical Collection, University of North Carolina, Chapel Hill, N.C.), No. 276. Gilmer mentioned to his wife that "Just at this point Sandy has come into my room. He is engaged to go with General Mackall as a servant. . . . He wears a grey coat with a military button and considers himself in the army."
107. Mason Papers, June 10, 1864. Four slaves from Chesterfield County were impressed to labor on entrenchments. D. O. Davis, for service of 10 slaves, 10 wagons, and 40 mules for thirty days, received $3,000. See *Confederate Records*, Manuscript No. 5402, June 1864.
108. Smith, *Executive Papers*, Oct. 1, 1864.
109. *Ibid.*, Oct. 5, 1864. The governor's aide was sent to Castle Thunder to take charge of the slaves and to discharge those unfit for service. He was

also expected to secure a receipt from the engineer who received the Negroes. Captain Lee was to provide a guard to take the Negroes to the Bluff.

110. *Ibid.*

111. Mason Papers, Dec. 7, 1864. On January 31, 1865, Mason was ordered by General Stevens to appear "at 10 o'clock before a committee of the Virginia House of Delegates to testify as to the treatment of impressed Negroes."

112. *Confederate Records*, Selected Slave Rolls. Eight slaves were also listed as laborers, and their owners received $300 for each one employed. William Johnson, a free Negro, employed because of his skill in making repairs on the capital and the state court house was exempted by Governor Smith "from service either in working on the public defenses or elsewhere." See Smith, *Executive Papers*, Feb. 5, 1864. David Patterson, another free Negro, was also permanently exempted. See the letter from Governor Smith, March 15, 1864.

113. Robinson, "The Confederate Engineers," 413. Not more than one fifth of any owner's able-bodied slaves should be taken without his consent.

114. *Ibid.* The Bureau of Conscription sent out Circular No. 60, Sept. 7, 1864, calling on the enrolling officers for returns of all free Negroes and slaves taken into the service up to September, with a statement of their assignments. See Register of free Negroes enrolled, 1864–1865, *Confederate Records*, Chap. 1, Vol. 241. Over four hundred free Negroes were assigned to labor on fortifications in Virginia. Approximately 1,818 free Negroes were assigned to arsenals, hospitals, railroads, ordnance works, quartermaster installations, and so forth.

115. *Ibid.*, p. 414.

116. *Ibid.*

117. *Journal of the Congress of the Confederate States of America*, IV, 257.

118. *Official Records*, IV, III, 839.

119. *Ibid.*, p. 899.

120. Charles H. Wesley, *The Collapse of the Confederacy* (Washington, D.C.: Associated Publishers, 1937), p. 158.

121. *Ibid.*, p. 160. See Richmond *Dispatch*, Dec. 9, 1864.

122. *Ibid.* Lee's opinion was that the Confederacy should employ the slave as a soldier without delay.

123. Richmond *Examiner*, February 3, 1865.

124. Freeman, *Lee's Dispatches*, p. 114.

125. Gilmer Papers, Sept. 7, 1863. See *Confederate Records*, Slave Rolls Nos. 317–845.

126. Richmond *Examiner*, Oct. 27, 1863. Slaves from Cumberland, Buckingham, and Appomattox counties were impressed to erect bridges to span waters in western Virginia. See Governors Letcher and Smith, *Executive Papers*, 1863–1865. Thirty free Negroes were impressed to build bridges over the Appomattox and Bannister rivers. In 1864 the Bureau of Conscription was asked to assign Negroes from Appomattox, Prince Edward, Amelia, Buckingham, and Cumberland counties to the Engineer Bureau for bridge construction.

127. *Confederate Records*, Manuscripts No. 3672, Sept. 24, 1864. Lieutenant J. S. Norrison was commanding officer of Company A.

128. *Official Records*, iv, III, 1084–1086.
129. Robinson, "The Confederate Engineers," p. 414. A field officer in the office of the chief engineer of each army or department was placed in general charge of the force allotted to that army or department. The Negroes were collected at the conscript camps and then forwarded to the rendezvous.

Bibliography

MANUSCRIPT SOURCES

ARCHIVES OF THE UNITED STATES, Washington, D.C.
  Record Group 45—Naval Records, Collection of the Office of Naval Records and Library.
  Record Group 109—War Department Collection of Confederate Records
  Record Group 156—Records of the Office, Chief of Ordnance.
ARCHIVES OF VIRGINIA, Richmond Virginia.
  Accessions, State Library
  Engineer Department of Virginia, Documents Nos. 62–787, Payroll of Slaves and Free Negroes, 1861–1862, State Library.
  Governor John Letcher, *Executive Papers*, 1861–1864, State Library.
  Governor William Smith, *Executive Papers*, 1864–1865, State Library.
  Governors' Letter Books, State Library.
  Legislative Papers, A Collection of Petitions Sent to the Legislature of Virginia, 1860–1865, State Library.
  Records, Counties, State Library.
  Registers of Free Negroes and Mulattoes, 1860, State Library.
  Tax Books, Land and Personal, Counties and Cities, State Library.
ARCHIVES OF CITIES AND COUNTIES CLERKS' OFFICES.
  Annual Reports of the Overseers of the Poor.
  Deed Books.
  Confederate Pension Board Minutes, Petersburg.
  Land Books.
  Minute Books, Petersburg Common Council, 1861–1865.
  Order Books.
  Registers of Free Negroes and Mulattoes.

GOVERNMENT PUBLICATIONS AND OFFICIAL DOCUMENTS

U.S. Bureau of the Census. *Seventh Census of the United States: 1850.* Washington: Government Printing Office, 1854.
U.S. Bureau of the Census. *Eighth Census of the United States: 1860.* Washington: Government Printing Office, 1865.
U.S. Bureau of the Census. *Negro Population, 1790–1915.* Washington: Government Printing Office, 1918.
The United States on the Eve of the Civil War. Washington: Government Printing Office, 1964.
The Official Records of the Union and Confederate Navies in the War of Rebellion. 26 vols. Washington, 1894–1922.

The War of the Rebellion: A Compilation of the Official Records of the Union and Confederate Armies. 128 vols. Washington, 1880–1901.
Journal of the Congress of the Confederate States of America, 1861–1865. 7 vols. Washington, 1904–1905.
Report of the Joint Committee on the Conduct of the War, 1865, 39th Congress, 2nd Session. 3 vols. Washington, 1865.
De Bow, J. D. B. *Compendium of the Seventh Census of the United States.* Washington, 1854.
Matthews, James M. (ed.). *Statutes at Large of the Provisional Government of the Confederate States of America* . . . . 5 vols. Richmond, 1862–1864.
Ramsdell, Charles W. (ed.). *Laws and Joint Resolutions of the Last Session of the Confederate Congress* . . . . Durham, 1941.

GOVERNMENT DOCUMENTS, VIRGINIA

Acts of the General Assembly of Virginia, 1860–1865.
Auditor of Public Accounts, Annual Reports, 1860–1865.
Board of Public Works, Annual Reports to the General Assembly, 1860–1865.
The Calendar of Virginia State Papers, 1652–1869. 11 vols. Richmond, 1875–1893.
The Code of Virginia. Richmond, 1860.
Cumberland County Miscellaneous Papers, 1861–1865.
House of Delegates of the Commonwealth of Virginia, Documents 1860–1865.
House of Delegates of the Commonwealth of Virginia, Journals, 1860–1865.
James River and Kanawha Canal Company, Annual Reports to the General Assembly, 1860–1865.
Senate of the Commonwealth of Virginia, Documents, 1860–1865.
Senate of the Commonwealth of Virginia, Journals, 1860–1865.

FAMILY PAPERS

Anderson, Joseph R. Papers, 1850–1866. Virginia State Library, Richmond.
Beauregard, Pierre G. T. Papers, 1862. Manuscript Collection, Duke University Library, Durham.
Bragg, Braxton. Papers. Manuscript Collection, Duke University Library, Durham.
Cloptom, Marea G. Papers. Confederate Museum Collection, Richmond.
Gilmer, Jeremy F. Papers. Southern Historical Collection, Library of the University of North Carolina, Chapel Hill, N.C.
Hammond, Isaac. Manuscript Collection, Virginia State Library, Richmond.
McGuire, Hunter. Papers. Confederate Museum Collection, Richmond.
Lamb, William. Papers. Confederate Museum Collection, Richmond.
Mason, Charles T. Papers. Virginia Historical Society Collection, Richmond.
Stephens, Alexander H. Papers. Library of Congress, Washington.
Tanner, J. S. Papers. Confederate Museum Collection, Richmond.

CONTEMPORARY WRITINGS

Alexander, E. P. *Military Memoirs of a Confederate.* New York, 1907.
Brown, William W. *The Negro in the American Rebellion.* New York, 1888.
Chestnut, Mary B. *Diary from Dixie.* New York, 1905.

De Leon, Thomas C. *Four Years in the Rebel Capitals*. Mobile, 1890.

Guthrie, James M. *Camp Fires of the Afro-Americans*. Philadelphia, 1899.

Jones, John B. *A Rebel War Clerk's Diary*. Philadelphia, 1866.

Kean, Robert G. H. *Inside the Confederate Government*. Ed. by Edward Younger. New York, 1957.

McGuire, Judith W. *Diary of a Southern Refugee, During the War, By A Lady of Virginia*, New York, 1867.

Olmsted, Frederick L. *A Journey in the Seaboard Slave States, with Remarks on Their Economy*. New York, 1856.

Russell, William H. *My Diary, North and South*. Boston, 1863.

Vandiver, Frank, ed. *The Civil War Diary of General Josiah Gorgas*. University, Ala., 1947.

Wilson, Joseph T. *The Black Phalanx: A History of the Negro Soldiers of the United States, 1775–1865*. Hartford, Conn., 1888.

NEWSPAPERS

DeBow's *Review*.
Lynchburg *Daily Republican*.
Lynchburg *Virginian*.
Petersburg *Daily Express*.
Petersburg *Index*.
Richmond *Dispatch*.
Richmond *Enquirer*.
Richmond *Examiner*.
Richmond *Sentinel*.
Richmond *Times*.
Richmond *Whig*.

PERIODICALS

American Historical Review. New York, 1895.

Civil War History. Iowa City, Iowa, 1955.

Confederate Veteran. Nashville, Tenn., 1893.

Journal of Negro History. Washington, 1916.

Journal of Southern History. Baton Rouge, La., 1935.

Military Engineer. Washington, 1920.

Mississippi Valley Historical Review. Cedar Rapids, Iowa, 1914.

North Carolina Historical Review. Raleigh, N.C., 1924.

Southern Historical Society Papers. Richmond, 1876.

Virginia Cavalcade. Richmond, 1935.

SECONDARY SOURCES

Aptheker, Herbert. *The Negro in the Civil War*. New York, 1938.

Aston, James. *Wrought Iron: Its Manufacture, Characteristics, and Applications*. Pittsburgh, 1939.

Bill, Alfred H. *The Beleaguered City: Richmond, 1861–1865*. New York, 1946.

Black, Robert C., III. *Railroads of the Confederacy*. Chapel Hill, N.C., 1952.

Blanton, Wyndham B. *Medicine in Virginia in the Nineteenth Century*. Richmond, 1933.

Bruce, Kathleen. *Virginia Iron Manufacture in the Slave Era*. New York, 1931.

Chisolm, J. Julian. *A Manual of Military Surgery for the Use of Surgeons in the Confederate Army*. Richmond, 1861.

Clark, Victor S. *History of Manufacture in the United States*. 3 vols. New York, 1929.

Coulter, E. Merton. *The Confederate States of America, 1861–1865*. Baton Rouge, La., 1958.
Cunningham, H. H. *Doctors in Gray: The Confederate Medical Service*. Baton Rouge, La., 1958.
Davis, Burke. *To Appomattox: Nine Days, 1865*. New York, 1959.
Dew, Charles B. "Southern Industry in the Civil War Era. Joseph Reid Anderson and the Tredegar Iron Works, 1859–67." Ph.D. dissertation, Johns Hopkins University, 1964.
Dowdey, Clifford. *Experiment in Rebellion*. Garden City, 1946.
Eaton, Clement, *A History of the Southern Confederacy*. New York, 1954.
Eavenson, Henry N. *American Coal Industry*. Baltimore, 1942.
Fairbairn, William. *Iron, Its History, Properties, and Processes of Manufacture*. Edinburgh, 1865.
Freeman, Douglas S. *Lee's Dispatches*. New York, 1915.
Harrison, M. Clifford. *Home to the Cockade City*. Richmond, 1942.
Henry, Robert S. *The Story of the Confederacy*. Indianapolis, 1931.
Hesseltine, William B. *The South in American History*. New York, 1943.
Jackson, Luther P. *Free Negro Labor and Property Holding in Virginia, 1830–1860*. New York, 1942.
Johnston, Angus J. *Virginia Railroads in the Civil War*. Chapel Hill, N.C., 1961.
Lesley, J. P. *The Iron Manufacturer's Guide . . . .* New York, 1859.
Mahan, D. H. *A Treatise on Field Fortifications*. New York, 1848.
Nichols, James L. *Confederate Engineer*. Tuscaloosa, Ala., 1957.
Phillips, Ulrick B. *American Negro Slavery*. New York, 1918.
Pollard, Edward A. *Southern History of the War . . . .* 2 vols. New York, 1866.
Ramsdell, Charles W. *Behind the Lines in the Southern Confederacy*. Baton Rouge, La., 1944.
Randall, James G. *The Civil War and Reconstruction*, Boston, 1937.
Schwab, John C. *The Confederate States of America: A Financial History of the South During the Civil War*. New York, 1901.
Simkins, Francis B. *The South, Old and New: A History, 1820–1947*. New York, 1947.
Stover, John F. *The Railroads of the South, 1865–1900*. Chapel Hill, N.C., 1955.
Swank, James M. *History of the Manufacture of Iron In All Ages . . .* Philadelphia, 1892.
Vandiver, Frank E. *Ploughshares into Swords: Josiah Gorgas and Confederate Ordnance*. Austin, Texas, 1952.
Waitt, Robert W., Jr. *Confederate Military Hospitals in Richmond*. Richmond, 1964.
Wesley, Charles H. *The Collapse of the Confederacy*, Washington, 1937.
———. *Negro Labor in the United States*. New York, 1927.
Wiley, Bell I. *Southern Negroes, 1861–1865*. New York, 1938.

Index